To Tom Go'
all the

May 2018

To my father, Panayiotis Leotsinidis

IN THE AFTERNOON SUN:
MY ALEXANDRIA

Julie Hill

Published by
THE SOCIETY FOR CULTURAL ENRICHMENT, INC.
Makati City, Philippines

Cover art by June Poticar Dalisay

Book design by Kurt Gloria

Printed by Kayumanggi Press

CONTENTS

ACKNOWLEDGEMENTS

In July 2014, my book *Privileged Witness: Journeys of Rediscovery* was published, and I thought that this third volume of my travel stories would put a close to my writings. But suddenly I now had time to leaf through family files, yellowing papers, the letters of my parents, and old faded photographs that chronicled important and interesting events in my life.

I stumbled upon letters my father wrote me nearly of sixty years ago, while I was a graduate student at the University of Minnesota, relating the events in Egypt following the Suez Canal crisis of 1956, the time of my departure. That opened the floodgates of memory, returning me to the place of my birth and my young life.

As the events I recount in this book do not always follow a chronological order, it might help the reader for me to provide, in broad strokes, an outline of my life. I was born in Alexandria in 1936, and grew up and studied there until I left for postgraduate studies in the United States in 1956. There I met my husband Arthur, who had come from Australia, and we were married in 1959. We then lived in and traveled to many places around the world, wherever Arthur's job as an executive with the Ford Foundation took us. I myself joined a major global telecommunications company and Arthur and I led a full and happy life until his untimely passing in 2002. We had moved to Rancho Sta. Fe in Southern California, and that is where I remain, writing accounts of my various travels and undertaking a few more for as long as my aching body will permit.

The editor of my previous books—Jose Dalisay, an award-winning novelist who has also become a mentor and a friend—felt that there was another book to be done in those meanderings of my mind, the voice of an Alexandrian Greek to be heard. It is his insightful approach which framed my story. He offered constant feedback that carried me through this undertaking, and without him this book would not have been accomplished.

Before his death in 2014, my brother Akis—the keeper of the family flame—provided useful insights into the world of Greeks. He volunteered many precious details and offered his recollections.

On the greatest joys of working on this memoir was being reunited with my childhood friend Aida Khalafalla, who provided useful details of our time while at the Lyçee Français and the Faculty of Science of the University of Alexandria. She was responsible for introducing me to the International Friends of the Bibliotheca Alexandrina.

I wish to acknowledge the input of Mrs. Chewikar Abdel Aziz, the former headmistress of the Lyçee, who reviewed the section on the school.

Lorenzo Montesini, an Alexandrian living in Sydney and a member of the board of the International Friends of the Bibliotheca, volunteered his own memories, providing exquisite details on the Esperia and the movie theaters of our beloved city.

I am grateful to the Bibliotheca Alexandrina for welcoming me back to my native city as a guest. Like Alexandria's ancient Pharos or light-house, the Bibliotheca today is a beacon of knowledge and hope, acting as Alexandria's window on the world, and the world's window on Alexandria.

I wish to acknowledge the input of Dr. Sahar Hamouda head of the Alexandria and Mediterranean Research Center of the Bibliotheca, and Dr. Muhammad Awad for his invaluable suggestions and his interest in my story.

And finally, my deepest thanks to my dearest friend Dr. Jaime C. Laya, former Governor of the Central Bank of the Philippines and former Chairman of the National Commission for Culture and Arts of the Philippines, for helping me see this project through.

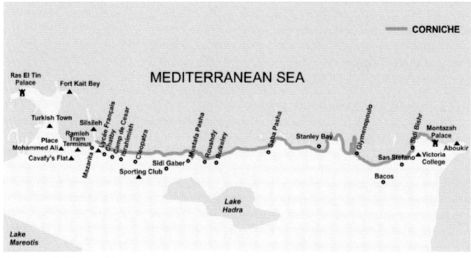

A map of Alexandria

A map of the Mediterranean

FOREWORD

by Harry Tzalas
Director, Hellenic Institute of Ancient and Medieval Alexandrian Studies

Fate decreed that I should not meet with Julie Hill, or Julia Leotsinidis as her maiden name was when we lived in Alexandria, Egypt, the city in which we were born within the same year, and whence our families flew to the suburb of Sidi Bishr to avoid the bombardments during Rommel's advance in North Africa. The coincidences do not stop here. Both our families had emigrated to Egypt from the mastic-and-lemon-grove island of Chios, we both went on to the same school, Lycée Français, trekked the same streets, walked the same alleys, come Easter and Christmas we attended the same Orthodox ceremonies in the same Churches, we probably rubbed shoulders, but we never met, face to face that is. And we both loved Alexandria as our very own city. Many years after our wanton expatriation from Egypt we still missed it, still longed for the carefree life we lived on that narrow strip of land stretching between the clear blue Mediterranean Sea and the stagnant, turbid waters of Lake Mariut.

Yes, it was with deep nostalgia that we looked back to those years of our early youth, which it so happened that for the city's cosmopolitan style of life were the last.

For many decades, tens of thousands of Alexandrian Greeks lived peacefully next to the indigenous population, mixing at the same time with Italians, Maltese, Jews, Armenians, and a smaller contingent of British, French, Germans, and Swiss. It ought to be said that cosmopolitan Alexandria has never been in modern times a melting pot of nationalities. Each community insisted on keeping its own identity, its own self-sufficient way of life, customs, language, schools, even its own athletic institutions. Each prayed to one's own God, Christ the Savior, Allah the Omnipotent, Jealous Jehovah, in one's own churches and synagogues that were often built in close proximity to the mosques. A church bell might be tolling as the voice of the muezzin would be heard calling the faithful to prayer from atop a towering minaret. The Europeans met and socialized in restaurants, movie houses, the famous and popular beaches, they went on excursions, hunted, fished, and celebrated Sham el Nessim, the Monday following Orthodox Easter.

Except for a few wealthy Greek magnates whose names and donations were commemorated on marble plaques at the entrances of community buildings, schools, orphanages, hospitals, churches and cemeteries, most of our countrymen were poor and worked as common laborers. Our grandfathers and grandmothers who had come to Egypt from the poorer regions of the Ottoman Empire were privileged to find in Alexandria, and become part of, a more prosperous middle class than the one they had left behind. Those few who had come from the big city centers like Constantinople or Smyrna fared better. Living among a distressingly poor and nearly destitute indigenous population they enjoyed the limited but important privileges of their new status. And so the poorest of Greeks who worked as clerks in shops, a bakery, a café, barber shops and an occasional book store could well afford a *doula*, a "slave." That was the usual appellation for a servant, a housemaid, a term that was in no way considered offensive or derogatory. They were unfortunate, destitute creatures who worked hard for a pittance, most of the time content to secure their board and lodging.

But when one is young, lives in Alexandria, and has his entire life ahead of him, such matters are of little concern or importance. There were plenty of lovely sights to see and enjoy. And yet, if one of us had ventured to visit the poorer neighborhoods of Karmoush, Bab Sidra, Gormouk el Adim, or Ahfushi, he'd be shocked by the dreadful living conditions that prevailed in those shanty-towns inhabited by the indigenous Alexandrians, their lives ever mired in squalor and despair. But Alexandria was their city; it belonged to them as much as it belonged to us. We, on the other hand, lived in spacious apartment houses, strolled the wonderful boulevards, had our ice cream at Pastroudis' patisserie, tasted *mille-feuilles* at Delices. On a Sunday we'd dance at Atheneos, would go to the cinema at the Royal, the Strand, theRialto, and the Gaieté; we'd swim at the beaches of Stanley, San Stefano, Sidi Bishr, and Agami. In the evening, we'd promenade at the Cornichewheresmiling Arab boys sold garlands of *foul* and jasmine that infused the air with their fragrance.

And then, in the fateful year 1952, and after centuries of colonialist suppression, a small band of officers, much to our and everybody's surprise, rose up to depose the powerless and corrupt king Farouk, who left Alexandria on his royal yacht, the Mahroussa. By 1953 the monarchy had been abolished, and when, in 1956, the World Bank refused to provide funds for the building of the Aswan Dam, in a historic speech at Muhammad Ali Square, Nasser announced to an astounded crowd and an astonished world the immediate nationalization of the Suez Canal. In defiance of the United Nations, the French and British launched a series of attacks aimed at the Suez Canal, Israel following suit.

The Jewish population of Alexandria had already left by 1948 when the Israeli state was created. They were followed by the English and the French who also fled in 1956. For the other foreign communities, and particularly for the Greeks and the Italians who constituted a majority among the Europeans, the world had turned upside-down. The great private estates were nationalized, property and tax laws were revised, and Egypt would never be the same again.

"Can you imagine such a thing?" protested Athenodoros Economides, my boss at the shipping office where I worked. "Now we'll be forced to keep our accounting books in Arabic." He couldn't fathom the truth that a day would come when such radical changes would be enforced, changes like the abolishment of the Mixed Courts. In these courts foreign judges adjudicated on the affairs of foreigners in the absence of Egyptians. No one could comprehend that the English, after a century and a half of absolute rule, would not control any more the fate of the land, that a more just and equitable tax system would be enforced, an agrarian reform would be passed, that Egypt, in other words would seize to be a protectorate. The foreigners just couldn't get it through their heads that the majority of illiterate locals were about to claim the right to an education, and to a better life.

The Greek community found itself "ungoverned," that is without leadership, since the rich, for the most part, had taken every precaution to secure their accumulated wealth by sending it abroad long before the crisis. The majority of the Alexandrines who had no problems with the locals and were not directly affected by nationalizations, felt uncertain and insecure.

So the time had come for us to leave. I left for Brazil, Julia for the United States. And the years went by, a lifetime full of joys and sorrows. Wherever we went,

Alexandria was following us, haunted our dreams. At some point we returned for a visit, but it was not the same city any more. Much in it had changed, we had changed too.

Many Alexandrian Greeks have written about the years they lived there, many have wanted to leave an account, a testimony of what they had witnessed. They wanted to express what they felt within themselves. To paraphrase Cavafy, they wanted to be "deemed worthy of such a city"; much like the aborigines who left upon the walls of caves the imprints of their palms.

Almost all of their works fall within the category of "nostalgic literature." Yet what they often describe is but a mirage—a trip to the outer boundaries of imagination where a nostalgic disposition corrodes and beautifies at the same time their concept of reality. Extremely few books dealing with the historical facts have been written by Greeks. Julie Hill's book is an exception, because in it she takes us by the hand and walks with us in the Alexandria of our childhood days, and she manages to do that within a historical framework that is both factual and well documented.

I.

STRANGERS AND EXILES

You won't find a new country,
Won't find
another shore.
The city will always pursue you.
You'll walk the same streets, grow old
in the same neighborhoods, turn grey in these
sane houses.
You 'll always end up in this city. Don't hope for
things elsewhere
there's no ship for you, there's no road.

From *"The City,"* C. P. Cavafy

I AM AN Alexandrian.

When I am asked where I am from, I would say Alexandria, which is not the same as Egypt. I am a citizen of that city. "Alexandria" is a word that is a key, opening up the imagination to a vivid dream that brings the ancient past and the more recent future together: and in that dream parade the Pharos—one of the seven wonders of antiquity—the great library, Alexander the Great, Constantine Cavafy, and Lawrence Durrell, to whom the city persists as the Capital of Memory.

The city, inhabited by these memories of mine, moves not only backwards into history, studded with so many great names, but also back and forth in the living present, to the familiar and the commonplace, to my family, to myself. That family, now long dispersed, is my connection to the past. Where did they come from, and what brought them to Alexandria?

My parents, Greeks from Asia Minor, were part of the Greek Diaspora, among the 1.5 million Anatolian Greeks exchanged with 366,000 Muslim Turks living in Greece, when in 1922 the Republic of Turkey, under Kemal Ataturk, the victor of Gallipoli, was founded. That ended the Ottoman sultans' rule—a genocide event. My father was born in Cesme, a small town an hour from Izmir, a daylong voyage by horse-drawn carriage on unpaved roads at the end of the 19th century. He studied accounting and commercial law in a French college in Izmir, a rarity in 1895. My mother was born in Istanbul—which she invariably referred as Constantinople, with its five thrilling syllables—so proud was she of her Byzantine heritage.

Our ancestral home on my father's side is Chios, a Greek island 25 miles from tip to tip, and five nautical miles to the coast of Asia Minor. This was where my grandparents and our family before them sank their roots, and where my parents are buried. This green mountainous island grows mastic, a semi-transparent sap drawn from evergreen bushes, the original chewing gum. The island is well known for its painted geometric façades and the fiery mosaics of the Nea Moni monastery, today a convent. It was founded in the 11th century by the Byzantine Emperor Constantine Monomachos—a character known to be strikingly modern in a way, and very likely neurotic—and is recognized as a Unesco heritage site.

Perched on a mountainside, with terraces looking down the mastic-growing valley and across the waters of the blue Aegean, Nea Moni is lovely and secluded. It represents the heart of folk traditions in weaving and embroidery. I visited it many times, taking peaceful walks around, touching its crumbling walls, viewing the austere frescoes renowned for their calculated symmetry, examining the icons in the little chancel, tasting the rose petal jam offered by the nuns, sipping cold water from the spring; but mostly it was to commission the weaving of a couple hand-spun cotton bedspreads, exquisite creations that grace the guest bedroom of my home in America.

On Homer's rock

Chios echoes with forgotten moments of history. Many great men—philosophers, astronomers, mathematicians, sculptors, and architects such as Homer, Glavkos, and Hippocrates—made Chios their home from time to time. As early as the 7th century BC, it was an independent naval power, with its own monetary system, minting its own gold coins with the Sphinx as its symbol.

Homeric rhapsodies flourished and many believe that the great epic poet was born there. Not far from the main town, on the fretted coastal road, is a huge boulder on which legend says Homer sat teaching. Years later I would sit with my husband Arthur on Homer's rock, sheltered by trees from the hot sun.

As well as the sunlight, Chios can harbor pockets of darkness and mystery. I have often wondered about the Franks—Christians following the Latin rites in the Eastern Mediterranean—who came to Chios; but they did not belong, and most of them were chased out by the Turks. But a few of their descendants remain in some of the Greek islands, especially the Gattilussis family in Chios whose ancestors had a tragic end, in 1566. The younger set—18 of them—were supposed to have committed suicide, to avoid the harem or the services to Janissaries. How could they have done what they did? I did go to meet that family, owners of a small apple orchard; they were a strange breed, a wild lot with roots from Genoa whose name meant "alley cats." Columbus must have known them, if he was not actually one of them! (Chios having been a Genoese possession from 1307 to 1566, the term "Genoese," when used in Chios, would come to mean something ancient, like a myth or a fairytale.)

Greece is a maritime nation by tradition, and shipping is arguably the oldest form of occupation of Greeks and the key element of Greek economic activity since ancient times. Greece has the largest merchant marine in the world, which is, after tourism, the largest contributor to the economy. Chios, with the tiny Island of Oinoussai off its northern shore, is the birthplace of many Greek shipowners. Forty percent of Greek ships are owned by Chian families with names like Rallis, Rodocanachi, Chandris, Lemos, Carras, Levanos, and Peraticos, among others. Michael Peraticos, a good friend of ours and a member of the Greek Shipping Hall of Fame, hosted my husband and me twice in his 90-foot catamaran, sailing among the Aegean islands. He would kid me about his origins in Kardamyla, a small town 15 miles north of Chios' city center, where my grandparents had their home. "We are a different race up North!" he would boast.

An open Mediterranean

But like many of his countrymen, my father and his Greek friends would find themselves boarding a ship for a new home across the water, where there fortunes to be made amidst a welter of spoken languages. In the distant past, many nationalities lived in Alexandria, trading and communicating with each other. Arabs spoke with Turks, Jews with Syrians, Armenians with Italians and Greeks. "The shudders of monetary transactions ripple through and divide them.... Where else on earth will you find such a mixture?" wrote Lawrence Durrell of the vibrant cosmopolis, the city in which the world as we knew it converged.

The people who held office on the Rue de France, the commercial heart of Alexandria, were the builders of the city. They were wholesalers, tradesmen, exporters, stockbrokers, moneychangers, moneylenders, industrialists, and bankers. My father was one of them.

Durrell put it best in one of the most quoted passages from *The Alexandria Quartet:* "The Alexandrians themselves were strangers and exiles to the Egypt which existed below the glittering surface of their dreams, ringed by the hot deserts and fanned by the bleakness of a faith which renounced worldly pleasures. The Egypt of rags and sores, of beauty and desperation. Alexandria was still Europe, the capital of Asiatic Europe, if such a thing could exist. It could never be like Cairo where the whole life had an Egyptian cast, where every one speaks Arabic; here French, Italian, Greek dominated the scene. The ambience, the social manner, everything was different, was cast in a European mold where somehow the camels and palm trees and cloaked natives existed only as a brilliantly colored frieze, a black cloth to a life divided in its origins."

As Robert Ilbert and Ilios Yannakakis would observe in their study of *Alexandria 1860-1960,* "If there exists such a thing as the Alexandrian myth, it is because she stood, for the best part of a century, as the symbol of an open Mediterranean unlike the sea of today, sealed along all its coasts by petty nationalism. This openness was not simply cosmopolitanism.

Alexandria was neither New York nor Paris. What was important was not the multiplicity of nationalities represented in the town but rather the interaction between it and those various peoples who came from all the different shores of a sea nominally Ottoman but indelibly marked by western imperialism. Alexandria was one of the last places where one could marry individual expansion to liberalism to traditional community ties." (One should note that this interaction existed on a business but not on a social level, at least among the middle class; it was different at a higher level of society.)

Many of the people who arrived in the late 19th century and the beginning of the 20th came from the Ottoman Empire's lands, with both a history and a lifestyle in common. Alexandria emerged not just as a staging post nor a port city. That would be to reduce it to a function of commerce. It was at once an Ottoman city, an international refuge, a European economic center, and a cultural pole of the Mediterranean basin.

Builders of a city-state

What is contained in the word "Alexandria"? A European city, a cosmopolitan city, an international resort; in the 1940s, only the minarets reminded you that you were still in Egypt.

Alexandria was not built by the Arabs nor was it the seat of British rule (occupied by Britain in 1882, Egypt remained a "veiled protectorate" until 1956). Alexandrian foreign communities, in all their ethnic and religious diversity, built the city themselves. In certain cases, families had settled there for generations, exuding pride as citizens in their city-state.

The only other city which paralleled Alexandria in its cosmopolitanism was Shanghai in the 1930s. With the establishment of the Shanghai international settlement and the French concession, the city flourished as a center of commerce between East and West. It became the undisputed financial hub of the Asia and Pacific region. Tea, silk, and porcelain sailed to Europe and America, and opium came in to pay for them. Alexandria was founded by Alexander the Great in 331 BC. Upon his death the throne passed to the Ptolemaic dynasty under which Alexandria became an important commercial city and the center of the Hellenistic world. Its prosperity was based on the exploitation of its fertile hinterland along the shores of Lake Mareotis (called Mariut today) where wheat, vines, and olive groves grew in abundance. The Ptolemys' desire was to make Alexandria the intellectual and cultural capital of the world. Ptolemy I conceived of a place that would bring together all the learning of the world as he commissioned the most important library of the ancient world: the Library of Alexandria. It held 900,000 papyrus scrolls written in many tongues, reflecting the ethnic mix in the capital. Among the most famous items in its collection were the original manuscripts of the Greek classics such as the great tragedies of Aeschylus, Sophocles, and Euripides, and translations of the Jewish scriptures.

We do not know when the library was destroyed and how. We know it was part of the Mouseion but do not know where exactly it stood. During the Roman civil war, a depot of manuscripts near the Eastern Port, known also as the Lesser Library, was destroyed by fire.

Ptolemy II followed his father's vision, completing the Pharos or lighthouse, one of the Seven Wonders of the ancient world —a symbol of Alexandria's economic power. It was also destroyed, this time by an earthquake in the 4th century. There is little trace remaining today of the ancient city. The Roman persecution of Christians and various epidemics, including the plague, decimated Alexandria.

(An intriguing member of the Ptolemaic dynasty who would fascinate and inspire numerous writers including Shakespeare and George Bernard Shaw was, of course, Cleopatra, after which one of the city quarters is named.)

Alexandria was invaded by the Persians at the beginning of the 6th century, and later in 641 by the Arabs who brought Islam.

Alexandria lost its position as Egypt's first city when Cairo became established as the country's capital. Alexandria was marginalized, its vitality destroyed, its population shrunk. On arrival, Napoleon found a miserable fishing village of five thousand people.

By 1805, Muhammad Ali arrived on the scene. He was an Albanian from Kavala, a small Ottoman town in Northern Greece, who proclaimed himself khedive and made himself master of the country after Nelson forced Napoleon's withdrawal. His ambition was to renew Egypt's links with the Mediterranean world, an aspiration that the country's rulers had lost sight of since medieval times. He greatly admired Bonaparte and France, and called in French engineers to oversee his construction schemes and summoned French experts to train a professional military and bureaucracy. He organized the administration, nationalized land, and planned new irrigation systems. Among his major achievements was the restoration of the Mahmoudiya Canal which, when completed in 1820, provided Alexandria for the first time in five centuries with a regular supply of drinking water and reconnected it to the Nile, thus giving the Egyptian hinterland access to the sea. Alexandria's port was expanded and the entire trade between Europe and Egypt passed through the Western harbor.

To attract capital and expertise, Muhammad Ali encouraged foreigners to settle in the city, especially Greeks and Syrians from the Ottoman Empire. He granted their own areas of the city, inside the desert city walls. Besides Greeks, English, French, Armenians, and other communities settled in the center of the new city, developing its European core.

The birth of a cosmopolis

The inauguration of the Suez Canal in 1869 marked the beginning of the cosmopolitan era of Alexandria.

Architects were hired to shape a city with broad avenues and parks, and as expansion continued, the walls were taken down and the suburbs extended, and by the mid-19th century a railway system was built, the oldest in Africa. A municipal council was later established with Egyptian nobles of Ottoman origin, leading Coptic families, and representatives of the foreign communities.

By the early 20th century Alexandria's population reached nearly half a million, about what it had been in Cleopatra's time. Thanks to Muhammad Ali, businesses grew, the city expanded, trade boomed, and immigrants flocked in.

Alexandria became Egypt's summer capital for five months of the year, from June to October. During King Farouk's time the entire court, the government ministers, and the entire diplomatic corps, including the British High Commissioner, descended from the sultry heat of Cairo (this has changed with air conditioning) to Alexandria for its Mediterranean breezes. The newspapers recorded the arrival of the King at Sidi Gaber in a ceremony elegant and snappy with plenty of military pomp. The judges of the Mixed Courts were among those who welcomed the King at his arrival at the train station at Sidi Gaber and who each autumn bade him farewell.

Cairo was, as is the case nowadays, visited in winter for its mild dry climate and abandoned in summer because of the great heat. In Alexandria, sea breezes blew without interruption and maintained the temperature at a moderate level.

The new Promised Land

Not without irony, Egypt became the new Promised Land. At the beginning of the19th century, Alexandria's population was13,000; by 1927, this had grown to 527,000, swelling further to 800,000 (about 500,000 of whom were foreigners) when I was growing up during the Second World War. The population stands over 6 million today. (Statistics vary according to the sources.)

Why did those immigrants come? Importuning them, besides economic opportunity, was the stability and the security of the region. In effect, the direct or indirect presence of the Great Powers during the Eastern Crisis (the decline of the Ottoman empire led to the emergence of a nationalistic movement by the Christian provinces of the Balkans) and the Britishoccupation of 1882 reassured the non-Muslim populations of the Ottoman Empire that Egypt was a stable country protected by the occupying power of England.

The men and women who landed in Alexandria were not true exiles. Here they found something of their previous life. Many had family connections, like my father; all had at least, acquaintances, and none were forced to lead a life according to different norms. Alexandria mirrored the complexity of

Ottoman society.

Foreigners were employed in administration and in construction, but mostly they were in commerce—the importation of industrial machinery, iron, weapons, and clothing for soldiers. The export trade consisted of agricultural products, notably cotton.

During the American Civil War from 1860 onwards, the cotton plantations in the southern states were destroyed, their exports to England blockaded. The drop in American sales created a boom for Egyptian and Indian cotton. Long-fiber cotton from Egypt, renowned for its quality, took a leading role in the global trade, and demand for it rocketed.

Greeks, Italians, Armenians, and Syrian-Lebanese arrived, but tended to remain within their own groups, where they had language and religion in common. There were also numerous Maltese, who were British subjects; in fact, the 1882 riots that ended with tragic bombardment of Alexandria by the British fleet stated with a quarrel between Egyptian and Maltese donkey owners. To supplement the consular authorities, each community elected representatives to look for its members' interests and help the needy. The community would own land, sometimes whole quarters of the city, the income of which was used to finance common enterprises—schools, places of worship, hospitals, theaters, clubs, and newspapers—and to care for the underprivileged through such means as orphanages and old people's homes.

The architects employed by the city were mostly Greeks and Italians. Some of those buildings have survived, neo-Byzantine or neo-Venetian in style, expressions of national sentiment. There were effectively two towns side by side that were unaware of each other. The Turkish town close to the port—with its enclaves of alleys, culs de sac, dotted with mosques, seedy hotels, and overhanging houses—was a town almost exclusively Egyptian, with a few poor immigrants. Surrounded by its colorful bustle, with smell of spices, the cries of men pushing handcarts and the stalls blocking your way, you felt very remote from the European city, even though that was just a few streets away. Few Europeans ventured into the Turkish town and few even knew it existed.

To the East of the port stretched the Corniche, the beaches which made Alexandria a seaside resort. On that thin tongue of land between Lake Mariut and the sea, known as Ramleh, the European town was built. Villas arose, and gardens and avenues sprang up. The Sporting Club with its race track and modern amenities was infinitely more attractive than the port of the Turkish town. Some of the city's villas reflected the taste and the wealth of that select group of Alexandrians whose villas offered spectacular panoramas of the city and the sea. Lawrence Durrell described those villas with their "long beautiful reception rooms pierced with alcoves and unexpected corners to increase their already great seating capacity and sometimes as many as two or three hundred guests sat down to elaborate and meaningless diners." The exclusive enclaves were Laurens, Rouchdy, and Glymenopoulo. The more modest enclaves such Camp Cesar, Ibrahimieh, Cleopatra, and Sporting were populated by middle-class Greeks, Italians, Jews, and a few aspiring Egyptians. The Greek community schools were established at Chatby in Ramleh, where stood the College Saint-Marc and the Lycée Français, while the Victoria College (renamed Nasser College) stood at the end of the Victoria tramline in Ramleh.

The economic growth of the port and cotton exports were responsible for the emergence of a wealthy class of merchants, who became benefactors—or philanthropists as they were well known at the time. They were the real builders of Alexandria.

This mercantile elite was fascinated by modernity. Within their community, they spread knowledge, ideas, skills, fashions, and ways of life which compared favorably with the great cities of Europe. These rich merchants and industrialists developed the cultural and social activities of the community and held privileged positions among their compatriots.

Europeans in Egypt

Prominent writers on Egyptian affairs such as Madame Jehan Sadat have provided interesting statistics on Europeans in Egypt.

At the start of World War II in 1940, Egypt's population stood at 15 million, half a million of them foreigners. Between Cairo and Alexandria the number of Greeks was reported at 300,000, the Italians 100,000, and another 100,000 persons of various nationalities, otherwise known as stateless. Most of the Greeks lived in Alexandria. Alexandria's population stands today at about 6 million with less than a thousand Greeks left, a paltry handful compared to hundreds of thousands 75 years ago.

Citizenship and ethnic origin did not always coincide. About 25 percent who considered themselves ethnically Greek, for example, were not Greek citizens. With the outbreak of wars grew the number of inhabitants who had been Ottoman subjects, including ethnic Greeks, Armenians, Syro-Lebanese and Jews from Asia Minor, Georgians, and those born in Greek settlements on the Black Sea: they were all communities cut down like branches of trees, lacking a parent body, dreaming of Eden. They were now considered stateless or were counted as Russians, Bulgarians, Persians, North Africans, or Egyptians. They lived in the poor quarters of the city among the locals. They bore no relation to the lovely streets and the beautiful villas decorated by foreigners, where wrote Durrell, "brokers sit and sip their morning papers."

Europeans who lived in Egypt enjoyed special rights. To attract foreigners, Khedive Ismael allowed the establishment of a judicial institution, the Mixed Courts (1875-1949) to bring a European-based legal order to foreign investments. It provided a venue to liquidate private debts but mainly to secure an environment for the continuing expansion of European investment in Egypt.

In reality they were European courts with European lawyers to prosecute and defend people. The court language was French; the codes were a modified version of the French civil code and British common law with some Islamic and local principles. A judge at the Court of Appeal at the Mixed Courts occupied one of the highest positions in the land as he was deeply immersed in Alexandrian affairs. Most of the time the head was British, although an American Judge, Jasper Yeates Brinton from Philadelphia, headed the court during the war years. The judges were Europeans: English, French, Italians, Greeks.

Europeans born in Egypt had the right to acquire Egyptian citizenship, but most elected to remain under the umbrella of their country of origin and thus be protected by the Mixed Courts. These tribunals were abolished in 1949, making Europeans subject to the Egyptian judicial system. Changes were coming to that cosmopolitan city.

A community of contrasts

I cannot dwell too much on the foreign communities as I had little exposure to them, but anyone who has lived in Alexandria would recognize two prominent names: those of Baron Felix de Menasce, the head of the Jewish community, and Oswald Finney, the unofficial head of the British community.

The Menasces, the wealthiest members of the Jewish community, lived in a huge, rambling house in the Moharrem Bey area of Alexandria. Their splendid garden was covered with palm trees, and their Tuesday afternoon piano concerts were an Alexandrian institution. The area they lived in was an upper-class neighborhood comparable to the Quartier Grec.

Of Hungarian origin, the family had served as the private bankers of Khedive Ismail. They remained through generations as merchants and moneylenders, but they diversified beyond banking into road construction, waterworks, and landholdings in Upper Egypt, primarily for the cultivation of sugar cane and cotton. Their involvement in arms smuggling prior to the establishment of Israel is well documented.

The Jews were strongly represented in high positions in the social world of Alexandria. They were conspicuous in the city's intellectual life. It was more likely, according to Judge Brinton, to meet at Jewish homes the luminaries of the European literary world.

Glymenopoulo was where the Finneys—Oswald and his wife Josa—lived; they were the richest foreigners in Egypt. Oswald was a major player in the cotton trade. He had his finger in every pie, according to his wife's memoirs. He had diversified businesses: oxyacetylene, the making of yeast (my brother would work for the Finneys after the war as a chemist in their yeast factory), and the distribution of milk. He had wide investments in property, and was the town's top publisher, as proprietor of the leading English and French language newspapers, the *Egyptian Gazette, the Egyptian Mail, Le Progrés Egyptien,* and *La Bourse Egyptienne.* The Egyptian Gazette, a four-page weekly tabloid, would fold by 1952 with the departure of English troops. Finney also served as president of the Alexandria Commercial Company, the Alexandria Insurance Company, and the Filiature Nationale, the leading textile company, and was member of the Minet El Basel stock exchange. He endowed the Victoria College with a prestigious scholarship.

The Finneys' fabulous and legendary wealth epitomized the gilded age of Alexandria prior to the war. Their spectacular balls, recounted and photographed in the local papers and tabloids, became part of Alexandrian lore and gossip. The world's finest tapestries hung on the walls of their ballroom. Laurence Durrell described the Carnival Ball in *Balthazar,* the second volume of the Quartet. A documentary titled *Aleksandrike,* produced in 2011 by a Slovenian director, recounts some incidents in Finney's life. Oswald Finney died in Cape Town in 1942, and his wife returned at the end of the war. Their enterprises and house—as those of all foreigners—were sequestered by Nasser in 1960; years later President Sadat returned the house to Mrs. Finney. Empty now, it stands on the Corniche at Glymenopoulo, dusted by a faithful retainer.

The Italian community had a long history, and was large but less well organized. They had a smaller elite and were generally of a more humble social level. While the Greek middle class was quite independently minded as entrepreneurs, making their way in businesses large and small, this was less true of the Italians, who for most part were manual workers and clerks. Many Italians were of Egyptian birth but claimed Italian nationality simply to enjoy the protection of the Mixed Courts. With the Italian occupation of the Dodecanese, a number of Greeks held Italian papers, and so many were interned during the war, including a good friend of my father. Many Italians were receptive to Mussolini's dream of a fascist Mediterranean.

The Swiss, another small community, had their wealth based in cotton. Alfred Reinhardt, a widely respected gentleman whose company traded in cotton yarn, headed the community for over twenty years. The Swiss played crucial role in the Filiature Nationale d'Egypte, the cotton spinning community sponsored health projects and was founder of the Red Crescent organization for Alexandrian youths. The Swiss were also active in hotel management. There was hardly a hotel in Cairo or Alexandria where one could not find a Swiss staff member—the Shepheard Hotel in Cairo, the Mena House at the foot of the Pyramids, the Windsor Palace in Luxor, the Cataract in Aswan. The Beau Rivage in Alexandria, owned by a Swiss, hosted many glamorous receptions and weddings. Though bearing an Italian name, Groppi, the famous café, had been founded in the early 20th century by a Swiss pastry chef and chocolatier. Also eminent members of the Swiss community were the Allemans who undertook to build the Swiss School.

While at university, I was often a guest of our friends Renzo and Louise Alleman at their Rouchdy residence. Renzo was a cotton *classificateur*, someone who graded the quality of Egyptian cotton. Their villa was luxurious—the first home where I saw a walk-in closet, as we of the middle class had armoires. Their garden was something exceptional; a dash of colors from the dahlias and zinnias stood against the green backdrop of fan-shaped traveler palm and tall clumps of graceful bamboo. It had a flowering forest of violets, ginger lilies and fragrant frangipani. The papyrus —the oldest and most emblematic of Egyptian plants—graced an orna-mental oval-shaped pond. The Allemans gifted me with the first novel in English I ever owned: *Gone with the Wind*, the widely acclaimed work of Margaret Mitchell. It was the talk of the town, the long-running movie being so popular.

Years later in 1961, on our way to Australia, my husband Arthur and I stopped by Zurich and were hosted by the Allemans at their stunning home overlooking the lake. Renzo as a hobby was growing cacti which he exhibited around the world, including what was then the Soviet Union. Until his death Renzo remained the major shareholder of Swiss Air. It was Arthur's first encounter with a multilingual household where the conversation was carried in German, French, Italian, and Greek according to the participants; English was used with us their guests, while they communicated in Arabic with their Sudanese household.

The Greeks in Egypt

The Greeks had a thriving presence in Egypt from the Hellenistic period until the aftermath of the Egyptian Revolution of 1952.

Herodotus visited Egypt in the 5th century and claimed that the Greeks were one of the first group of foreigners who ever lived there. Greek culture and political influence continued and perhaps reached its most influential times during the Ottoman Caliphate. On the eve of the 19th century it was reported that a knot of Greek families lived close to the patriarchate.

In 1907 the official census showed 62,400 Greeks. The number increased to about 300,000 during the Second World War; they were mostly located in Alexandria, while smaller communities emerged in Cairo, Port Said, Mansurah in the Delta, and Upper Egypt. Greeks were flocking to Alexandria at a greater rate than to Cairo, accessibility to the port being the magnet.

Muhammad Ali, who had been born in Greece, maintained a strong connection with the Greeks and encouraged their settlement. Initially they put roots around the church and monastery of Agios Savas, the seat of the Patriarch. In time, the community began to organize itself, and as their number increased the need was soon felt for schools to cater to their children'seducation.

The contribution of the Greeks in the financial life of Egypt was very important. The first banks in Egypt were created by Greeks, like the Bank of Alexandria, the Anglo-Egyptian founded by the Synadinos family, and the General Bank of Alexandria.

Also, it was the Greek agriculturists and farmers who were the first to syste-matically cultivate cotton and tobacco. With improvements in both quantity and quality, the opportunities for export increased. Initially Greek business-men enjoyed a virtual monopoly, but other Westerners followed soon.

It was after the American Civil War in the 1860s that Greek migrants flocked to Alexandria, and they continued to arrive in great numbers until the mid-1920s. (I believe my father came in 1922, in his late thirties.) The social composition of the first Greeks was very mixed. Alongside the bankers, the cotton landowners, the exporters, and the industrialists were a mass of artisans, small shopkeepers, street peddlers, hawkers of newspapers and lottery tickets, waiters, and taxi drivers. Until the tobacco industry was mechanized in the 1920s, most of the skilled workers were Greeks.

Among the most prominent families who dominated the commerce were the Salvagos, the Benakis, and the Choremis—those three families were interrelated by marriage, and all dealt in cotton—in addition to the Rodochanakis and the Zervoudakis families. One of the Zervoudakis sons was my brother's classmate.

Many of the prominent Greeks had come from important Greek commercial centers under Turkish rule, where they were part of the mercantile bourgeoisie trading between the Ottoman Empire and Europe—"the remnants of Byzantium," as someone called them.

The development of Alexandria was not limited to cotton but spread into food manufacturing, such as the business of our friends the Melachrinos family, who made Italian pasta. Others made wine such as the Gianaklis, while the Drakos family (Eleftheria Drakos before her marriage *née* Kouk-las was my primary Greek schoolteacher) manufactured carbonated water; yet others produced or were engaged in the Sinalco orange juice, soap, oil presses, breweries, wood crafts, and printing industries.

The cotton profits financed most of Egypt's infrastructure. The "white gold," as it was called then, made notable families extremely wealthy, and Alexandria's prosperity as a whole depended on it. The elite class comprised the cotton landowners and growers, the cotton exporters, the cotton brokers, the cotton classificateurs, the cotton seed oil manufacturers, and the bankers who financed them. They were the few people besides the pashas and courtiers who owned an automobile and who enrolled their children in private schools. This does not imply that everyone was well off, but there definitely was a prosperous middle class within every foreign enclave. Even the less affluent could have a maid for a pittance.

An aristocracy emerges

Thus emerged an aristocracy among the Alexandrian Greeks. Among them, the Salvagos family was reported to have owned 900 fedans (i.e., 1,450 acres), cultivating cotton in the delta in addition to their extensive real estate investments in Cairo and Alexandria.

The generosity of the wealthy families was unparalleled. Having made their fortune in Egypt, they stood at the heart of the city. They created a broad network of communal institutions, schools, orphanages, hospitals, nursing homes, food kitchens, and a variety of leisure and athletic societies, most of them run by the city-based community organizations which were often also headed by them.

The support of social and philanthropic works excited the pride of all Greeks and drew the admiration, perhaps even the envy, of the other foreign communities. Their contributions led to the great legacy of Greek-Egyptian philanthropy.

This does not imply that there were no rivalries or tensions among the elite leaders vying for the presidency of the Greek community. Where pride was involved, much money was spent.

Take the tram along Ramleh today—as you pass through Mazarita and Chatby, you will notice imposing structures such as the Salvagion, a vocational school established by Miké Salvagos, who held for 25 years the presidency of the Greek Alexandrian community; the Benakion, the girls' orphanage established by Emmanuel Benaki; the Kaniskerion, the boys' orphanage built by George Kaniskeris, to which my father was a minor contributor. Theodoros Kotsikas, a philanthropist from Cairo who built his wealth in the manufacturing of alcohol from sugar-cane, erected the Greek Hospital of Alexandria; although the name has disappeared, the hospital decades later is considered the best in the city. The signs of those buildings may have faded but they still stand.

Some Greeks in Egypt gave back to Greece itself. Michael Tositsas donated huge funds for the building of the University of Athens, in addition to a

Greek school in Alexandria; Georgios Averoff, a renowned benefactor, established the Greek high school my brother attended and also built the National Technical University in Athens, a marble stadium which was still used in the latest Olympic games. He gave the Greek navy its first battleship. And again Emmanuel Benaki, an art lover and collector, the most stylish figure in Alexandria, built the National Gallery of Athens while his son Anthony founded the Benaki Museum.

The Benaki Museum opposite the National Garden in Athens on Queen Sofia Avenue is the repository of the art collection of the Benaki family who lived in Alexandria. Their collection of 37,000 Islamic and Byzantine objects was donated to the nation and is maintained by their foundation. More recently more artifacts were added with donations from other sources. I was eager to view that Alexandrian Benaki collection: the jewelry, the arms, the medals, the porcelains, the embroideries—almost every sort of art in the finest example.

In the 1950s, when I visited that museum, I focused on the ethnographic section with its stunning display of embroidered costumes from Greek villages and from the islands. While there, I noticed a portly, bald gentleman settledin a comfortable chair, drawing. A couple hours later as I was leaving, I noticed that he was still sitting sketching, this time in front of another exhibit. Photography then as now was prohibited. I was curious and inquired at the registration desk what that gentleman was doing, sketching for hours. "He is Mr. Christian Dior, the recipient of a special permit," I was told. The finest examples of Greek embroideries, of ecclesiastical patterns, were being copied, to be replicated for French *haute couture*.

The museum collection has traveled widely in the last few years to Canada, the United States, and Australia. Major renovations had been accomplished; the Islamic art and Chinese porcelains were moved to a satellite location; the Benaki Museum is today focused solely on Greece.

The social life of Greeks

The social life of Greeks revolved to a large extent around their clubs, their churches, their schools, and their associations. As with all Alexandrians,

Greeks spoke several other languages, particularly French and Italian with English added in the 1950s.

While the *fellahin*—the Egyptian peasant—picked the cotton and baled it under the scorching sun, it was the Greeks who served as the industry's backbone, employed as cotton ginners, insurers, accountants, and clerks in the exporting houses and the banking institutions.

The Greek middle class included teachers, journalists, commission-based merchants, restaurant owners, grocery shop owners, maritime agents, medical doctors, and lawyers. All made a good living in the city's cosmopolitan milieu, enjoying the privileges of the colonial life.

There was definitely an aura of snobbery among the cotton barons. They were, in wealth and culture, a world apart from the rest of the Greeks, the middle class who supported them. They spent their summer holidays in Greece; among them it was a point of honor to speak French, hiring only French or English nannies for their children. Glittering gatherings were held in their Alexandrian homes. Their names were Westernized or Anglicized. I recall my brother noting that Salvagos, Choremi, and Benaki had three syllables in their names, while ours, Leotsinidis, had six. The shorter the better—not Michalis Salvagos, but Michel or Miké Salvagos.

That Greek aristocracy lived in a special enclave of the city called the Quartier Grec, although they owned second homes in Ramleh, along the Glymenopoulo promenade on the Corniche or among the exclusive British and Swiss villas of Rouchdy. Ilias Yannakakis would note that the Quartier Grec, however, "was not a ghetto, it was porous, socially mobile and well inserted in the psychology of the town." Leading Greek medical doctors, including our dentist Dr. Frangoudis, had their clinic in the Quartier Grec. My godmother was a regular visitor to her husband's family, as a branch of the Karalis lived there. They are all gone now; the Salvagos house, a classical villa which with its gardens occupied an entire city block, is now the Russian Cultural Center.

The *Journal of the Hellenic Diaspora* would note that "The Greek community did not mix with Egyptians and other foreigners, nor did enjoy complete autonomy from the haute bourgeoisie which ruled over the official communities and philanthropic associations. The Greeks were closely integrated with their own ethnic community and within this community there was a critical mass of members whose jobs and livelihoods depended on the ruling industrial and business class."

Greek associations had an exclusive Greek membership; our Egyptian friend Ali el Kouni could not join one as a member, and was not allowed to enter; he had to be admitted as my brother's personal guest. Clearly, most Greeks still saw Arabs as inferior, potentially dangerous, and unreliable. This perception was not unique to the Greeks, and was shared by other communities.

At the same time, a purely Egyptian culture was evolving, a culture which achieved particular distinction in music, sculpture, architecture, film, and literature. But this was something I would learn about only much later. Growing up, both at school and at home, I never heard of an Egyptian culture except for the Pharaonic civilization of antiquity.

II.

A YOUTH IN ALEXANDRIA

NOW LET ME tell the story of my youth in Alexandria.

I was born in 1936 in a clinic located on top of the Delices pastry shop, which could be why I am so fond of sweets! Following Greek custom, I was named Ioulia, later anglicized to Julie, after my paternal grandmother who had died a decade earlier, overriding my mother's wish to name me Nicole. Ioulia then became Ioulaki then Laki, but the diminutive did not stick long as I entered the French Lyçée at the age of three as Julie. Still somehow I retain Laki as my favorite password on the Internet, with the addition of a few more numerals and characters.

My baptism, I would be told, was a grand event. As the daughter of wealthy parents, I was lavished with the finest that money could buy— blankets, hand-embroidered bibs, soft cottons, delicate voile dresses, and a golden cross with a large diamond in the middle that I still keep. My parents fussed over their little girl, who filled them with joy.

I learned to be thankful for my given name, which could have been one of those ancient Greek goddesses or another saint of the Greek Orthodox church. This does not mean that Julie as a name did not have its drawbacks. French literature of the 17th century—Corneille, Racine, Moliere—is filled with maids all named Julie. I often cried when my classmates teased me for being named after a maid. At least that was until Madame Heranger, our French teacher, advised us to wait for the next year, when we would study the 18th century and the dignity of the name Julie would be restored. Indeed, in Jean Jacques Rousseau's masterpiece *La Nouvelle Heloise*, the heroine was named Julie, and I felt vindicated.

I did not sport a middle name, and later in America that would prove to be a problem. From my Social Security card, to the admission application to the University of Minnesota, an "X" was inserted as my middle initial! Computers had to recognize a middle name. With marriage, I was able to substitute it with an "L", the initial of my family name (Leotsinidis) when I became a "Hill."

My brother Triandafillos was nine years older than me, and was also Alexandria-born. Named after our paternal grandfather, my brother did not like his name and preferred like so many Greek boys to be called by the diminutive of Akis.

In Greece, someone called Panayiotis becomes, as a child, Panayiotakis, i.e. little Panayiotis. It has an endearing intention (a bit like saying,in America, darling or beloved); then the name is shortened to something like Takis, and these diminutives fade as a child grows up.

But my brother remained Akis all his life. Our parents, family, and friends all called him Akis. He even wanted to use that name in his schoolwork, in exam papers, even on University registration forms. He sometimes succeeded but in his passport he remained Triandafillos, with Byron as a middle name. Where did the Byron come from? A literary reference? An important figure of that time? Although he adopted his middle name when he emigrated to America (as initially his employer and his American friends could not use Triandafillos, and called him Mr. "T"), for me he remained Akis.

Akis also anglicized his surname from Leotsinidis to Leonard. He appeared before a judge in his new hometown of Chicago to explain the change. Other applicants wanting to alter their names from Cohen to Coen or Kohen faced many questions from the judge, but when my brother's turn came wishing to change his from Triandafillos Leotsinidis to Byron Leonard, it took 30 seconds for the judge to say "Approved—next!"

I once asked my parents if we could claim any eminent ancestors. No one of significance, they answered, but there was emotion in their voice as they mentioned that their grandfather, Xenophon, had served as a seaman under Admiral Constantine Kanaris who gained fame during the Greek war of Independence. Might Xenophon have been a naval hero from way back?

Chios has always been renowned for its mastic gum favored by the Turkish sultans, who left the island mostly unperturbed during their four centuries of occupation. Was it the mastic gum or the provision of maidens for their harem that placated these rulers? They must have been beautiful women, as can be gleaned from a marble statue from 5 BC in a museum in Boston, known as the "Chios Daughters."

The family owned vineyards on both sides of the strait. My father's memories of his adolescence took him back to Asia Minor, to wine-rich Cesme, to the old house with a blaze of flowers on the beds, to the fig trees laden with fruit ripe by September. "We had thirty people sleeping in the living room," my father would recall, "in the days before the forced deportations, the expulsions, the executions…" and his breathing would pause in a trembling silence. That place in Cesme must have been very large; I heard him saying that the number of people staying was never constant, and expanded or contracted according to the help needed for grape harvesting. Sometimes visitors arrived for a few days and stayed for weeks, but no one minded. My grandfather—whom I never met—must have been well off at that time, taking in people who needed hospitality.

An exodus across the sea

Greeks of Asia Minor—settlers for centuries if not millennia—were driven from all over Anatolia to Smyrna, following Kemal Ataturk's cry "To the Mediterranean!" In 1922 more than a million and half Greek refugees converged in Smyrna; there were battles, the town went up in flames, and more than a million refugees fled by sea across the Aegean; tens of thousands more who could not escape met their deaths in fire and massacres. All their holdings, homes, and agricultural lands were now in the hands of the Turks. Their lives were in ruins, their world destroyed. My family was one of them.

Father held three birth certificates to avoid the Ottoman draft, although he could not recall which the correct one was! His Greek passport, issued years later, identified him as an "exchangeable." He held the key to the Cesme house, one of those old-pistol-spring types such as one sees sometimes in medieval English houses. It is in my person today, the only souvenir left from those times.

These days one takes the ferry to cross the strait from Chios to Cesme. It sails at dawn every day, at the same hour, at the same speed. You could hear the faint drumming of engines as it cuts through the water; half an hour into the voyage, as it reaches midway into the channel, the blue and white Greek flag is lowered, and the Turkish red and white flag is hoisted; the reverse procedure is observed on its return.

Michael Psomathakis—whom we affectionately called "Barbas" (uncle)—moved to Egypt after World War I. As the Ottoman Empire crumbled, many of its subjects fled to foreign shores, and to these migrants, Egypt represented a "Far West" rich in economic potential, just a short 36-hour hour voyage away. A Greek community already existed in Alexandria, and it would have been easy for Barbas to become part of it. Educated in Smyrna, he spoke Greek, Turkish, and French, he found in Alexandria the same climate, the same regime, and the same country organization as prevailed in Asia Minor. He possessed some capital from the family vineyards but also from comprador activities in Asia Minor and Constantinople.

Foreigners were protected by commercial treaties known as the Capitulations that exempted them from taxation and judicial control. For them, Alexandria and all Egypt was a veritable free zone and they formed a society which, though settled in Egypt, was always looking westward.

My father, Panayiotis Leotsinidis, was expelled in 1922 after the events in Izmir. Greece was impoverished, still a nascent country. Father did not consider alternatives but followed his uncle who had already settled in Alexandria a few years earlier.

Nephews and nieces

Barbas was an uncommonly able man, and with his import-export business, he held a seat in Alexandria's Greek Chamber of Commerce. Lively and cultivated, he moved in the higher social circles, and counted leading Egyptians as his friends. He remained resolutely single all his life, no matter how many eager matchmakers approached him and how many prominent fathers tried to lure him with attractive and handsome dowries. He was determined to support nephews and nieces and rebuild what the family had lost in Asia Minor. There were dowries to provide to his nieces Katina and Elpiniki, my father's cousins. Both were given in style; his two nieces were married off with lavish ceremonies. And so it was no surprise for Barbas to see his nephew Panayiotis, my father, well established.

I can imagine Father then—a small, thin man who in winter wore a dark suit, waistcoat, a shirt with a stiffly starched collar, and cuffs and cufflinks (the shiny gold ones for special occasions), and always a tie, even on hot summer days. His summer suits were tailored from lightest wool fabrics. Father traded in spices and grain, and his company had either a branch or a representative in Piraeus, Marseilles, and Calcutta; I knew that in Piraeus, he had an office headed by a Mr. Stefanidis. His accountant, a Mr. Kleanthis, was engaged in the mornings, and proceeded to another merchant office in the afternoons.

Aunt Katina, a sociable woman, had access to prominent Greek families due to the position of her late husband—a distinguished barrister and a graduate of Basel University in Switzerland—at the "Mixed Tribunals." She was also sought after for her embroidery skills. She embroidered dowries for the daughters of many wealthy Greeks. An avid needle worker, she bought embroidery patterns at the crafts store, but she also designed and traced her own patterns which give a touch of uniqueness to her work, an individuality appreciated by the discriminating ladies of the Greek elite. Her Byzantine, ecclesiastical-inspired designs were stunning, but what was most in demand were the flowery motifs in vogue in France at that time. She executed stitching, crewelwork, *petits points*, and appliqué meticulously, employing these techniques on tablecloths, runners, tray-cloths, pillowcases, handkerchiefs, and nightgowns. But Mother resented the fact that Aunt Katina never offered to embroider anything for me.

Her needlework opened doors to the Alexandrian elite, who invited her for tea—a stylish affair among the society hostesses—when an embroidered tablecloth was delivered.

Her elder sister Aunt Elpiniki—whose husband, a businessman and avid poker player, passed away recently—was my godmother, our most frequent visitor. She had an aristocratic outlook and demeanor, the product of a privileged upbringing by Barbas. Her husband, Uncle Dimitri, belonged to one of the prominent Alexandrian families—the Karalis, who were cotton exporters. With my mother, Aunt Elpiniki tried to enjoy the comforts that life in Egypt had to offer.

Aunt Elpiniki gifted me with a doll every New Year. For the Greek Orthodox, St. Basil is the equivalent of Santa Claus, bringing gifts, toys, and sweets to children on New Year's Eve—not on Christmas as in the Western world. I recall receiving a blue-eyed baby doll, so exquisite in its pink dress and pink bonnet. My parents did not give me any toys, but rather books of history, a children's encyclopedia, and even travel brochures. A black and white brochure with pictures of London inflamed my dream to visit that great metropolis. I read everything I could get my hands on with childish pleasure. My parents also gave me games such as Snakes and Ladders, Monopoly, dominoes, and a chess set. On New Year, however, I was gifted with a gold coin, a tradition that my husband preserved. Decades later I would find myself the recipient of a valuable gold collection.

A Greek from Constantinople

My mother Urania was barely educated—girls rarely were in Turkey; she completed only primary school, but she was such a bright woman. With her elder sister Aunt Aphrodite and younger brother Uncle Peter, she was raised by a stepmother, because their own mother died at the age of 22 at childbirth. Her father Nicholas was a charcoal wholesaler who brought his goods on a horse-drawn *araba* or cart from the coalmines to a warehouse from where it got distributed to Istanbul neighborhoods. Mother recalled how dark her father looked covered with soot as he returned from his weekly voyage. It took a day or even two, depending on the weather, to reach the coal mines close to what is now Bulgaria; back then the entire area was part of the Ottoman Empire.

Mother's most vivid recollection of Istanbul had to do with the fires that engulfed entire neighborhood of the city quite regularly. Houses were mostly made of wood and burned easily like matchsticks.

She recalled the Bekçi Baba, a fearsome-looking fellow with a dark cloak flapping behind him. He carried a large, thick stick, the bottom of which was bound with an iron rim, and with this he went *tak-tak-tak* on the cobblestones shouting: *"Yangivar! Yangivar! Beyoglu!"* or "Fire! Fire at Beyoglu!", spacing out his words carefully and clearly, so that no one should misunderstand.

Mother would jump out of bed and run to the window to see if the fire was at their neighborhood. Fortunately, their house was never affected, but the fear of fire persisted with her, especially with the raids during the war. She would shout the word "Yangivar!" as an expression close to "Oh my God!"

The Bekçi Baba was attached to a police station, and years ago had many and varied tasks. During the day he brought vats of drinking water to the houses, and during the night he patrolled a street as a watchman. He beat the drum during Ramadan or any other religious holiday like the Bayram. He announced important tidings and knew the residents of every house under his patrol, but mostly he gave warning if there was a fire in any part of Istanbul. There is still a Bekçi Baba in Turkey, but the "Baba" has been dropped and his duties are less onerous than they were in the old days.

My mother was 28 years old when she married my father Panayiotis, who was by then 42. She patiently waited ten years for him, which was part of the Greek tradition to see female siblings married and established first. (My brother in America would follow that tradition, marrying three months after me although he was nine years older.) My father provided a hefty dowry to his sister Aunt Argyro, in addition of financing his brother-in- law's medical specialization in Paris. Upon his return to Chios, Uncle Michael Nyhas became the chief medical doctor of the island. A philanthropist, he built wells in the countryside and fountains in village squares, and renovated the primary school of the village of Elata where my ancestors came from; he treated monks and nuns at the island's monasteries, and provided for their medication. Most significantly he emerged as a leader of the resistance against the Germans during World War II.

Not knowing of his activities, the Germans consulted him on medical issues; years later Germans who were stationed in Chios returned to the island as tourists, wanting to meet the doctor. The war having ended, Michael Nyhas graciously opened his door to the German visitors.

Uncle Michael persuaded my father to invest funds in Egypt, in ventures that Nasser's regime would sequester later. Because of this, some friction would arise, not with my uncle but his wife, my father's sister, Aunt Argyro. I would be the one years later to heal the rift.

The heritage of Byzantium

Although my mother left Istanbul when she was seventeen, its culture was so powerful, almost mystical, that it remained indelibly in her mind, which was not unusual for anyone who traced their roots to Byzantium.

The textbooks note that Istanbul, the largest city of Turkey in the northwest part of the country, stands on both sides of the Bosphorus at its entrance into the Sea of Marmara. Founded in 660 BC as Byzantium, it was re-founded in AD 330 by Constantine the Great, and under the name Constantinople it became the capital of the Eastern Roman, or Byzantine, Empire. The city was sacked by Crusaders in 1204 and taken by the Turks in 1453.

Istanbul was chosen as the city's official name in 1930 after the founding of the modern Republic of Turkey, the successor state of the Ottoman Empire. Interestingly, Istanbul's three syllables comprise three Greek words —in stin poli—meaning "to the city." But Turks do not like to hear that the city's new name has a Greek origin.

Greeks have emotional and historical ties to that famously rich city on the Dardanelles, the only city situated in two continents; the Greek presence there lasted two millennia, only to end abruptly in the 20th century.

To be a Greek from Constantinople meant obeying a set of social and religious conventions that dated back centuries and almost never changed with the times—rules that spelled precisely how to live and how to die, how to be stoic, never showing emotion and never crying as though one were from ancient Sparta, how to marry and raise children. Traditions observed during the holidays adhered to rigorous rules: baking the *tsoureki*, a brioche-like bread, formed in braided strands of dough and sprinkled with almonds and sesame seeds to be served with Easter eggs; the eggs were dyed red, as they represented the blood of Christ. The rules also prescribed the making of the Sign of the Cross with a lit candle, the flame carefully transported after the Easter Resurrection service, at the front entrance of one's door, a practice that went back for centuries to Byzantium. They called for the placing of a gold coin inside a wine goblet—a fluted champagne glass in later years—on New Year's Day, to bring prosperity to the years to come.

Traditional sweets were always baked for the holidays. *Kourabiethes*, shortbread cookies covered with powder sugar, were customarily made for the New Year, although they were prepared for other celebrations such as baptisms, birthdays, and weddings; the sugar signified something sweet and desirable, i.e., prosperity, but mostly a long life so the celebrant 's hair would turn white.

My father was not religious, being too inquisitive to accept Christian teaching, suspecting that God must have flirted through religion with a hurried nod in his direction. The only time I can recall him going to church was at the Easter Resurrection service at midnight, as it was too late for us children to go alone, with Mother in the kitchen preparing the festive midnight meal.

Was my mother religious? She was adamant, very strict about Lent during Holy Week; Father abstained but made an egg salad, as I shall later explain in greater detail. I also recall that, at Epiphany, the priest from the Taxiarchis church and the deacon would come to bless our house and the three or four icons we had in the bedroom. I still have one of those icons, which I would write about in a book and count among my most treasured possessions.

Did my mother invite the priest, or it was part of the priest's duties to visit Greek homes and pocket a contribution? I do not know.

Mother also faithfully went to Cairo at St. George's festival on April 23rd and spent the night in vigil at the church. St. George's Church was one of the most beautiful Orthodox churches in Egypt, and it still functioning; Nasser left it alone as, for some reason, many Muslims visit and even pray there. There must be some connection between Muslims and St. George's, but despite inquiries with those who might know, I still have no clear answer to this mystery. While visiting St. George's in 2015, I learned that a large number of Copts and Muslims visited the shrine of Saint Georges on Fridays and Saturdays. The Holy Family is said to have taken shelter in a place now covered by the church. Mary is the only female mentioned in the Koran, and neither the Prophet Muhammad's wife or his daughter Fatima is mentioned, hence for Muslims it is a place of veneration. The church has been destroyed and burned many times. Renovations were undertaken and it finally reopened in 2014. It is culturally interesting, for amidst a fury of burning candles, scenes from Saint George's valiant fight for Christianity are depicted through the art of many different styles, periods, and media.

Did Mother go to the festival because she was religious, or was she just taking the luxurious bus once a year to Cairo to visit her friends, with the church providing the excuse? My brother and I often talked often about Mother's religion, and we concluded that she was just following tradition more as a part of her Byzantine heritage rather than a matter of faith.

Sometimes the line between religion and folk belief got blurred. During the 12-day battle of Alamein, with the German army only 60 miles from Alexandria, Mother declared one morning: "The Germans will never reach the city. I saw Agios Minas in a dream last night, and he held his palm in front of me like a stop sign." Agios Minas was not one of those saints whose name day was celebrated, but was one of many miracle-working saints venerated by the Greeks. Born in Egypt in the 3rd century AD and often invoked by Kazantzakis, Minas was considered the protector of cities and patron Saint of Heraklion in Crete. When a German bomb hit the cathedral of Heraklion and failed to explode, the miracle was attributed to Agios Minas, bolstering my mother's confidence in her dream.

Indeed, for my mother, brought up in Istanbul, religion represented tradition. We attended Christmas and Easter celebrations and church festivals commemorating a particular saint whose name was associated with that particular church.

The rites of Easter

Easter is the most significant and sacred time on the Orthodox calendar. We fasted during Holy Week, as Mother observed the rules she grew up with, not questioning the myriad prohibitions imposed by the Greek Orthodox Church: no meat, no fish, (i.e., fish with spines; shell fish was permitted), no eggs and dairy products, and no vegetable oils or anything of animal origin. In the spirit of Lent and abstinence Mother created a slew of enduring recipes, named for what they were not, such as "Lenten fish" which was nothing more than simmered leeks, as they resembled small fish, forbidden during the fast. Dinner consisted mostly of lentil soup sprinkled with vinegar or cooked with orzo and topped with caramelized onions. Mother would bake a *tahinopitta*, a cake using a *tahina*, a sesame-based paste, and Lenten pies filled with raisins, all-spice, and sesame seeds which we devoured. Wine was permitted in my family during Lent, except on Good Friday.

Father asked if any of the colored Easter eggs were cracked—you needed perfect eggs for Easter Sunday—and it was the only time I saw my father engrossed in preparing a meal. Patiently sitting in his dining room chair, using fork and knife, he cut the eggs into tiny morsels, then mashed them with his fork before adding a few drops of olive oil; this was his egg salad, his way of refusing to observe Lent. My brother and I were green with envy.

When we asked Father why he did not adhere to the fasting rules, he commented that the monks, priests, and bishops had their own interpretation of those rules, and he had his. While visiting Mount Athos, where he spent couple of nights at the monastery, he was offered a delicious bean soup. The beans were simmered with a huge quantity of black olives, oozing with oil, giving the soup such a great flavor—after all olives were a interpretation of those rules, and he had his. While visiting Mount Athos, where he spent couple of nights at the monastery, he was offered a delicious bean soup. The beans were simmered with a huge quantity of black olives, oozing with oil, giving the soup such a great flavor—after all olives were a fruit. There was even a rumor that our local Archbishop gorged on lobster tails or other shellfish, expensive items beyond the means of lay people. There were so many exceptions to the rule, Father would say, and so as to not upset my mother, he would add that, without judging what others believed was appropriate, he would stick to eating "simply and modestly."

On Good Friday, with my mother, I attended the services at Taxiarchis, the neighborhood Greek Orthodox church, and we stood among the faithful as the touching and beautiful procession went on.

> *When I go there, into a church of the Greeks,*
> *with its aroma of incense,*
> *its liturgical chanting and harmony,*
> *the majestic presence of the priests,*
> *dazzling in their ornate vestments,*
> *the solemn rhythm of their gestures…*

From "*In Church*," C.P. Cavafy

Easter is always a joyful celebration; the Paschal matins, the Paschal hours, are followed by the divine Paschal liturgy. At its completion all lights in the church building are extinguished and we wait in darkness and silence for the stroke of midnight. Then a new flame is struck at the altar, or the priest lights his candle from the perpetual light kept burning there, and then lights candles held by the deacons or other assistants, who then go to light candles held by the congregation (this practice has its origin of the Holy Fire at the Church of the Holy Sepulcher in Jerusalem). Then the priest and the congregation go in a procession around the church, holding lit candles and chanting "*Christos Anesti*"—Christ is risen! The bells are sounded, and firecrackers explode in the church courtyard. We return home with paper lanterns in hand (today made in China), and with the candle lit from the "holy light"— a symbol of the revelation from Christ's sepulcher after his resurrection—we make over the door the Sign of the Cross, its black outline clearly visible at daylight the following morning. Among others, the priest blesses Paschal eggs and baskets brought by the faithful containing those foods that had been forbidden during Lent. We never brought any eggs to be blessed, and instead rushed home.

Much later, when we went to America, at Saints Constantine and Helen Church in San Diego and St. Andrews in Chicago where my brother served as a board member for years, it was customary for the congregation to share a meal—an *agape* or love dinner—that went on until 3 am, but I never stayed for it.

A. N. Wilson would explain these rituals thus (*Financial Times*, April 3, 2015): "The light of Christ is handed from neighbor to neighbor not only in the Easter ceremony but down the ages. The huge majority of Christians derived their faith not from reading books but from contact with other people. One of the things that liturgy or public prayer does is link you and me now with all the many who had gone before us; not as a club, or a party or a political movement is linked—collectively—but as a series of flickering candles-flames, each distinct, each ablaze with a different light, though touched by the common source, which is Christ. Those of us who count ourselves (even if, as in my case, wishy-washily) among the Christian numbers do so because we have shown the light by other Christian lives—by friends or family, or by lights in history."

I saw and took part in numerous Easter Resurrection services at Taxiarchis. What was more mesmerizing was celebrating Easter in Athens, at the little church of St. George's on the top of Lycabittus Hill, a vantage point overlooking Athens. The Acropolis would be floodlit; a procession of thousands of people, candles in hand, would emerge from various neighborhood churches, congregating towards Syntagma Square in the center of the town, like a giant, pulsating, illuminated octopus.

An Easter feast

From the kitchen came the encouraging smell of food, which we sniffed appreciatively. Mother had not joined us for the Easter Resurrection service, immersed in the kitchen preparing *mezes*—appetizers—and the time-consuming *mageiritsa*, a hearty soup, or rather stew, of chopped lamb liver and wild greens seasoned with egg-lemon sauce. Greece is a culture of ritualistic foods. The soup was made once a year, as it was the occasion to slaughter a lamb or goat; it was to be served only after the midnight Resurrection Service.

As we cracked Easter eggs, we exclaimed the Paschal greeting *"Christos Anesti!"* (Christ is risen!), to which the response was *"Alithos Anesti!"* (True, He is risen!). It was a greeting offered to every Greek Orthodox on Easter day.

The soup was excellent, and the *tsoureki*, fresh from the oven, would become my favorite bread from my childhood. The red wine put everyone in good humor; even I was offered a little wine diluted with water—it was Easter!

The Catholic and Orthodox observance of Easter coincides only every four years. The Orthodox observance correlates to the Jewish Passover. Because the death, burial, and resurrection of Jesus Christ happened after the Passover, the early fathers wanted Easter to always be celebrated subsequent to the Passover. And, since the Jewish holiday calendar is based on solar and lunar cycles, each feast day is movable, and the dates shift from year to year. Some years Greek Easter comes one week, and at other times three or five weeks, later. We anticipated with pleasure the basket of colored eggs prepared by Madame Zabé, our Armenian Catholic neighbor, which came a few weeks earlier than when we could reciprocate. Try to explain to a youngster why Christ resurrects twice! Another difference was the way we crossed ourselves. In the Orthodox fashion, the first three fingers are held tightly together, starting with the forehead and touching the shoulders first on the right and then the left; Catholics do it with an open hand, going from left to right.

We painted hardboiled eggs in the Western fashion, using different colors: blue, yellow, green, and orange beyond the traditional bright red of Greece, which symbolized the spilt Blood of Christ and the promise of eternal life.

Easter Sunday was when the festive gathering took place. The house was enchanted, with the glasses polished, the silver striking a note of glory against the mellow walnut color of the buffet; an embroidered tablecloth graced the table; neatly pressed napkins were efficiently laid out, and fine shell-thin china, dishes rarely used, appeared for that occasion. Nothing less would have done, for proper ladies used only the best. I have one of Mother's embroidered tablecloths, which deserves to be at the Victoria and Albert Museum.

The aroma of roast lamb permeated the house, as a variety of side dishes and Greek appetizers—a limitless array of small savory pastries filled with greens, cheese, meat, and other ingredients—had been prepared; innumerable glasses of wine were served. Pastries and almond tarts from Athineos, the best pastry shop at that time, had been delivered. Aunt Elpiniki brought an enormous crème caramel, a custard quivering and shaking in its dish, all brown and gold ivory. Besides my aunts, there were two friends, Philia and Dimitri, sister and brother, who came as my father did from the small town of Cesme. They spoke of their homesickness for the old country. Dimitri studied in Russia before the Revolution, and he presented me with a book in French, Tolstoy's *Anna Karenina*, which dwelt on issues of divorce. I was too young to follow the arguments.

My favorite guest was the old Dr. Skamnakis, a physician from Crete, a well-traveled man; he talked about life in Egypt compared to life in Vienna where he studied. I listened attentively to his evocations of old times. Vienna? "You should go there one day, it has such a different life!" He raised a glass of wine to his lips, then turned to my mother: "You should add few drops of arsenic in the wine, it is good for digestion. Give it to the children, daily." Did he want to poison us? As I Google "arsenic" today I learn of its unique medicinal attributes. The doctor learned them long ago in Vienna! "A very good Easter indeed!" he would exclaim on his departure, and then walk six miles to his apartment. I was moved when, visiting in later years the Greek Orthodox Cathedral in Vienna, the name Skamnakis appeared on a plaque identifying the family as major donors. The son and grandson of the old doctor, both physicians, made Vienna their home.

The smells of spring

One of my favorite secular holidays as a child was Sham El Nessim, the Smelling of the Breezes. It marked the beginning of spring and always fell on a Monday, the first after the Eastern Christian Easter (following the custom of the largest Christian denomination in the country, the Coptic Orthodox Church.) Despite the Christian date, the holiday was celebrated by Egyptians regardless of religion. In his annals, Plutarch noted that, at the start of spring, the ancient Egyptians offered salted fish, lettuce, and onions to their deities.

Many rituals of Sham El Nessim were handed down intact, although my family did not observe them. On that holiday Egyptians took to the streets, setting out from the distant poor suburbs until they reached the coast, the public gardens, and the grand squares. Many locals, especially women, started the day by breaking an onion and smelling it, or sleeping with an onion under their pillows; that way, tradition had it, the nose could smell the air better. Generally children had bright new clothes to wear on that day and the Nouzha public gardens were crowded with families having picnics. They ate traditional foods that symbolized the new life, spring: colored boiled egg reminiscent to our own Easter eggs, scallions or green onions, lettuce and *feseekh*, a pungent fish which had been buried in the sand to ripen. Although I never tasted it, Egyptian friends still claim it is delicious although the fish smelled awful. The zoo was another popular destination, always too crowded.

For us, the tradition was to set out for the long ride to the Domaine de Siouf in the countryside. The trams, the buses, and the roads were jammed, but we did not care, as it was a lovely spring day to spend with our friends.

A home of many languages

At home we spoke Greek with my mother, while Father talked to my brother and me in French, the language I used with my school friends. The morning newspaper, the *Journal d'Egypte*, was purchased daily from young boys who ran howling though the streets. I did not dare to interrupt Father's daily communion with his newspaper as he plodded through the business page; it was left at home so I could read after I returned from school. The Greek newspaper, the *Tahydromos,* was published later in the day and was bought in town.

We spoke demotic Greek at home but my parents felt that my education was deficient if I did not master modern and classical Greek. A tutor was hired to instruct me a couple of times a week. I never gained masterly proficiency in Ancient Greek, but I learned it well enough to appreciate the rhythmic pattern of the lines of Sophocles' *Antigone.* Could a translation capture the rhythm of the original?

The Arabic we all spoke was known as colloquial Arabic, more or less a dialect with many Greek, Italian, and French words intermingled. It was sufficient to communicate with servants, office staff, and bazaar shop-keepers. We never learned "classical" Arabic, which would be mandatory years later when I entered an Egyptian university.

Home was a two-story villa in the middle-class suburb of Camp Cesar, at 25 Rue Memphis. Our living room—equivalent to what in America would be the family room—on the second floor opened to a large balcony which echoed on many weekend nights with the clink of ice in tall glasses; it overlooked a flowering garden and two fruit trees, a lemon and an apricot. Father was boastful of his lemons, which he gifted to his friends at the café at a time when ripened lemons were the least expensive in the market!

In the formal living room—it was typical in Egypt to have a formal room to receive guests—sat my piano, dark as night; dotted around the room were two or three intimate clusters of sofas with exquisite carvings. Their rich velvet brown winter fabric was replaced with a lighter floral design in the summer months. Lamps stood adjacent to them. Three paintings purchased at auctions, poor imitations of Watteau, hung on the wall. A chandelier blazed over a carved and polished coffee table on which an enormous arrangement of flowers stood. (I inherited my mother's passion for fresh flowers, and they always grace my home, in every room!)

In my room stood a beautiful, heavy, and ornate desk meant for a businessman, a castaway from my father's office. A shelf held rows of green leatherbound Victor Hugo novels gold-stamped for "Basil Misserlis." Maps of Africa and Asia on the walls inflamed my wanderlust.

Our most precious possessions were carpets; they came from Anatolia, India, Persia, even from Greece; the colorful ones were my favorite, knotted in the Caucasus. Father was a collector; his advice on carpets was sought by friends and acquaintances, and he was happy to oblige. Four carpets were later sent to me through intermediaries in America; the most precious one, an Anatolian, was gifted to relatives in New York years later. My parents often attended auctions, sometimes to buy a painting, and sometimes out of curiosity, just wanting to see a house. Once we acquired another armoire—one of those large carved walnut monstrosities. I was with them when they purchased my piano, the bidding taking place between my father and our otolaryngologist. It needed tuning, but my parents were proud to cart it home, where it would become an important part of my cultural upbringing.

Our neighbors were Greeks, Italians, Armenians, Swiss, Maltese, and Jewish. Their children attended neighborhood schools: The Greek primary school, the Armenian school, the St. Mark school for boys, or the French Lycée. They were good times for an almost nine-year-old to remember.

The predominance of French

Language and religion were the basis on which Alexandria was divided into different communities, each of which received support from a foreign government or from patrons. The French state contributed to the needs of the Lycée Français, whereas the Greek schools were funded privately by rich cotton merchants.

Somehow the very idea of assimilation or integration into the surrounding society and culture was foreign to the community spirit. Importantly, Alexandria never became a melting pot as happened in America; rather, it remained a mosaic of people.

The Salvago Theater was one of the Greek community's cultural haunts just as the Alliance Française was for the French. Talent was appreciated and encouraged within the community, and there were annual prizes awarded to encourage talented people. Dailies, weeklies, literary reviews, publishing, lectures, amateur drama, and art exhibitions formed a rich tapestry that expressed the spirit of cosmopolitan Alexandria. There were newspapers in all the languages, and each community read its papers.

The French language acquired a dominant position. In Christian schools, lay missions, and Israeli Alliance schools, the teaching was conducted in it. In all community schools, French was chosen as the first foreign language, and thus a linguistic causeway stretched between the communities. What could be more normal than that French should be the lingua franca of the Eastern Mediterranean? French and foreign-language newspapers, whose number had expanded by 1890, trumpeted French culture.

It was the social language of the city when I was growing up. French newspapers—*Progres Egyptien, the Journal d'Egypte, La Bourse Egyptienne*—proliferated. The French denomination schools were mostly tuition-free, while the Lyçée, the English Girls College, and the Victoria College were expensive private schools.

At the Ibrahimieh market where we shopped, you could hear Greek from a Jewish vendor or an Arab baker, Italian at the Armenian greengrocer's, and Arabic at the butcher's shop, all in the same Alexandrian bazaar.

But French tended to predominate with all foreigners, because at some point it became the official language of the administration and of a large number of consulates, as well as of the Mixed Tribunals. Announcements to the public, meant to be understood by all, were made in it. This was why it was on every storefront, on street names, on advertisements, and on the plaques of professionals. All the shopkeepers spoke French; in the elegant downtown stores, one would have said it was Europe.

My father's business

My father was in the export-import business, and although I do not remember the details, a license renewed annually was required for his trade. I recall spices such as black pepper, imported from India. Was he the agent of the powerful Ralli brothers of Calcutta—from among the diaspora of Greeks from Chios? Spices were stored in a warehouse in the Suez Canal free-zone, then shipped to Europe according to world prices. From England he imported bolts of cotton and woolen fabrics, while from Egypt he exported cotton oil—or was it Barbas who did that?

Were any taxes paid? I asked my father years later. Foreign nationals were exempt from many taxes, particularly taxes on income and profit, but there were indirect taxes such as customs duties, purchase taxes on properties, license fees, and stamp duties. I recall those brown and dark blue stamps—today collector items on eBay—that were affixed on documents giving them legality and authenticity, as they were submitted to the authorities; their value differed according to the documents' importance.

Sometimes I would visit my father at work, going up a circular marble staircase leading to his suite of offices. My father's office was located in the center of town in an imposing building on the Rue de France, past the Square on the way to Alexandria's port, close to the old town. The Square, as the English called it, was the very heart of the city, with the Bourse containing the stock and cotton exchanges, the Mixed Courts, the Anglican Church of St. Mark's and, in the middle, the bronze equestrian statue of Muhammad Ali, the founder of modern Egypt. He was not identified in deference to the Islamic prohibition against representing human or animal forms.

The rooms in his office were huge, with large detailed maps of Greece and Egypt hanging on the walls—Egypt with its green central spine bounded by deserts, Greece with its blue waters dotted with islands. There were dozens of islands on those maps, not the few marked these days on tourist brochures. I was fascinated by those maps, which would encourage my wanderlust from childhood.

Father once received an offer to purchase the Petalouthes, the Butterfly Islands (not to be confused with the Petalouthes Valley in Rhodes). "Uninhabited rocks!" interjected my mother. The purchase was debated, although I was too young to participate. The islands were part of the Dodecanese, Italian territory at that time; with warnings and war threats on the horizon, the opportunity sank from view. The islands would revert to Greece after the war.

Years later, the maps would become a source of suspicion. "With such detailed maps, you must be up to no good!" Government representatives, some dressed in military uniforms, would scream at my father. The times had changed.

Also to be found in the office were Underwood typewriters, a cast-iron, wheel-operated book press, carved wooden desks, shelves lined with green leather-bound books engraved with golden initials, an armoire filled with documents, and a solitary telephone. Manual calculating machines had not yet appeared in Alexandria. In those days, carbon paper was used to make purple copies of letters.

There was always a water glass, freshly replenished, beside a finger-moistened pad, an inkwell, and three rubber stamps in the merry-go-around holder. I wondered what he was supposed to use them for.

My father always carried a small notebook with him, attached to the back of the tram *abonnement* (the yearly tram pass), in which he wrote numbers. His handwriting was identical to mine.

Father would have liked to own a telephone whose number was 12345, but he settled for 23145. Mail was received at the central post office where he rented Box Number 112; telegrams, the most reliable mode of communications, were delivered in his office.

I do not recall receiving mail at our home address, perhaps as the post office box was more reliable. All transactions were done in cash—a system that would backfire years later with the closing of the Mixed Tribunals, as I will recall in another chapter. Utilities were paid for in cash, with a proper receipt issued. Such documents were kept for years, a useful reference identifying us as long-time residents and not recent foreign arrivals; they would be required for the issuance of a residence permit under Nasser. By 1955, my father was already in Egypt for 37 years, but even so a residence permit was still required of us by the government.

Not infrequently packages disappeared, never to be delivered by the post office. What a treat we had when, one day, Father brought home a box of Swiss chocolates. As it turned out, they had been put by mistake in his post office box—we were not the right recipients! But we enjoyed that rare treat.

The office windows were shaded with wooden horizontal blinds painted green, so different from the wooden shutters, the norm of the time. When they were open, and above the clamor of a crowded street, one could catch the whistles of the steam engines rolling from the dark goods yards.

One prominent tenant of that building was Fritz Hess, an eminent Alexandrian—his son Rudolf rose to prominence under Hitler in the Nazi regime — who ran a prosperous wholesale business on the Rue de France, a floor above my father's, importing Bordeaux, Rhine, and Moselle wines, and acting as the sole agent of several English, Austrian, and German firms, among them the Krupps.

Moneychangers, the old *sarais*, were prominent on the Rue de France together with craftsmen jewelers, mostly Armenians, and embroiderers.

Decades later, in 2007, walking in that neighborhood, I saw that the building still stood where I had remembered it to be, but its majestic appearance was gone; the ground floor had been converted to little shops selling woolen blankets and bolts of textiles. There was rubbish strewn at the entrance. As I spoke with the local merchants occupying those street-level stores, I thought back, with a pang of longing, to when one of the building's tenants was King Paul of Greece, in exile during the war. The green wooden blinds of my father's office remained visible up there.

Father also owned a small tannery in the semi-industrial area of Mex, an outer suburb of Alexandria. We occasionally went as a family to the fish restaurants that stood on piles above the sea. The owners of the restaurants were mostly Greeks; the errand boys, young Egyptians, would jabber in all the many laguages of Alexandria. Little things stand out from those Mex outings, details that seemed unimportant then but now, remembered, bear an almost painful clarity: the vendors and the fishermen squatting behind baskets laden with sardines, red and gray mullets, *loufaria* or bluefish, prawns, and crabs.

I never visited father's tannery—it was not for children, I was told. The pungent, petrified smell of the tannery was suffocating, agreed my brother, who had been there once.

Tragedy however struck the family when Barbas, our beloved uncle, committed suicide. Afflicted with diabetes, his body was covered with boils. Although discovered in the early twenties, insulin was not yet available in Egypt. In a deep depression, he took his revolver and shot himself. The tragedy was never spoken about; within the community it would be acknowledged as an accident, as the Greek Orthodox Church would not conduct burial rites for anyone who committed suicide.

My father assumed responsibility for the family business. The Great Depression paralyzed economies all around the world, but his business prospered and even expanded; he purchased two commercial vessels of eight and ten thousand tons each, mostly to carry his commodities. Life was good for a decade until the start of the Second World War.

My mother's jam

Spoon sweets are customary prepared all over Greece, and it was not an exception in our household. Muhammad would sometimes trail behind my father in the Ibrahimieh food market, watching silently as my father selected the fruit, picked the best one, left the damaged one, and made sure the guavas were ripe enough for mother to make jam.

Jam preserves were my mother's specialty—apricots, marmalade made with Seville oranges or grapefruit, and figs, but mostly quince. Making quince jam required the peeled fruit to be scraped and julienned before being simmered to the necessary consistency so that a light orange pink coloration was achieved. If you simmer too long, the sugar will caramelize, my mother instructed me. Color was as important as the aroma in making that jam. It took me years of trial and error to capture the magical translucency of quince jam, earning at the end an award at the San Diego county fair! Rose petal jam is usually available at Greek monasteries. I recall once, in Chios, reading the sign "rose jam factory," and I knew I was on the right road leading to a monastery.

Rose petal jam was another of my mother's trademark confections. Most people looked for the alabaster-white-petaled roses, but Mother preferred the red petals, the more aromatic the better. At summertime, one could find in the market bushels of rose blossoms, at the cost of a few piasters. The petals were covered with a damp cloth, to retain their freshness, to keep the dust away, and to hold them down. Mother simmered them in a mixture of sugar and lemon. She was renowned for her *confiture des roses*, a light flavored jelly which was considered to medicinal properties (a laxative!) and was always appreciated as a gift. At other times, Mother would mix in a jar equal amounts of sugar and petals, then leave them for ten days in the sun. They would then be ready to be eaten, a sort of crystallized candy which lasted for months.

In the fruit market, the oranges, the cucumbers, the apples, the bananas, the custard apples, the dark brown dates, and the sweet seedless grapes glowed in the light while the Arab vendors moved like magicians; all were products of the fertile Nile Delta. I always stopped to admire the pyramid-shaped mounds of gleaming pomegranates. There was always a bit of haggling in colloquial Arabic involved. Muhammad would intervene only if things went out of hand. His job was to carry the huge wicker basket, load it with purchases, and ferry it from one vendor to the next until he reached home, where Mother sorted things and did the cooking.

The miracles of morning

Pork was not sold in Muslim markets but it was available in wintertime at an Italian specialty store in the city. Pork roasts, pork sausages, smoked pork chops, Mortadella. What a treat it was, until one day both my mother and Akis my brother got *taenia*, a pig tapeworm. There would be no more pork served on our table. The Prophet Muhammad must have known something, forbidding his followers to eat any hog.

In addition to the small food shops such as those of the butcher, the fishmonger, and the baker who sold both French baguettes and Italian loaves, and the Arab bakery with its wheat flat pita bread, there were also workshops in which you could get things made or repaired. There was the tinker who regalvanized cooking pots. At that time cooking pots were made of copper and had to be refurbished as they wore down. The loud hammering of the *sankari*, the plumber, would be heard all over the street, his services in high demand in view of the poor quality of plumbing, especially the toilets.

Once a year we brought our cooking utensils to be tinned at the Ibrahimieh bazaar. The fellows there had an extraordinary collection of strangely shaped hammers and anvils. They sprinkled a white powder over the copper, repeatedly wiping it over with a cloth wad that they dipped in molten tin that bubbled over a brazier. But we never tinned the large copper cauldron used for boiling the sheets before washing; those copper cauldrons may be worth a fortune in antique stores today,

At the baker's, the breads were layered on giant black tin trays, lying one on top of the other with no covering whatsoever, not even cellophane; flies hung around, sometimes landing on the baguettes. You chased them away, then picked a baguette and squeezed it, then another one, until you found that golden crusted one that you made your choice. Who knew how many other hands had touched it? Still warm, wrapped in news-paper, you took it home intact, unless you nibbled of the corner of that bread. No one in the family ever got sick from the market's bounty, so we must have developed an immunity like the locals.

The small miracles of every morning happened when the fruit and vegetable vendors arrived. I sat in the verandah or at a corner window, a pile of cushions placed on my chair when I was little so I could see better and watch the street vendors leading their donkeys or mules up and down, hawking their wares and shouting obscenities at each other.

They would station themselves outside the house, balancing baskets with the vegetables and fruits of the season—zucchini, cucumbers, eggplants, tomatoes, okra, potatoes, and my favorite fruit, the black figs in autumn. Figs remain my favorite temperate climate fruit, surpassing even the delicious tropical mangoes of the Philippines, which I would discover later in life. From our balcony, we could point to what we wanted, adding an extra bunch of sweet seedless grapes, a small cantaloupe, and those marvelous purple figs; Mother had an entire cookbook devoted to fig recipes. Then it was the turn of the iceman, from whom we purchased a block of ice carried in a burlap bag. Basil, mint, and parsley from the vegetable vendor permeated the air.

And what about the fresh grape leaves which my mother would stuff with ground meat, rice, and herbs, and then simmer in a lemony broth? As the vendors moved along our street, either carrying their baskets or pulling theirwagons, they made their presence known by shouting advertisements of their produce; occasionally there was a mule that pulled the wagon.

Milk in glass bottles and freshly made yogurt in round brown pottery containers were delivered every other day, with the empty containers to be retrieved the next time around. Father stopped once a month at the milk shop to pay the bill. The milkman was Greek, but deliveries were handled by a young Arab on a bicycle.

Who needed to go to a supermarket? Years ago, in Alexandria, the super-market came to us.

Familiar faces

Muhammad was but one of many people who became a familiar face to me and to my family when I was growing up. He worked six days a week, from morning till early afternoon. Muhammad and his wife had seven children, but all of them died before their first birthday, likely the result of poverty and poor hygiene. He had been with us for more than twenty years when he approached Father and confided his ambition. He wanted to own a shop and become his own proprietor. Was it advisable? He did not ask for any financial help, as he had saved some money. Would he make it? What could you say to someone who was illiterate but was able to count?

Muhammad set up a little shop at the corner of Rue Memphis, were we lived, and a major thoroughfare, Rue Eleusis. Father gifted him with his first stock: a selection of stationery, brightly colored wooden penholders, steel pens for different styles of lettering; Waterman ink in blue, black, green, and red; and various paper items. He later expanded his wares to include sewing items, including regular threads and embroidery threads —of the Mouliné brand—in a variety of colors. We often patronized his shop. Muhammad confided that most of his earnings came from selling cigarettes and local candy. With foreigners in the neighborhood, he made a living; with their mass exodus in the 1950s, his business collapsed. With our own departure, his fate would remain unknown.

Kyria (a term of address to a city woman) Argyro, a seamstress, came a few times a year for a day or two to make beautiful dresses for us. If she did not finish them—a hem or a buttonhole—my mother would complete the job. Kyria Argyro was as an elderly woman, gray-haired, hard of hearing, and very quiet but also very efficient. She had a family but preferred not to talk about them. Her son-in law was Italian, and was interned in a desert camp, probably contributing to her reticence.

A woman named Aziza came every other week to do the family laundry in our washing room on the terrace. Water was boiled first in huge copper cauldron, then enough cold water was added to bring it to a lukewarm temperature. Aziza squatted in front of a large copper basin, in which she washed the clothes. Her feet were flat on the floor; sometimes she wore wooden clogs about two inches high and would squat on those. Washing meant kneading, slapping, and wringing the sheets, until she had squeezed the very life out of them. She ended the washing by adding an agent that gave the sheets a slight blue tint.

Aziza was in her early fifties but looked much older, so wrinkled was she. She wore the traditional black *galabiyeh*. Her arms and hands were so white, having lost their pigmentation because of the heavy bleach she used in her laundering.

There was a gridlock of clothes lining the terrace, sagging gray cords frayed with use and, along them, a cluster of unused pins which sat like little sparrows idling in electric wire. My mother helped Aziza to uncoil the clothes after the wash, bedsheet after bedsheet, and to hang them in a row one next to the other; then another row on a line opposite thus creating a scented passage where I could run and lose myself as in a heavenly corridor, of clean sheets drying in the sun.

A few hours later Aziza would bring down the fragrant and sundried laundry in a giant wicker basket. Some clothes would be folded, others ironed. The following day Kyra (a term of address to an elderly country woman) Despina would come to do the ironing. Two heavy black irons were placed one after the other over the Primus for that purpose. Electric irons were not yet available in Egypt. Kyra Despina sprinkled father's shirts with the lightest of starch, and did a marvelous professional job. Looking back at the division of labor, there was obviously a sort of caste system at work, with ironing, a higher skill, allocated to a Greek who undoubtedly received higher wages than Aziza, the Arab washerwoman.

Kyra Despina's apartment overlooked the Sporting Club racetrack, and she invited me there a couple of times. Ignorant about horses, I did not understand the thrill that people got from horseracing, nor had I ever heard of betting, although I knew there were prizes and a trophy for the winning horseowner. To me those horses were like meteors shooting across the turf.

Spring mattresses were unheard of when I was growing up. What we used was the equivalent of a giant pillow filled with cotton; the mattress case was made of thick cotton material, often with black stripes.

Once a year we hired Moustafa for the maintenance of the mattress up, as he knew his trade. He carried an instrument resembling a harp, which had a single taut cord. He set himself up on the flat roof of the house, the terrazza as we called it, first to undo the case, pulling out the cotton fibers that over time had formed large compact lumps. With the help of the cord of his instrument, he would separate the lumps one by one until the cotton fibers regained their original consistency and flexibility. The case of the mattress would be filled once again with the separated cotton. For a month or two those mattresses would be heaven, but by the end of the year they would be lumpy and the process had to resume again.

Always a lady

I rarely entered the kitchen to help. During the holidays, I'd stop to see Mother and Aunt Katina making traditional breads or cookies. I was an observer, never really a helper.

But one morning Mother put me to work, not just to look. Father's friends were joining us for dinner that evening. She gave me a pretty apron—which later in life I would be taught was not for ladies but for maids.

Did I have to peel potatoes?! I loathed that job just a little less than I loathed the taste of potatoes. "Why don't you have Muhammad peel potatoes? Give me something easier to do!"

She asked me then to rinse the polished silver cutlery and dry them. "Bring the crystal glasses, put them on the buffet and do not break any. And fill the Galle bowl with *kourabiethes*." She meant the sugar-powdered butter cookies. She went on with her homily. "Have you inscribed in your book all the recipes you like to keep? It was my stepmother in Istanbul who taught me how to cook. One day you shall have your own home. You may not have to peel potatoes but you must cook for your husband a real meal. Although the piano is very nice, you better learn to set a table properly. For celebrations, for friends, always use the best, the best crystal, the best silver, always polished. Even if you do not serve a biftek, the table has to be set properly, with fresh flowers befitting the season. Do not forget the silver candlesticks. Always a lady—a lady uses only the best!" At that we both chuckled.

A special treat

Kyria Philia, our friend from Chesme, had a small olive grove in her large property in Siouf, 25 kilometers from Alexandria. Once a year she brought us a hamper of four to five pounds of lustrous plump green olives from her property, prompting the start of a major project in the kitchen. The olives were washed first, then Mother slit them horizontally with a sharp knife in one spot, making sure not to cut all the way to the pit.

They were then placed in a large container and covered with cold water. They remained there unperturbed for six weeks. Mother tasted the soup after the fourth week to gauge its bitterness. The degree of desired bitterness was subjective; once they were debittered, they were rinsed and returned to the container in an 8-10 percent solution of brine. At this point, they could be flavored to taste with sliced fresh lemons and the juice of several lemons. Olive oil, around two inches deep, was poured to cover the top of the container and left to steep for at least six weeks but preferably three months. This way we always had green olives at our dinner table to last us for a year!

Mother had an even more special treat for me. In the tiny pebble-shaped pasta that is the *trahana* lie all the reasons why I am still, after all these years, completely in awe of my mother's cooking.

Behind a food so trivial lies a complex history that throws light on the past of a whole region from the Balkans to Persia. Whatever its origins, the ancient and modern versions of the *trahana* evolved from pastoral traditions. Shepherds needed food that was quick to prepare and easy to carry between their lowland abodes in the winter and their highland homes in the summer. The granular little pasta could be boiled with plain water to produce a filling and nourishing meal. It was made with semolina or wheat flour or bulgur or cracked wheat, kneaded with milk, yogurt, buttermilk, or a vegetable pulp.

I still recall my mother and Aunt Katina sitting in the family room taking the dough, cutting it into very small pieces, then twisting it. When the pieces were almost dried but not yet brittle, they were passed through a special sieve and rubbed along the grates so that the *trahana* took on its characteristic pebbly texture. Plastic storage containers were not available at that time, so it would be stored in muslin bags in the pantry or another cool place.

Trahana was used to make soup cooked in water or both, and it was delicious mixed with a little tomato or meat or sometimes milk. Mother occasionally substituted rice with *trahana* in rolled vegetable dishes, a meal then reserved for special occasions, or used it as savory pie filling.

What a surprise when recently in America, at the home of a Hungarian neighbor, I was offered *trahana*! He did not make it, but those tiny sour granules, vacuum-packed, were available at a European food market!

Around the neighborhood

An elderly mysterious woman took a walk every afternoon dressed in her black, moth-eaten dress adorned with a string of pearls. The rumor was that she was a White Russian—a member of the Imperial Family, perhaps? She lived alone like a dethroned Empress. Occasionally she attended the service at the Greek Orthodox Church of our neighborhood. She did not talk to anyone, never smiled; she looked at nothing in particular, and seemed unaware of her surroundings. Whatever the secrets of her past were, like a masked veil, they were never revealed.

A lavish villa at the end of Memphis Street served as home to Theodore Moshonas, the chief librarian of the Patriarchal library; a man of letters, he was friend of Durrell with whom he exchanged many letters. His son Dimitri often joined my brother for a game of chess.

Across our home, in a vast tree-covered compound, stood three villas. The owners, the Valvis family, were Greek entrepreneurs, owners of hardware stores in Khartoum. They came to Alexandria during the summer months to avoid Sudan's oppressive heat; their two boys boarded at the prestigious Victoria College. Occasionally a couple of shiny black limousines could be seen parked outside the compound; cars were a rarity among the Memphis street residents. We were all curious until we found that one of the classmates of the Valvis boys was none other than young Prince Hussein, the future King of Jordan.

A special day

Some days were more special than others, and one of them was when the Annual General Meeting of the Greek Community of Alexandria was held. At 7:30 in the morning, the chimes of Taxiarchis, the Greek Orthodox church, would echo in our neighborhood. The liturgy had begun.

On one such morning, I selected a small violet from the garden and offered it to my father; smiling, he put it in his boutonnière, always happy to accept a flower from his little girl. He did not take the tram; today, he flagged Michalis, the Greek taxi driver at the Camp Cesar taxi stand, to take him to the meeting.

Kyra Despina arrived early that morning to iron the family laundry. Those Egyptian cotton sheets were finished wrinkle-free.

Angela—a hunchbacked, toothless, and white-haired woman from Asia Minor—was mumbling to herself; she wandered up once a month to receive a pound or two, a small token of charity. I did not know where she lived, or if she had a family. She pleaded for help in a mixture of Greek and Turkish, and came knowing that there was a contribution waiting for her. She regaled me with stories, fairytales, and I wished I could record them, as they were most absorbing, better than any I had read. She was illiterate, but what a fertile imagination she possessed! Where did she hear them? Was she making them up? How she ended up in Egypt remained a mystery to us. Was she tortured by the Turks before escaping? Father wanted to help and have her admitted at the Antoniadis old folks' pension home, but she resisted, enjoying her freedom. She may have been right, as she would have been ostracized in a place meant for well-to-do retirees.

I happily accompanied my father to that pension home one sunny day. I had never visited the place before, and I was excited to see it as it lay within the lovely Nouzha Gardens, but I was also fearful, to be seeing so many old people in the sunset of their life.

In the garden, on a reclining chair, sat an old balding man who looked to be a hundred years old—none other than Antonis Antoniadis, the son of Sir John, a living, walking embodiment of all the legends of the Greek aristocracy.

How did he make his money, I asked my father innocently—was he staying here? "His father must have been among the first cotton barons, knighted by Queen Victoria!" I muttered.

And then Father said: "He made his money by providing women to the Pashas, to the court, to the King." To my fifteen-year-old mind, the gods had come crashing down to earth.

Mother read the *Bouqueto*, her favorite periodical; there was a recipe there which appealed to her, a savory rustic pie made with shredded leftover meats combined with cheese, eggs, and herbs, traditional fare from the island of Zakinthos. She cut the recipe and stored it among others in her cookbook, the *Tselemende*, the cooking bible of every Greek housewife. She liked to experiment; those recipes reflected a different way of cooking, a contrast from the sophisticated, urban, fragrant cuisine of the Byzantine Greeks.

A kind of black art

Mother viewed cooking as a kind of black art, part skill and part magic. She was able to maneuver from pot to pot, stirring a bit here, adding a spice or condiment there, tasting from one pot, and with a clean spoon tasting from another.

She needed to get sour cherries to make *vissinatha*, a refreshing summer drink. They were unavailable at the local Ibrahimieh market, so Father would dispatch one of his staff to an upscale neighborhood to buy a kilo of cherries, which were a great delicacy and hard to come by. They were also needed for the making of meatballs with sour cherries, a dish that took hours to prepare, and something she learned from her stepmother back in Istanbul. She would knead half a dozen spices into the chopped meat—including cinnamon, of course, along with salt and pepper. The effort was worth it and we devoured dozens of the miniature meat balls which were sweet and tangy at the same time. So unusual! —for years I would wonder if I could savor this delicacy again—and I would, more than six decades later, in a restaurant in old Damascus.

Food shopping was done twice a week at the open market of Ibrahimieh, but we also patronized two grocery stores of our area, both run by Greeks. The one of Mr. Marangos was located on Rue Eleusis, the more upscale one of Mr. Papadopoulos at the Camp Cesar tram station. He even sold something unheard of: cereal from America! In both groceries there was a telephone—a luxury many people still did not own—so they also offered the facility of a calling and messaging service.

Mother called Aunt Katina to ensure her availability for the following week as she required assistance for kneading the traditional Easter breads. These were always made within the family, and Aunt Katina always participated in that effort.

Mother would make the starter the day before. She would dissolve the yeast in warm water in a ceramic bowl, let it stand few minutes, then add some flour and sugar to activate the yeast, until the dough was smooth. Covered, the starter stood at room temperature overnight.

Aunt Katina arrived early in the morning to prepare the dough for the bread. The starter was combined with eggs, flour, sugar, and whatever else the recipe called for, in addition to *mahlepi*, a favorite aromatic condiment. For about twenty minutes, they kneaded it on a flour-dusted marble surface until the dough was smooth and soft, adding more flour to achieve the proper texture. Covered and let to rise in a warm, draft-free place, the dough doubled in bulk in about three hours. Then they pinched the dough down and divided it in two. Mother and Aunt now shaped the dough into twisted loaves. A couple of hours later, the loaves had swollen, almost doubling again. With no electric blenders or Cuisinarts, the entire process was handled manually, an easy process but so time-consuming.

The twisted loaves were now carried by Muhammad on a *sania*, a tray on his head, to the Greek Hamos bakery in Ibrahimieh. Mother accompanied him, not only to pay the owner but to tip the attendant to ensure that the breads were baked to perfection.

A doctor makes house calls

When I fell ill, Father called our physician Dr. Ghazis. Like everyone else we associated with, he was Greek. Dr. Ghazis had lately enhanced his reputation by traveling for a month to New York at the request of one of his former patients who migrated there, as if there were no good doctors in America. He made headlines in the local Greek newspaper. The doctor made house calls, arriving in his chauffeured black Ford automobile.

He did not use a stethoscope, but simply put his ear to a clean, white handkerchief that he placed on the chest or back of his patients; he concentrated, eyes closed, checked heartbeats, the workings of the lungs; he took the pulse, examined tongue and throat, evaluating any vital digression.

His fee for us was two Egyptian pounds. He charged different rates according to the socioeconomic status of his patients, an indication being the neighborhood they lived in. His orders were taken literally and zealously implemented.

His clinic was also his home, where he lived with two spinster sisters who were always wearing black, on fashionable Rue Fouad. It was always crowded, with a long queue of people waiting for consultation. He was late again. After a round of house calls and hospitals in the morning, he took a late lunch. When the wait to see patients took too long, a rumor spread that many small bones were contained in his fish dish.

For a patient to be hospitalized, the choice was the Greek hospital, the Kozzica, staffed mostly by Greek doctors, where every specialization known at that time was represented. As in so many places elsewhere in the world, physicians had an extraordinary cachet in the community, revered by everyone, rich or poor.

They sent their children to the private French or British schools. Dr. Stergiou, the leading urologist, had registered his daughter as an "observer" at the Lycée. She occasionally attended my French literature class, the only person I knew who played golf and was a member of the prestigious Sporting Club.

Summer afternoons

Summer afternoons it would grow so quiet in our home and all over Rue Memphis in Camp Cesar. In the heat, Mother would take a nap, and Father would doze on the sofa. I practiced my piano exercises enough to lull everyone to a restful long sleep.

At 4:30 in the afternoon, for the second time in the day, the chimes of Taxiarchis echoed in the neighborhood. There was no mosque around our area, and we did not hear the muezzin calling Allah's faithful to prayer; those chimes were, for us Christians, a reminder that the evening Mass was starting. By five, Father departed for his café to meet friends, while Mother's visitors started gathering in the family room.

It was a daily open house. My godmother, a well-traveled woman, was the first to arrive, followed by an acquaintance or two from Asia Minor, a couple of neighbors, and two schoolteachers. They were all part of my mother's entourage, all Greeks, although Madame Christine Rustelhorz hailed from Izmir, her late husband a Swiss businessman, and Madame Pangalou came from Rome, married to a Greek. Madame Pangalou loved opera to the point of obsession, and would relinquish through the years many necessities just to be able to purchase season tickets when La Scala performed once a year at the Muhammad Ali theater.

Miss Alexandra, an imposing big woman dressed at her best, was the local principal of the Tsoumbion, the primary school my brother attended. Mrs. Yannoulatou joined occasionally; she was a high school teacher, an attractive lady in her late thirties, and divorced, a rarity. She was a hardcore Communist and wanted to lure my mother into her camp, but you could not find a more conservative Greek, more faithful to the royalist cause, than my mother. (A secret Communist organization at the heart of the Greek community recruited volunteers for the armed struggle which was raging in northern Greece.)

The freshly baked walnut cake, the *karidopita*, was served along with a roster of cookies and biscuits on old porcelain dishes with a glass of cold water. Coffee would follow. Some of the women were accomplished embroiderers and knit away as they talked, their metal needles click-clacking like tiny swords. No one smoked, which my parents would have discouraged anyway.

I was cloistered in my room studying, to be interrupted only by the arrival of Miss Ftiara, my private tutor for modern and ancient Greek.

Mother visited other friends in the morning while I was at school. For clothes shopping or for items for the house, she was always accompanied by Father.

Egyptian neighbors were a rarity in our neighborhood. On our street, the majority were Jewish. On the first floor of the three-story apartment next door lived an Italian artist, Mr. Caselli; on the second resided a Coptic family, and on the third the Rustelhorzes. My father's acquaintances, clerks, or official associates were never invited to our home, as it was simply not done then. My brother and I were the ones with Egyptian friends.

Ali El Kouni called from time to time. After savoring a piece of my mother's delectable cakes, he drove with my brother along the coast to one of their favorite hangouts. Aida, my school friend from the Faculty of Science, was warmly welcomed. My mother was particularly fond of her, and occasionally the two of us took lunch sitting in the balcony. Those two westernized Egyptian friends opened their home to us, inviting us to their Bayram festivities, to birthdays, to family gatherings. Ali invited us to his *ezba* or estate to take part in a colorful village wedding, a hallmark of Egyptian hospitality. The only get-together with Egyptians in our home took place when I invited the five honor students of my class after graduation to a simple celebration.

From doctors to hospitals, from clubs to schools, from churches to festivals, from grocery stores to taxi drivers, and from friends to neighbors, our entire life revolved around a Greek milieu. Ours was a fairly closed society whose members married among themselves—a pattern I would break away from—but today, I am who and what I am, my parents' daughter, an Alexandrian Greek.

Sea, air, and land

There were many ways of getting into and out of Alexandria—by sea, air, and land.

Lorenzo Montesini, an Alexandrian living in Sydney whom I met at the Bibliotheca, would recall that in the late 1940s and the 1950s, there was not one Alexandrian who did not know this ship—the Adriatica Line's *SS Esperia*, which did the Alexandria-to-Venice run, ferrying vacationers, honeymooners, students, and business people. The *Esperia* was joined in the mid-1950s by a sister ship, the *Ansonia,* also a beautiful liner, but she came too late to dislodge the much-loved *Esperia* in the public's affections. The Adriatica Line once held pride of place in a corner office at the Rue Cherif, with the beautiful maquettes of their ships in the windows. Their office later became Thomas Cook and then Misr Travel.

After the war, Trans World Airways or TWA—also known as the Howard Hughes line—became known as the smartest airline to fly on. They flew Super Constellations from Cairo to Athens, Zurich, Paris, and New York, with connections to the West Coast. As you passed their office, you always stopped to see who had flown that week, as they displayed photos of celebrities boarding or descending the planes: Ali Khan arriving in New York, Zsa Zsa Gabor in Paris, Cole Porter in Zurich, Frank Sinatra and Ava Gardner in Los Angeles. Among the other airlines, Air France was the most prestigious; BOAC also served the region, and its office stood opposite the British Consulate General on the Corniche. We had a lot of fun making up names for the airlines: Air France was Air Chance, TWA Teeny Weeny Airline, BOAC Better On A Camel or Built On American Credit.

Instead of taking the train that ran through the delta for Cairo, my parents and I once took the melon-colored Pullman, the luxurious motor coach linking Alexandria and Cairo; it must have been around 1947, as my brother was in Europe. I felt important taking the Pullman; in addition, I was wearing a pretty new dress.

For a little girl, going to Cairo was a treat surpassing all others. Alexandria had its stellar attractions, but Cairo was the capital and its Khan Khalil bazaar surpassed all other bazaars of the Middle East, worth hours of exploring. Cairo meant the Pyramids, the Sphinx, lunch at the Mena House, a felucca sail on the Nile, the archeological museum with its Tutankhamen treasures, the Citadel with the stunning Mosque of

Muhammad Ali, and lighting a candle at Saint George's Church. But the real treat was Groppi (before it was burned down in 1952) to sample one of their divine pastries with Groppi's signature Chantilly cream.

Writing for *Aramco World* (March-April 1994), Hassan Eltaher would recall his own boyhood fascination with that very special bus: "The buses that crisscrossed Egypt in those days were just like all buses everywhere—except for the Cairo—Alexandria Pullman. This motor coach was quite futuristic for the times, and not only was it air-conditioned, but it also was specially imported form the United States. No one operated a bus like it anywhere in the country or in the wider Middle East; even the famous Narin trailer bus that linked Beirut to Baghdad via Damascus was no match."

The ride wasn't cheap—a ticket cost a small fortune—but it meant traveling in unaccustomed style, as it featured that rarest of midcentury Egyptian luxuries, air conditioning.

Crossing over to Asia

For a fourteen-year-old it was an exciting journey, a dream, as my father was taking me to Asia!

Father had a warehouse on the Suez Canal for storing spices from India, and I was joining him on a business trip. Crossing over from Port Said to Port Fouad on the Sinai Peninsula, on the other side of the canal, was technically reaching Asia. I was also intrigued by the prospect of watching the vessels plying the canal.

There was only one major street at that time in Port Said, a small town of around 160,000 people. And how could I forget the street name? It was Palestine Street. On a jetty protruding from it, on a concrete base, stood the colossal, 33-foot bronze statue of Ferdinand de Lesseps, the diplomat engineer, the "Father of the Canal." His right hand reached out towards visitors and vessels entering the canal, while his left held a map of the canal. It was, of course, a display of de Lesseps' pride in connecting the Red Sea to the Mediterranean—a formidable feat by any measure.

The statue was partially destroyed in 1956 after the canal's nationalization by Nasser, but it was later restored and is now located in a shipyard in Port Fouad.

As John Brinton would write in *Aramco World* (September-October 1969): "The building of the Suez Canal has always seemed like a great engineering challenge; a man-against-the-desert epic of formidable magnitude. The major problem was not engineering, as by the 19th century huge new steam dredgers were available; the real problems were in politics, finance and diplomacy, fields as it turned Ferdinand de Lesseps excelled."

The canal had been opened in November 1859 by Khedive Ismail with with flags flying, cannons thundering, bands playing, and Empress Eugenie presiding as a special guest, together with a thousand dignitaries including representatives from most of Europe's royal families. Few seemed to know or to care that the canal would bankrupt the country.

Palestine Street was full of commotion when we arrived. As in any other port, peddlers were waiting for disembarking passengers from Australia or South Africa or India or that emerald island then called Ceylon. Their cacophony made a kind of music.

Writing for *Aramco World* (September-October 1977), Elias Antar would recall for me the very same cries I heard: "Hey Mister, come and see my camels, small camel only 20 dollars!... Hey, *ragazza*, look, look! This real scarab... Mister! Mister! This way visit Bor Saeed. Fast horse, go quickly, quickly! Hey lady! *Buon giorno!* You want cheap Frigidaire? Very good Frigidaire only 900 dollars! Hey Mister! Hey Mister!" And so on the litany went.

The city as any port was alive, tumultuous. From our hotel window we could see the ship convoys which appeared to be floating across the desert as if by magic. (The canal is a single lane and contains no locks.) Antar noted that when a ship anchored, passengers disembarked, and "tugs hooted in the roadstead, cranes rattled on wharfs, horses neighed and coins tinkled. The air crisp, crowds gathered to watch, and the vendors in full cry moved in."

My big reward of the trip was going to Asia. With tickets in hand, priced at one millieme (at that time less than a quarter of a cent), we climbed the ferry. The return was free. "It should be free both ways," said my father, but charging that tiny sum prevented the peddlers and urchins from plying the crossing all day back and forth. Today there are three ferries moving passengers continuously and free of charge. It was no more than a ten-minute voyage then, and I do not remember anything else, except my excitement crossing Africa to Asia, I reached another continent.

The canal was blocked after the Suez Canal crisis in 1956 for a year and later again blocked by the Egyptian authorities from 1967 to 1975 after the Six-Day War with Israel. War brought heavy damage, with vessels clogging the waterway and rusting for eight years. Cities as Suez, Port Said, and Ismailia, and dozens of villages along the canal were rendered wastelands by the war—scarred, deserted, silent.

The canal reopened during President Sadat's time after the peace treaty with Israel was signed; the cities were reconstructed, light industries restarted, and the canal zone bustled with life anew.

In 1981, Arthur and I drove along the highway parallel to the Suez Canal and stopped overnight in Ismailia. While only a single shipping lane exists in the canal, there are two major turnouts for passing. Typically three convoys transit the canal daily. We witnessed a southbound convoy which had departed from Port Said proceeding to Bitter Lake in Ismailia, where the convoy awaited its northbound counterpart before continuing to Suez.

A new Suez Canal parallel to the old one for half of its distance was inaugurated in August 2015, and sailing on that new canal added another eventful episode to my lifelong engagement with Egypt.

Outings at the beach

Every summer for six years, my brother returned from Europe. There was always a trinket, a souvenir of his travels for me: a miniature Eiffel Tower, a painted wooden windmill from Amsterdam, a crystal Easter bunny from

Norway, my own little radio. I always anticipated that special treat, a box of Swiss chocolates.

One summer Akis arrived from Italy by seaplane. I had never seen that type of aircraft landing on water and I was excited by this novelty. We drove to the Lake Mariut airport and found a large number of onlookers, journalists, and photographers gathered; there was even a cordon of police to control the crowd. Why were there so many people? Why such an entourage? An important dignitary had to be on that seaplane. To our great surprise, we saw the mystery passenger, climbing down—none other than Cheeta, the monkey of the Tarzan movie fame! She was on her way to the jungles of Africa for another film shooting. Her picture made the front pages of Alexandria's newspapers next day.

With my brother in town for the summer, there were always outings to the beach. Greek friends had rented a cabin in Stanley Bey, and my piano teacher in San Stefano and I found ourselves invited. The myriad of multicolored umbrellas from Chatby to Sidi Bishr through San Stefano and Stanley Bey resembled a field of gaily colored mushrooms.

The waterline was the site of an old promenade where groups of teen age boys and girls would stroll past each other, heading in opposite directions, attempting their first flirtations, away from the watchful gaze of parents who sat somewhere in the shade of a beach umbrella, absorbed in a game of backgammon.

The waterline was also a favorite place for photographers whose equipment bore witness to the evolution of photography over the years. Tripod-mounted square boxes with attached black cloth sleeves that made them into portable developing chambers as well as cameras gave way to the smaller and more sophisticated twin-lens Rolleiflex and the rangefinder Leica.

While my brother studied in Lyon, he befriended an Egyptian student, Ali el Kouni, a Victoria College graduate, a landowner with 200 hectares in the delta planted with cotton. Ali became a family friend and often invited my brother to his country estate; occasionally I tagged along. From those visits come recollections of the slow-moving Egyptian village life.

A village wedding

I have witnessed many Muslim weddings in the Middle East, in Afghanistan, in the Caucasus—with guests sipping their vodka, dancing in a circle with other women—precious memories that I penned in one of my travel books.

In accordance with local custom, such weddings always take place after sunset and always on a Thursday, the start of the Muslim weekend. The well-off hold costly receptions in a hotel with music, food, a juice punch, and a performance to make it a merry event. To avert the evil eye, it is customary to toss confetti or gold-foil chocolate coins, to draw guests' eyes away from the bride. Those coins however would be quickly scooped not only by children but by the tourists who happen to be billeted at that particular hotel.

Nothing however rivals the commotion of a village wedding which I was privileged to witness six decades ago as a guest of our friend Ali el Kouni in his *ezba* (private agricultural estate) in the delta.

With the other women of the village I crowded into the home of the bride's family to pay my respects on the morning of her wedding day. I felt very uncomfortable, not knowing any of the women. Being the guest of the wealthy landowner, attention was now focused on me, and with my limited Arabic I had an overwhelming desire to depart. Every bride looks beautiful and it was no exception for Egyptian girls, *fellahin* or not, to look at their very best. The bride was so young, perhaps just sixteen.

I understood that the night before, the bride's sisters and friends had come to bathe her, to lay out her clothes and jewelry, and to stain the palms of her hands and the sole of her feet with henna. Henna has been used as a cosmetic since the time of ancient Egyptians, its color being considered not only beautiful and good for the skin but also a sign of purity. I did not see the actual process but the village women insisted that I should use henna as well for good luck and have a design on my hands. I do not recall the pattern, but it was executed expertly with a toothpick, a rich orange-red diluted with water or tea. It took ten days of vigorous scrubbing to remove it.

Though only women visited the bride before her wedding, it seems that every one of the village men—village officials, the local policeman, from the richest landowner to the poorest beggar—and of course children gathered to see the bride move into her new home.

First came the beating of drums, accompanied by trumpets and tambourines, as special songs were sung to celebrate the marriage by the young girls of the village. The biggest excitement however was the bride's trousseau— shiny pots and pans, a mattress, a mirror, a brightly painted wooden chest, a bed, a chair, a sofa, a new wardrobe all put on donkey drawn carts and shown off to the crowds. We all shouted our congratulations and the shouts were even louder when members of the bride's family carried large round trays with food: ducks, geese, meter-wide pots of meat, overcooked vegetables, beans, bread. All these had been cooked over propane burners. Then came the sweets, fried pastries, and honey-drenched *kunafa*, making up the wedding feast. Ali's staff had prepared four pigeons filled with fresh cracked wheat for the couple's evening diner.

But the loudest shouts came when the bride and groom paraded in the village street. The bride was seated on a cart drawn by a flower-bedecked donkey. I asked Ali why he did not lend his car. "It will be a precedent," he told me. "I should then offer my car for every bride in the village and neighboring villages." Throughout the procession there was noise and merriment, ensuring that everyone knew there would be a new family in the village. Young girls in the country wore very bright colors especially pink, and plain kerchiefs edged with glass beads.

The bride and some of her women relatives headed the procession. Some men fired ceremonial shots into the air while others threw firecrackers, filling the village street with smoke. As the bride passed we threw a few pinches of salt in the air to ward off the evil eye.

Every country has its traditions, and this wedding reminded me throwing rice or rose petals in Greek and Western weddings, a symbol of good luck.

The bridegroom emerged from the house of his best friend and followed the bride. He wore an impressive turban, a white *galabiyeh* of the finest cotton, and held a sword in his hand. He had also been bathed by his friends and had applied a light touch of henna to his hands and feet. Now, carrying torches and lit candles, his friends surrounded him, making a tight circle until he reached his bride who was waiting at his family home.

Following tradition, the groom and the bride's father clasped hands; the sheikh then covered their hands with a clean white handkerchief and read a passage of the Koran, confirming the commitment of the parties. Legally the couple was now husband and wife. The handkerchief was removed, or rather whisked away by a single young man for good luck. It was time for every one to celebrate, and singing filled the night with traditional Eastern strains.

What has not changed through the years and, remains characteristic of Egyptian country houses, are the pigeon towers, two clumsy columns built of earthen pitchers glued together with mud and cement. They supplied the choicest dish of Ali's table: *pigeon au Ferrik*, pigeon stuffed with fresh roasted wheat, onion, and cinnamon, one of Egypt's great delicacies.

Reading the coffee cup

In those years after the war, life resumed at a normal pace. Our summer holidays in Sidi Bishr were now a thing of the past. Akis was studying in Europe. No more talk of war threatened our peace of mind, but another fear had emerged, and dark clouds were hovering over Egypt.

My mother scheduled her dental appointments and visited her friends in the morning while I was at school. She stayed at home in the afternoons to ensure that I was not disturbed by visitors. Our living room was always crowded with visitors—my godmother, and Italian and Swiss neighbors coming over for tea or Turkish coffee, *petits-fours*, and homemade biscuits; they loved my mother's baking.

The conversation was mostly plaintive, with a repertoire of unflagging complaints about health, children, the servants who robbed you, the daily reminders of unrest and turmoil in Egypt. Madame Pangalou, the Italian neighbor, missed the opera; another complained about why I practiced the piano so late in the evening, and as if it was at a typewriter. She was right; I was not musical. Madame Maltezos, a saleslady at the Sistovaris fur store, the most famous furrier of the city, regaled the others with stories about the latest purchases of Mrs. Finney, whose husband was the wealthiest foreigner in the country. (Looking back, l would note that all those ladies had lived in Egypt for thirty, forty years, certainly most of their life, and in all that time, they had never learned more than thirty, forty words of Arabic, not even one for every year.)

The beverage of choice was Turkish coffee—*café Turque*, although today it is referred to as Greek coffee. It was always brewed in a little brass pot, never a tin one. The coffee was strong, black with extra sugar to camouflage the bitterness. One of the ladies would turn the cup upside down and read fortunes in the coffee grounds.

I can still hear Madame Pangalou's voice as she argued about the ability of one psychic versus another and their accurate interpretation of coffee grounds. At times, the conversation got quite heated, depending on who was involved.

Among my mother's friends was Mrs. Konstantina Cosmas. She came occasionally but when present she held court among them, all five fingers decorated with exquisite rings, jewels blazing about her neck. She was a big woman, arrogant, despotic, and commanded royally. I could hear her say "Let's read the cup!"

We knew families where the husband would not start his working day until his wife had read his morning cup and given her prediction for the day. Coffee reading could become an addiction. It was amazing to see how people from all walks of life—from the poor to the rich, from the wise to the simple, from the literate to the ignorant—craved having their futures foretold though these readings. Are there any biscuits left for me, I asked after the visitors departed. Mymother kept them under lock and key in one of the many cupboards in the pantry.

Over time, I learned how to prepare a cup for reading, how to hold the cup and cover it with a saucer and, holding both securely, turn them up-side down. You let the overturned cup rest over its saucer for 20 minutes.

You knew that it was ready to be "read" when you cautiously lifted the cup and nothing dropped from it. The longer a cup was left to dry, the easier the reading would be. You never read the back stump of the coffee cup. Whether it was Spode or local pottery did not make a difference.

I learned through osmosis—listening to the ladies, observing the coffee patterns—the meaning of certain symbols: good fortune, love, travel, stress, caution against diversity. In later years, among students at the University, I amused them by reading a cup and interpreting the pictures. My imagination ran wild, and it was fun, but they took it seriously and started believing me. I could see the excitement, the thrill of deciphering symbols. Once, completely out of the blue, I made a prediction; my friend whose cup I was reading was galvanized, sounding excited beyond words; I had made her so happy. A few days later, my prediction came true!

My husband knew that it was my wild imagination at work and he put an end to it in our first year of marriage. You step in perilous waters, he cautioned me. I stopped reading the cup fifty-five years ago.

III.

CARPETS, COFFEE, AND CULTURE

MANY OF MY happiest memories of childhood have to do with the market, a place I would return to and seek out for the rest of my life, in nearly every city in the world that I have ever been. I visit markets both for the fresh produce and the dry goods, but also to relive the days when my father took me along, thereby imparting to me the knowledge and the bargaining skills that would serve me well in the decades to come. It is in bazaars where one experiences the pulse of the country, getting a view of local life—the customs, the food, the laughter, the fashions. Bazaars are unique achievements of Islamic culture, inspiring trade and barter for profit, which is of course as old as the human race.

From the Rue de France one entered, through winding alleys, a teeming, working-class Alexandria. This was where poor Europeans lived: Greeks, Maltese, and "local subjects." The Jews of that area congregated at the old Jewish quarter; clad in *galabiyeh*, they blended in perfectly with the Arabs. From there you could hear a sniff of a sound from the siren of a commercial vessel negotiating the tortuous fairways as it set off for India.

Standing there was an exquisite bazaar—which was covered until 1922—filled with treasures from the Orient. What a joy it was when I was allowed to accompany Father in the food market; I loved my father and loved being with him. I often joined him as he purchased another carpet to add to our collection, honing my bargaining skills from childhood. My mother bought bolts of soft Egyptian cotton to have sheets made, and hand-embroidered pillowcases. I was engrossed by the colorful native quarter; holding my father's hand, we aimlessly meandered around, looking for whatever else was offered in the souk.

We usually started with the butcher shop of Ahmet, who had only one good eye and who welcomed us with his large grin. The halved carcasses of a cow and a lamb hung near his shop entrance. A red stamp on each carcass signified that it had passed the government health inspectors. Flies buzzed around those carcasses, especially during summertime; a young assistant with a whisk in hand chased them away.

Ahmet knew my father's shopping days and the special cut of meat he favored. There was a large wooden cupboard in the back of the shop where he kept special cuts for his customers. I doubt there that he had any refrigeration. Father bought only veal, and as I tagged along I would ask a few extra scraps for the *otah*, the cat. No pet food was available and our cat Boutzoukos lived on scraps and leftovers. Meat would be ground at home as many Greek dishes required minced meat; we never purchased it from the butcher as he usually incorporated inferior cuts with too much fat.

Price controls were put in place during the war years but the butcher was well aware that better cuts commanded higher prices and the *hawaga* (the title given to a foreigner, like "sir") would purchase it without reporting the infraction to the inspector.

At the end of the bazaar past the carpet and bolts of clothing section were the spice and the candy shops. As we strolled, we always paused, like bloodhounds with our noses in the air, to sniff out the spices, the seasonings, and the herbs. My mother would take a pinch of oregano or sage and crush it in the back of her palm for the pure pleasure of smelling it; she would buy a handful of cloves, another of star anise, and she would walk away with tears in her eyes because the smell of the cayenne made her sneeze so much. She would purchase a small amount, always very small, as the spice aroma deteriorated rapidly (unlike the spices sold in America, kept in hermetically sealed glass jars for months, sometime for years).

Father always asked for discounts, arguing gently as part of the repartee, the haggling so common in Arab marketplaces, until he got the best price. He paid with pieces of silver that the shopkeeper tested for the sheer pleasure of hearing them clatter against the marble counters.

We would then proceed to the candy section, where the merchants sat behind huge open jars or hemp bags filled with local candies: licorice strings, sesame candy, coconut candy, lemon or orange scented candies, brown sugar loaves, and sheets of *kamar el din* made from dried apricots. Often they would buy me a piece, sold by weight, to chew on. At other times mother would take a large sheet home, soak it in water, then simmer it in her Primus, ending with apricot juice or a substitute apricot jam when the fresh fruit was not in season.

In this part of the market there were not only edible things but others too with strange smells that spread out from right and left like exotic elves thrusting themselves upon us: camphor from China, naphthalene from Turkey (which we always purchased, to chase off silver fish from woolens), local fish glue, hemp ropes, and spools of string from India and wicker work items from Upper Egypt.

A little further one could see traditional Egyptian cosmetics: kohl to enlarge and beautify the eyes as in the time of the Pharaohs; henna to color the hair and to strengthen and protect it against lice, and to color the palms and soles of village women. All kind of perfumes were available, as well as brilliantine –a glossy hair pomade—inexpensive powders and face paints, and scented soaps in all shapes and colors.

Indifferent to the uproar of the bazaar, I was captivated by a paper seller who was demonstrating magic inks, red inks with a strain of blood, inks of a sad aspect for messages of condolences, phosphorescent inks for reading in the dark, invisible inks that revealed themselves in light, and then gold ink. I wanted all of them; my fascination with these inks would later lead to a degree in Chemistry. From the bazaar we proceeded to Muhammad Ali Square where I was treated to an Arab sweet called *arissa*—semolina-based, it oozed with a delicately flavored syrup. We referred those shops as the Syrian patisseries. There was always a stack of trays of bougatsa (that delicate phyllo concoction filled with semolina and sweetened goat cheese) and baklavas, their oiled surfaces and wrappings glittering in the light.

There was a vast selection of fish at the fishmonger: sea bass, *loufaria* (blue fish), red and grey mullet, giant crab, octopus, shrimp, lobster, and crayfish with huge menacing pincers. Here and there was the odd shark's head lying next to an expensive sole. Shrimps were inexpensive; only in later years when the canning factory was built would shrimp achieve an elevated status.

Father would look at the gills, not the eyes, of the fish to ensure its freshness. Otherwise he would not buy; there is always the possibility that the fishmonger smeared red ink in the gills of fish no longer quite fresh.

Chickens, rabbits, and pigeons were piled in huge cages hand made from palm fiber. Chicken for us was expensive, nearly a luxury to be enjoyed at Christmas time. It was an operation undertaking to purchase a chicken, and one needed to be patient. After selecting what was supposed a large one, the poultry owner would take it out of the cage, and cut its throat with a sharp knife or wring its neck with a single sharp twist. Mortally wounded, the bird would briefly flap its wings until it became perfectly still. After splashing water from a bucket to wash off blood, he shoved the heart, liver, and gizzard back inside the chicken, which he then trussed up and bundled in a newspaper. Placed in Muhammad's wicker basket, it was then taken home.

It was no surprise when, after purchasing a large chicken, by the time the feathers were plucked and the corn the bird had been stuffed by the merchant was removed, you ended up with just half of its initial weight.

Chicken would be roasted; it was a holiday meal for us unless one was sick, for which chicken soup would then be a recommended remedy; Campbell's soup had not yet arrived in Egypt. (I would not taste turkey until I came to America—and then it was so different from how others described it in their memoirs, as the fowl ordered by people at Pastroudis.)

The sugarcane man stood next to his cart at his usual spot at the end of the bazaar street. He was well aware of the pattern of the pedestrian traffic (there were no cars in the market). With his hand-cranked machine, he squeezed the cane, selling the frosty sticky sugarcane juice to the passersby. Father would buy me a small cane stick to chew on putting my jaws to a test. I chewed for a while before the spit out the cane's woody fibers, as the sweet sap was dribbling down my chin. Chewing sugarcane was strongly recommended by dentists in Egypt.

(Sugarcane is widely available in Alexandria's streets these days, sold by fruit vendors at many of the city corners. What is new are the number of "juice" stores that offer, besides freshly squeezed oranges and grapefruit, sugarcane. The cane is squeezed by a giant electrical operated juicer, and a large pitcher is filled with that sugary liquid, to be dispensed in a large paper cup, straw included, for just a few cents.)

As we walked from one merchant to another in the market, I would stop by the blind beggar who sat cross-legged in a corner of the pavement; he was always in the same spot day after day, reciting his misfortunes and begging passersby for alms. Encouraged by my father, I would place a piaster or two in his tin begging bowl. What a delight it was to see his warty, sour countenance soften with pleasure for just an instant.

The market was never quiet, and was always teeming with people. Carts laden with fruits or vegetables crowded the sidewalks. The shrill horn of a passing car got attention—cars were not permitted on that market street—followed by vendors swearing at the driver. A donkey cart heavily laden with clay water jugs avoided colliding with a cyclist vendor who skillfully balanced a board covered with *semit* on his head. (*Semit* was similar to giant pretzel or bagel covered with sesame.) Farther on, a policeman chased a boy who had stolen a guava.

The genesis of a carpet collector

A laughing voice came from Ibrahim el Mohair, the leading carpet shopkeeper of Alexandria's bazaar. "Come on, come on!" he would cry as he unpacked his treasures and spotted my father.

I accompanied my father on his bazaar outings, seeking out carpets. We already owned a few from such faraway places as India, Anatolia, and Persia, but Father was always looking for more. Was it another addition for our home or was he prospecting for one of his friends? I gazed at my father with admiration, my eyes shining with pride when I heard one of his friends say that Panayiotis knew his carpets; the reposing of such trust meant much to me. Even so, he admitted the mistake he made when he once purchased a Romanian carpet; it was of inferior quality, worn unevenly in the center. He loved the design and the colors were appealing, but it had been made with "dead" wool.

As he looked at a carpet from Ibrahim's newly arrived inventory, he turned it over and scratched it with his fingernail, giving him a rough estimate of the number of knots. A count of 144 knots per square inch was considered a base mark of quality, but he was not overly enumerative as some new designs were coarsely knotted. Slightly irregular knotting was not a defect but a characteristic of handmade manufacturing; highly uniform rows might betray a dreaded, machine-made carpet posing as genuine.

Although Father did not smoke, he carried a box of matches in his pocket, a precaution if the shopkeeper could not locate any. Ibrahim was a bonafide dealer and did not object when Father asked to extract a thread from a carpet he selected and set it alight. It was a simple test, as wool smolders and emits an unmistakable smell when lit, whereas artificial fibers burst into flames. The oily, ovine odor could easily betray a supposed silk carpet as being in fact made of boiled wool.

There was always the question of color, which I learned could be tested simply by rubbing the carpet with a damp cloth. I completely ignored that test when, in America few years later, we purchased a small entrance-hall carpet. It was the perfect size, an Isfahan design handmade in Pakistan. When our carpets were professionally cleaned, it was the only one that leached. Natural dyes do not leach, but cheap alkaline dyes do.

The colors Father was looking for were, besides the browns, various hues of red. Red pigments were extracted from pomegranate, cinnabar, onion skins, beet root, cochineals, beetles, and while the browns came from walnuts, apple leaves, and a variety of barks. Natural dyes took a month or more soaking to imbue the wool with their subtle shades, compared to boiling the wool for two hours with chemicals. Why don't we choose carpets with cheerful yellows or orange, I would ask him—after all, saffron was a natural product. Those colors have a tendency to glare within the overall pattern, my father would reply—use your aesthetic judgment!

Ibrahim flipped the carpet back and forth, as my father kept his eyes out for "abrash," the slight change in background color along the length of the carpet that indicated a change of skein. This irregularity is now sometimes faked but it remains a worthy indicator of natural dyeing.

We did not purchase any carpet that day. By osmosis I was absorbing a smattering of knowledge. Foreigners patronized the European stores of Alexandria's Rue Fouad, but it was while lingering with my father in the dusty corners of the carpet shops that I learned the trade. I got hooked and became truly intrepid when I ventured years later into the bazaars of Kabul in Afghanistan, the source of the finest Bukharas, pricey but durable weaves typically in an enveloping warm red color and distinguished by a traditional elephant foot octagonal pattern. Sheer poetry! My odyssey of carpet searching would put me on the trail of the Uzbeks, the Turkmen, and the Kazakhs, and I would walk through the stunning carpet collections in the palaces of the former Shah of Iran and the museum of Ashkhabad in Turkmenistan.

All that began in those forays with my father into Alexandria's bazaar.

A Little Paris

Beyond the market at Ibrahimieh, Alexandrians shopped in a variety of other places.

On the Rue Cherif stood the most elegant stores in town. How can I forget the reputed Old English shop which sold the finest quality of tweeds and woolens for elegant winter tailoring? If it was not for the staff speaking Arabic, French, Greek, and Italian, you could think you were on Regent Street. Fine Wedgwood china and Sheffield cutlery were prominently displayed at the shop, and if you needed Imperial Leather soap, you could find it there.

For everyday purchases there was a choice of several department stores. The Grands Magazins Chalons and Oreco both resembled French department stores. Those stores were elegant; it was like a Little Paris. Cicurel, a Jewish-owned department store, had slightly less expensive merchandise and was among the first to be burned down during the 1952 uprising.

We patronized mostly Hannaux, an elegant store with an old-fashioned grilled and caged elevator and parquet floors. (Those grilled elevators still exist in Alexandria, and were at my hotel, the Windsor Palace, in 2015— spacious, made of solid wood and artistically worked wrought iron, still functioning and still safe.) An attendant in white gloves pushed the button for the second or third floor. Once, on Christmas Eve, we went to view the store's festive Western decorations—artificial Christmas trees with decorations, manger scenes with tiny figures, Father Christmas, reindeer, and angels. Many shops would decorate their windows with cotton-wool snowflakes the size of plums, trying to create a Christmas atmosphere. Hannaux was packed that evening, with a well-heeled crowd. The sisters of King Farouk were shopping for toys to be distributed at local orphanages.

Patisseries and sweets

I remember the patisseries, a great monopoly of the Greeks. From the old stock exchange all along Saad Zaghloul, the roadside was studded with them: Pastroudis, Trianon, Athineos, Delices. The cakes were thick and fat, unlike the skimpy French pastries: *millefeuilles*, éclairs, madeleines, chocolate cakes, coconut cakes, macaroons, opera cakes, almond and walnut tarts with or without Chantilly cream, and then the baklavas, *trigonas, kataif, mamouls* stuffed with dates, and *konafa*. The sweet shelves were laden with stuffed dates, *marrons glacées*, crystallized fruit, chocolates in velveteen or wooden boxes, and biscuits in huge tins. The sweets of the Ottoman Empire stood side by side with the sweetmeats of Europe. Buying was done in French, Greek, or "Alexandrian." Sweets were essential to the conviviality of Alexandria. They standardized the rites of visiting a friend, which required a dozen little cakes, at least; a box of bonbons was always at hand to be presented on arrival.

Two of our neighbors were pastry chefs, one from Tornazaki, the other from Athineos. They were willing to impart to Mother the secrets of their pastry making, recipes I treasure decades later. How can one duplicate the hazelnut Daquoise of Athineos?

In Muhammad Ali Square stood a couple of Syrian pastry shops which we patronized. Over the glass-fronted shelves bearing all manner of sweets and savories were mounds of cheese or custard-filled *bougatsas*. Those shops sold exclusively a variety of Ottoman delicacies, among them *arissa*, a semolina-based sweet displayed on giant round trays and golden as the sun. There was a sweet called *ekmek kataif* in Turkish and *ech saraya* in Arabic, meaning "palace bread"; it remains my very favorite in the world—a mouth-watering desert, a bread pudding soaked in syrup and topped with clotted cream, if you do not count the calories.

Turkish specialties such as *loukoums* were piled high, forming a pyramid; they were made from gelatin, lots of sugar, coloring, rose and orange essence, in pistachio and pomegranate flavors. Next to these were the traditional pastries such as baklava with walnuts or pistachios drenched in honey; grilled pistachios soaked in syrup, dates filled with almonds, dates filled with strips of candied orange. No matter how often I went as a six- or sixteen-year-old, I knew that they could be mine for a couple of piasters.

The pretty wooden boxes—some inlaid with mother of pearl for well-heeled customers—were filled with dates stuffed with walnuts, almonds, and candied citrus fruit.

When I returned decades later the sweets were as delicious as ever, but did not hold the same attention.

Café Groppi based in Cairo was the most famous of all. Groppi was the chief purveyor to the court and pashas throughout the Middle East. Its Alexandria branch was purchased by a Frenchman whose daughter was two years ahead of me at the Lycée. His wife attended the Finney ball with a white fur cap purchased from the Sistovaris fur shop, whose saleslady regaled my mother with stories of their clientele. Until Nasser's revolution, Groppi in many ways symbolized Egypt itself, a cosmopolitan crossroads, a meeting place where new ideas could be vigorously discussed. "Cairo at that time was the center of the world, and Groppi was the center of Cairo," according to Marco Groppi, the fourth generation of his family to live and work in Egypt.

Bloomberg News would note that "Groppi was the scene in which to be seen, where political aspirations were born, business deals stuck, marriages and divorces negotiated." It was famous for its mouthwatering delicacies like fresh croissants, chocolate-covered dates and ice cream smothered with crème Chantilly—light whipped cream, the only establishment that offered it. A visit to Groppi demanded your finest fashions. It welcomed families and women, so different from the traditional male-only coffeehouses. Here, Bloomberg reported, British administrators, titled British diplomats, and French bourgeoisie rubbed elbows with Cairene dissidents and politicians.

More cafés than minarets

The European Alexandria where we lived stretched in all its modernity for 20 kilometers along the Corniche from the Square to the royal palace of Montaza. Cafés and patisseries were spread out along this spectacular promenade.

As evening fell, Europeans and Egyptians of the middle class would gather at the cafés, staying there for hours in tables of two or four, sipping their Turkish coffee accompanied by a glass of water, or waging a game of backgammon, or reading the papers and exchanging stock market tips.

There were more cafés in Alexandria than minarets. (There was a distinction between cafés frequented by men and pastry shops for women and families, although the famous Groppi in Cairo was labeled as a café.) Coffeehouses in Egypt were known for their vibrant nature. The patrons may have been intellectuals or merchants or spies or politicians. This was where friendships were forged, screeds written, plans hatched, alliances forged, discussions held on what was published in the morning newspapers stock market tips exchanged. Cafés in the Arab world were then and now places where people got together and sat down to have a conversation, so different from the Starbucks where hyperactive Americans grab their caffeine and run.

Young *bouyaggi* would polish customers' shoes. Vendors peddled their wares, and with a piaster or half a cent, one could purchase a lottery ticket, the nightly prize nothing more than a jar of jam. Father, occasionally a winner, brought home a preserve of Rosella quince jam from Australia (my husband Arthur would tell me in later years that it was a most inferior brand. How I remember the name of the brand is a miracle!)

The Egyptians did not patronize the same cafés that Europeans frequented; or they would sit at another section of the café where they smoked their personalized water pipes. A constant to and fro of waiters supplied them with glowing coals to relight their tobacco.

The most affluent gentlemen, usually dressed in tailor-made suits, met at Athineos or Pastroudis. The later was patronized by the elite of Alexandrian society. The atmosphere was animated and elegant, the moldings and paneling in the Art-Deco style. When I visited it again in 2014, it was rundown and somnolent.

As you walked along the Corniche a waft of Greek music emanated from the cafés, while every hour on the hour the triumphal march of *Aida* played from the radio station—Verdi had been commissioned to write an opera with Egypt as its setting for the inauguration of the Suez Canal. The opera was *Aida*, for which he was paid one thousand golden sovereigns, an enormous fee at that time and the equivalent of $3 million in today's money. He did not attend the premiere of his work, nor did he ever visit Egypt. The *Aida* march is still broadcast every hour, every single day, from Cairo's European station —a concession given by Verdi to the Egyptian government in perpetuity.

Incidentally one of the most memorable performances of Aida I ever witnessed was in the shadow of the great Pyramid of Gizeh. It seemed the entire Cairo zoo participated; and the triumphal march was repeated as an encore—a first!

From Chatby to San Stefano one could find restaurants built on pillars above the water, grandly called "casinos." As a university student, I would attend wedding receptions at those casinos. At Bella Vista in Camp Cesar, my parents would sit sipping a glass of cold Stella beer, taking the view of thecity and the stunning Mediterranean panorama. The Beau Rivage at Glymenopoulo, owned by the Bolange, a Swiss family, was an oasis of tranquility; its beautiful garden was a perfect setting for society ladies' afternoon tea, which included small mounds of sandwiches carefully cut to the prescribed thickness, golden brown scones warm with clotted cream and strawberries, and deliciously aromatic, inviting cakes. It was English tea, responsive to the British taste, unlike the Chantilly-filled French gateau of the patisseries, or the syrup-soaked Egyptian sweets. My parents would stop occasionally on a Sunday afternoon for tea. The Beau Rivage was a traditional venue for wedding receptions for the moneyed class. The flowering gardens shed fire on the lawns, and their magnificence made a perfect setting for a wedding. At night the Corniche was lit up like day, sparkling like a bejeweled tiara.

Love on the double-decker

Memories flow through Ramleh. There were two tramlines, the Victoria and the Bacos. The Victoria with its red emblem had double-deckers like London buses. During the war most of the drivers and inspectors were foreigners while the clippers were Egyptians. And what could be more cosmopolitan than the names of the stations spaced out along the terminus of Victoria?

As a teenager the double-decker was your favorite, as it allowed you to meet— by "accident," of course—your date, and to enjoy together the hour-long ride to Victoria terminus. As the upper deck was "second class," there was little chance of bumping into someone who knew you and who would report you to your parents. It was a perfectly innocent encounter by modern standards, in those pre-cellphone days. At that time, in the early 1950s, it was unusual for a young man and woman to go out together openly. Tittering remarks, disapproving stares, and unwanted advice always followed, but these did not prevent those "chance" encounters on the Victoria double-decker streetcar.

I recall travelling along that route, a half-day's back-and-forth journey, loafing and lingering in the tram. The conductor got angry when he caught us travelling without a ticket once.

Along those tramlines there was a clashing mixture of Arabic names, reminders of history, foreign business families, and European resorts: Mazarita, Chatby, Camp de Cesar, Ibrahimieh or Sultan Ibrahim, mostly populated by Greeks, Cleopatra, Sporting Club (mostly populated by Italians and Jews), and Sidi Gaber. This was the last station of middle-class Alexandria, where all nationalities and religions lived together. Past the next stop of Mustafa Pasha, opulent Alexandria spread out its villas and gardens, greenery scented with jasmine. Here were Carlton, Saba Pasha, Bulkley, Rouchdy (an Egyptian minister), and Glymenopoulo (a wealthy Greek).

The Bacos line, with its blue emblem, split towards Fleming (a wealthy English gentleman), Bacos (the birthplace of Gamal Abdel Nasser), and Gianaklis (a Greek wine manufacturer). Palm groves concealed private mansions and little palaces, but also outcrops of mud brick houses. Once a year, we took the Bacos line to visit Prophet Elias' Church for its annual name celebration and festival.

"What other town could offer such a motley parade of sights and symbols? What other town could boast such a bewildering roll-call of names?" exclaimed Ilios Yannakakis in *Farewell Alexandria.*

A visit to the yacht club

As a member of the Greek yacht club, Akis found himself frequently sailing solo a single mast-cutter and participating in numerous dinghy races. The yacht club, with heaps of regatta cups on display, held frequent dances for its members and their friends. I would take part in these dances in later years.

During a visit to the club, I noticed the *Rudder,* a venerable British sailing magazine, warped by the weather, lying on a table. Competition among the yacht clubs was fairly common. The French, the British had their boat clubs, of course, but even the landlocked Swiss had their Club Nautique Suisse. Each one belonged to a distinct ethnic community. The Jewish yacht club was known as the "International." They all still stand fifty years later, a bit run-down, under a different name and local management. The clubs owned canoes, skiffs of various size, large boats, cutters, etc., all purchased from overseas.

Another favorite outing took place when Akis joined a classmate, escorted by his father, for duck shooting in Lake Mariut. The lake was a land-locked sea, separated from the Mediterranean by a narrow isthmus on which the city of Alexandria is built. The main basin of the lake spreads blue and vast to the south of city, its surface broken by reeds. Not much has changed five or six decades later, although the lake is much smaller today. Fishermen follow in their ancestors' steps, poling their boats across its shallow and melancholy waters.

In autumn, innumerable duck, geese, and quail would migrate from Turkey to the warmer marshes of Lake Mariut. September was hunting season. Getting ready for the shoot meant packing and unpacking guns, getting cartridges, preparing a wicker basket of sandwiches and a thermos of hot coffee; it would be cold at dawn on the lake, and a heavy coat was carried for protection. I do not know if my brother was any good as a shooter, but he always returned with a bag full of birds, followed by gloating commentaries; the dead ducks were mostly courtesy of Mr. Papadakis, a family friend and the father of his companion. A few days later, a festive meal was prepared, consisting of roast duck stuffed with prunes and an exquisite paté—Mother was such a talented cook. It was a joyful get together as the Papadakises join us, recounting endless duck-shooting stories.

It is strange now as I sit here and look back to the past, and see my parents and the rest of the family clearly before me—people who molded me and are partly responsible for whatever I am today; the people who are now dead and forgotten by all who knew them, forgotten by me too until I started to look backwards to my far-off childhood. I did not know I was capable of remembering so much, but now that I have begun, the subconscious yields secrets and the memories come back from the buried years.

> *This fugitive memory.... I should so much*
> *Like to record it, but it's dwindled...*
> *Hardly a print of it remaining...*
> *It lies so far back, back in my earliest youth,*
> *Before my gifts had kindled.*

From *"Far Away,"* C. P. Cavafy

The flower festival

Every May, as flowers were in full bloom, the Greek community through its members, clubs, and associations sponsored the flower festival—the Anthesteria, a yearly fundraising event. Scores of carriages were decorated with multicolored flowers, adorned by the prettiest girls of the town. There was music and revelry in the evening, and dancing until dawn on the open-air terrace of the Athletic Club, which adjoined the parade grounds, the stadium in the west.

The Athletic Club was where, on Saturdays, Akis headed out as a guest of friends whom he would regale with stories of his adventures as a student in Europe. The young men sat around at the tables set out in the garden above the sport grounds, listening to Greek music and drinking lemonade. The chatter would revolve around the sporting events that were to be held the following day, about the film they would see on Sunday evening, the competition among the yacht clubs and, in furtive whispers, about the girls.

The festival was a friendly competition, with much effort put into the event and prizes bestowed on the prettiest floats; the judges were among the dignitaries of the Greek community. It was strictly a Greek event, and no other community organization was invited to participate or to exhibit their own float.

Here, let me digress about the Flower Cup event held earlier in April at the Antoniadis gardens. Princes, pashas, wealthy foreigners—Greeks, Italians, British, Jews—employed large teams of 30 to 40 gardeners to manicure their vast garden estates in anticipation of winning the Flower Cup. A committee of experts—Egyptians and foreigners from the Ministry of Agriculture—would inspect every flower and every plant, and interrogate the gardeners on how it was planted and taken care of. Some of the flowers had been bestowed with the names of past winners in the community: the Pastroudis carnation, the Prince Muhammad Ali hortensia, etc. They were costly shows, with thousands of pounds spent and days of preparation ending in a feast, a sort of fiesta with much pomp, food, and drink, all for the prestige of winning the Flower Cup.

We were not involved, as we did not belong among this rarefied elite. The local press was full of the event proceedings, accompanied with photographs. News filtered to us through my brother's classmate, a Zervoudakis whose family was always a Flower Cup participant.

Anna, a neighbor, one of the Flower Festival organizers, asked me to volunteer at a game kiosk. I was excited to be part of the event; I was just sixteen; my parents, however would not permit me to go alone. "Nice" girls in Alexandria were very strictly chaperoned, not so much allowed a step on their own, not even to a movie, without a female companion or a governess. (If the girls had fun, they did it discreetly. We were brought up to think that sex was a mortal sin.) Staying out until midnight was out of the question. I particularly did not want to join Aunt Katina, the elderly aunt who often served as a chaperon. I had to persuade my brother to accompany me; he was attending the festivities with his friends, and was not all that eager to have his young sister tag along; I pleaded, but mostly he obliged our parents.

I recall, early the morning of the festival, I joined my father at a nursery to purchase large bunches of purple dahlias, and had them delivered to the Chios club for their float. I wanted so much for them to be awarded the first prize!

Later that evening, my brother and I took the tram to Mazarita and walked to the high school stadium where the event was taking place. I wore a pretty white dress, with white being the unofficial uniform for volunteers.

The stadium was crowded mostly with carefree young people—it was a chance for young girls to meet boys of their age—but also there were families with children, even some elderly couples. We all took our seats in the stands and waited for the parade to begin. The procession moved slowly; girls sporting stunning colorful outfits lead each float. There was applause, cheering, and general rejoicing. Mothers waved proudly as they recognized their daughters sitting along the beautiful carriages.

When the parade was over the crowds began to stroll up and down as if the stadium was a park; the food kiosks were most popular offering simple fare, cold drinks, coffee, and mouth-watering pastries furnished by the leading Greek patisseries. I treated myself with a pistachio ice cream before moving to my games kiosk; there participants tried their skill at throwing loops, with the successful ones awarded a token prize.

Thinking back, it was an amateurish show, with carriages pulled by young men, and nothing motorized; there was even a flower-bedecked donkey pulling a float. This was not California's New Year Parade of the Roses, but it was genuine, and not commercialized. The festivities were conducted with spontaneity, with a certain *joie de vivre*, a joyful folkloric spectacle.

Besides the game kiosks were those offering bundles of flowers, including some inexpensive ones made with sweet-smelling jasmine. The food kiosks did a brisk business, but some families brought their own snacks, having already paid a hefty entrance fee of 25 piasters, five times the price of a movie ticket.

By midnight the dancing was still going strong, although the crowd had thinned. It was time for us to head home as we carried proudly to our parents a beautiful May wreath.

The flower festival was as exclusively Greek and as middle class as an Alexandrian event could be, one meant only for us to participate in and enjoy. I suppose it wasn't unfriendliness or malice that kept us away from other people so much as custom—others like the British and the Swiss also solidly kept to themselves. The elites of every foreign community reached out to their Egyptian counterparts for business and political reasons, but for the rest of us, there seemed to be no need. It was hardly the world we expect to live in today, one of racial harmony and active intermingling —but in its own way, it worked at that place, at that time.

Opera and theater

After the war, cultural events illuminated life in Alexandria, soothing some of the anxiety of the preceding years. Although there were a number of recreational activities for the various classes, those activities took place within individual communities and were based on their particular language or religion. Neighbors of different nationalities met at private homes, but I do not recall ever attending a dance or a masked ball at the Swiss or British club; nor did any other national attend the dances and the flower shows of the Greek community. As for the elite class, at that level, there was a closer interaction, mostly business.

Alexandrian society did meet at certain events. At the opera, the Italian repertoire always drew the most enthusiastic response. The brightest stars of

La Scala performed. How privileged I was to be exposed to the opera as a teenager to hear Gino Bechi or Tito Gobbi, great baritones whose renditions remained standards of many operas. There was great theater, a succession of plays from Paris and London performed by visiting companies. If the visitors were the Comedie Française, you could guarantee a full house. What a thrill to attend a performance starring Louis Jouvet at the Muhammad Ali theater in a Moliere play—Louis Jouvet was to France what Laurence Olivier was to England, at the very pinnacle of the performing arts—where he was able to infuse into classic repertoire modern interpretations. The National Theater of Athens with its great star Marika Kotopouli—the Sarah Bernhardt of Greece— performed Sophocles classics in the Antoniadis gardens. For my mother it was the most anticipated event.

But another kind of theater fascinated me. Long before the days of television, radio, or even cinema existed a different form of entertainment derived from folkloric traditions: the shadow-play, or Karaghiozis in Greek, an art form of a special kind. I had never seen such a performance before and would never see a Karaghiozis ever again, despite the many other forms of theater I would witness in my subsequent travels around the world.

For this performance, on a Saturday evening, I typically wore a flowery-print dress crafted for the season by Kyria Argyro, our local seamstress, as my Greek teacher would escort me for a unique outing, a rarity even those days nearly seven decades ago in Alexandria.

Was it an amateur group or a semiprofessional company from Athens that descended on Alexandria after the War?

Karaghiozis, the shadow-play's main protagonist, came to mainland Greece, probably from Anatolia, in the 19th century, during Ottoman rule. His name reveals its origins, as in Turkish *kara* means black and *gyoza* means eyes.

Karaghiozis is an ugly, hunchbacked Greek, his right arm always long, his clothes ragged and patched, his feet always bare. An irrepressible trickster, he stands for common people and for their cleverness in the face of injustice, which explains his popularity.

On Saturday evenings, kids from the Greek school and their parents crammed themselves into the small Luna Park theater at Ibrahimieh, in our neighborhood, to attend the show. We had good seats in the front row. A brisk trade in Sinalco—a fizzy orange drink—peanuts, and ice cream took place around us.

The orchestra—two violins and a drum—kept up a squealing sort of overture, punctuated by the giggles of the children and the pop of Sinalco bottles.

The screen was nothing more than a white piece of cloth, a plain sheet perhaps. Acetylene lamps on the hedge were extinguished and our eager faces were lit only by the light of the brilliant screen with its scarlet dado. The actors took their positions; now and then a shadow crossed the light, teasing us with the possible appearance of our hero. The orchestra plodded on with the awkward monotony of a squeaking shoe. Our expectancy reached its maximum intensity when sticks were rattled together from behind the screen. This was the sign for the play to begin.

The succession of figures on the dazzling screen glowed with a kind of brittle life of their own, and the voices—whose volume and pitch betrayed their human origin—crackled. All Greece was in the story, the marketplace, a row of Turkish figures, Albanian figures.

The story reached its peak with a faked election, in which Karaghiozis, in order to win, manages to resurrect all the corpses in the local cemetery who pass in a grisly single-file across the stage to the polling booth to vote for the hero.

And then, abruptly, Karaghiozis appeared to recite a short epilogue to thunderous applause. The screen went out, the orchestra packed up, and we stumbled yawning from the theater into the darkness.

Nights at the cinema

A very fashionable place to meet was the cinema. Movies were first shown in Alexandria, then in Cairo, then in the rest of the Middle East. It was the Hollywood studios who built those glamorous movie theaters, all air-conditioned. The Rialto, a very interesting Art Nouveau building, was built by Warner Brothers, the Strand by Paramount Pictures, and the Royale by Columbia Pictures; the last, long closed, was huge and modern and catered to the Anfushi public with a great rooftop salle. The Ferial, which was the old Metro located opposite Santa Lucia restaurant, opened with great publicity with *Gone with the Wind.*

In my area there was the Gaité (where once I viewed a silent movie with Greta Garbo, the dialogue projected on the right in red letters), the Odeon, and the Riviera. In those neighborhood cinemas two movies were shown as a double feature—what a bargain!

I cherished the moments to go to the movies to watch Cary Grant and Greta Garbo, Humphrey Bogart and Vivien Leigh, and the glorious world they inhabited.

One had to buy tickets ahead of time; always the seats were numbered, and an usher with a flashlight indicated your seat. I recall that once, at a Greta Garbo festival, I went with Aunt Katina to buy tickets at the Metro, and they were sold out. The Metro, owned by the powerful Metro-Goldwyn-Mayer, had huge mahogany panels, colored marble floors with geometric motifs. In 1950, it was the most modern and luxurious cinema in town.

My favorite however was the Muhammad Ali, as it was used for cinema and also for live theater performances. It was here where I saw *Hamlet* starring Laurence Olivier, one of the few English-language films my mother watched. In the summer, in San Stefano, we had access to an open-air movie theater, which as children we all loved. I recall the laughter from an Abbot and Costello film. Alexandria had never been merrier, more carefree than those years.

It was very different for the royals, who watched films at Montaza from an elevated lodge across the courtyard from the palace. King Farouk loved movies, especially those of Rita Hayworth, and he would have her films shown over and over. All the princesses would copy their clothes from those of screen stars like Gene Tierney and Marlene Dietrich. There were also

Arabic, Italian, Greek, French, American films, and we all partook of that feast.

I was envious of the other girls in my school, whose sweet parents took them on Fridays, the Muslim weekend, to the movies. It was Aunt Katina who escorted me and paid for my ticket. She did not speak any other language besides Greek and I became her interpreter during the performance. I did not know how to explain when I introduced her to my friends; she smiled, not uttering a word. I would avoid greeting them all together. During the intermission, I would try to put some distance between us or wrest my hand free from hers, or suddenly stop talking to her when I caught sight of a familiar face from school—which almost always happened, since everyone in Alexandria went to the movies on Friday. Because I lacked the courage to say she was my aunt, all I could do when I spotted a classmate coming toward us was simply to freeze, put a vague and absent look on my face, and pretend I had not seen her.

As soon as the film was over, I wanted to out of the theater, away from the crowded lobby where people were milling about trying to decide where to go next—we always went to the Delices pastry shop or A La Kefak for pistachio ice cream. But instead of hurrying, Aunt Katina always dawdled in her seat, talking about the film and asking questions, because despite my efforts at translation, she had missed quite a bit of the plot. Her real interest was in looking at what the ladies were wearing. She kept finding excuses to linger, to look under the seat, claiming she may have dropped something, invariably waiting for the aisles to clear before leaving and telling me to stay where I was, when all I wanted was to vanish.

Besides going to the cinemas, I recall Sunday afternoons with Aunt Katina at Athineos. Having been told to behave, I would wear my prettiest dress, and while eating chocolate cake or ice cream, I would observe the young couples dancing, watching many excellent dancers whirling lightly around the floor. Apart from the tango, they would dance the swing, the foxtrot, and also older dances as the Charleston and the waltz. The bands played the hits of the '40s and '50s such as *"Les Feuilles Mortes"* sung by Juliette Greco, Edith Piaf, or Yves Montand. During the war people asked the band to play "Yupee Yaya" or "It's a Long, Long Way to Tipperary."

An explosion of literature

Artistic societies abounded, endowed by the cotton merchants, and numerous amateur theatrical groups emerged.

At the Ateliers and at the Amis de l'Art, French cultural centers, were held exhibitions, lectures, concerts, and painting *vernissage* (private viewings) that as a student of the Lyçée I was entitled to attend. All these cultural activities were presented (i.e. financed) "by old business firms which had built the city's prosperity and whose families brought to the city the culture and tradition of foreign lands," as Judge Jasper Yeates Brinton would recall in his memoirs. Alexandria was "a city of great distinction, sophisticated, fond of music, art and literary interests, a city of beautiful homes, many of them veritable museums." Benaki, one of the wealthiest Greek cotton barons, was the Vice President of the Amis de l'Art. Along with the Atelier, those two institutions still flourish under Egyptian leadership and the city remains an artistic and cultural center.

The Greek International Society invited celebrities to lecture; George Duhamel received a standing ovation; Jean Cocteau was brought in for a series of lectures in conjunction of the opening of his masterpiece The *Beauty and the Beast*, a movie he directed and wrote the screenplay for. The "Beauty" was played by Josette Day and the "Beast" by Jean Marais. Cocteau visited the Lyçée, and honored me by signing my poetry album.

There was an explosion of literary activity in the form of newspapers and countless periodicals—literary, historical, political, some of high quality, written in all the many languages spoken in Alexandria. Newspapers were legion in Greek, Armenian, English and French. Typical among those we had at home was *Le Phare d'Alexandrie* and the Greek *Tachydomos*. Lectures were held on a variety of historical and literary subjects and the fine arts were catered to by several art schools.

The "old poet" (as Durrell called him) of the city, Cavafy, had passed away in 1933 but yearly lectures were given to commemorate him and his works, sponsored by the Greek Alumni Association. I recall that one year, I introduced the guest speaker at a Cavafy event, and received in turn a gift of the poet's book.

Many books, few readers

I knew of Cavafy's work—"The Barbarians" was my favorite poem of his then—but my family was not part of the intellectual life of Alexandria; there was never a literary discussion at our dinner table nor in the afternoon gatherings of my mother's friends, not even a commentary on a recently viewed movie.

There were lectures held at the Greek Hellenic Alumni Club and the Ibrahimieh Greek Club on a variety of historical and literary subjects, but it was not a pastime that attracted my parents' interest.

Intellectual pursuits within the Greek community were practically non-existent, and my parents were uninformed of the activities of other foreign communities activities. As for Egyptian culture—despite its formidable achievements the realms of music, sculpture, architecture, film, and literature—it remained largely a blank page for us then.

But this does not mean that we lived completely in an intellectual vacuum, as there were books, lots of books, in our home library—the Greek classics, translations from Goethe, Ibsen, Tolstoy. I wonder now if they were ever read. Where they accumulated through the years? Inherited from Barbas? Bought at one of the auctions my parents attended?

I, however, had a passion for reading. I was often gifted with French fiction—Dumas' *The Count of Monte Cristo*, St. Exupery's *The Little Prince*—supplemental reading, at the suggestion of the Lycée. Those novels were available at the school library, but often remained on long-term loan to other students. Green leatherbound books with golden labels graced a shelf in my study. I was so proud of the forty volumes the entire works of Victor Hugo, a gift of Aunt Katina.

The poet Cavafy was never talked about, completely dismissed in our home, although his subtle artistry was praised by the intellectuals of the town. My parents were more likely to be aware of Dionysius Solomos who wrote the

"Hymn of Liberty," the first two stanzas of which became the National Anthem, or of Costis Palamas, informally known as the "National Poet" of Greece.

Nikos Kazantzakis was also ignored in schools, viewed as a communist, a taboo subject. At home, we owned in Greek the author's *The Last Temptation*. Most surprisingly, years ago, my mother and her sister, a schoolteacher, called on Kazantzakis at his home at the island of Aegina, where he lived. Mother did not remember anything about the writer nor about their conversation, but was awed by the extensive and exquisite collection of small demitasse coffee cups he owned.

It was a painful yet also comic reminder of my mother's limited education, but perfectly understandable given how her social life revolved around family, friends, and church activities. She did, however, love the theater, and looked forward to the summer months when the National Theater of Greece arrived from Athens and mounted the classics at the Antoniadis gardens, in addition to attending the local productions in Ibrahimieh.

IV.

SCHOOL DAYS AND WARTIME

I WAS NOT even four years old when I entered kindergarten at the Lyçée Français at Chatby, a private French school, the flagship of all other French schools in Egypt.

It was run under the auspices of the Mission Laique Française, a lay mission, a non-profit organization located in Paris' 5th Arrondissement. Its aim was to spread the French language and culture. Its motto was "two cultures, three languages," with French and Arabic being the cultural anchors for Egypt. It offered a choice of languages—Latin, Greek, Italian, German, English, and Arabic—besides French, the medium of instruction. There were two sections: the French section leading to the French Baccalaureat, and the Egyptian section leading to an Egyptian high school diploma. I was enrolled in the French section, opting for Italian as a foreign language; English would be added in high school. I regretted entering an Egyptian university years later without having taken Arabic earlier. In my parents' home, no one took learning Arabic seriously. Arabic would become compulsory after 1960 in all foreign schools.

We did not own a car, like most of the other kids in school. We came from varying social backgrounds. Some were on scholarship, while others paid a full tuition of 100 pounds a year (at least US$10,000 in today's money), a prohibitive fee at that time; some rode the school bus and others took the tram, but most walked, as I would do by the time I was eight. We were envious of my schoolmate, the chauffeur-driven Sylvia Peta, whose father was the leading physician of the Italian community.

Would the school bus run in the morning after a long raid? Or would it be Muhammad, our live-in servant, who would carry me gently, virtually in his arms, to school? School started on time; there was no delay even if we had spent part of the night at the shelter, as there was another raid.

A mosaic of people

Half a dozen nationalities, a mosaic of people, were represented in my class: French, Greek, Italian, Swiss, Maltese, and Egyptian. No one asked where you came from, or if you were a Christian or a Muslim. It did not matter in those days. We all spoke French, the social language of the country; we followed the curriculum established in France, and we mixed freely among ourselves. There was a general consensus that despite or because of the incredible diversity of people, at least at the school level—and the school level only—there was a luxuriant tolerance in Alexandria.

The Lycée was totally different from so many other schools; it seemed to have an abundance of teachers—all expatriates from France—and classrooms. From kindergarten, I learned to say *Bonjour Mad*ame, *Bonjour Mam'selle*. In Egypt, all European ladies of a certain age and station were then called Mademoiselle or Signora.

Not a single English girl registered in my school, as they attended the private English Girl's College, and the boys the prestigious Victoria College, or the VC as it was better known; those schools were run on English lines.

Our school uniform was navy blue for winter, and off-white for the summer months; both were emblazed with the embroidered red crest of the Lyçée. In class we wore a gray *tablier*, a linen smock, which was brought home for laundry every Saturday. Classes were held six days a week from 8 am to 1 pm. On Saturday the class hours were shortened to noon. Monday morning started with the collection of few coins to be donated and dropped into the *boite des pauvres*, the box for the poor. Civic duty was instilled from first grade at the Lyçée.

The *chapeau* was obligatory: like our dresses, they were navy blue in winter and off-white in summer, festooned with a bright red ribbon. How much I disliked that hat; the *chapeau* got crushed in my leather briefcase the moment we were out of sight of the school supervisors. *"Le chapeau sur la tête,"* hat on your head, was a refrain that would echo decades later.

Each school had its distinct uniform, by which we recognized, on the streets and the trams, the school the students attended; mostly there were Catholic Mission schools—the College Notre Dame de Sion, the Mére de Dieu, Besançon, etc.

The Greek schools

When I was growing up in the '40s and '50s, many Greek primary schools were present in Alexandria. Some were private, while others were tuition-free, sponsored by the community. The bulk of the budget of primary and secondary schools came from donations and rents of community property.

My brother Akis attended the Tsoubion, a primary private school headed by three schoolteachers, a brother and sisters who came from Asia Minor. All classes were taught in Greek: Geography, Natural Sciences, and Arithmetic, with French as the foreign language.

There was a primary and a high school (which closed after 1956) run by the patriarchate, but the bulk of Greek education was provided at the Averofion, the high school in Mazarita, an outstanding institution at that time; it even became a model for all schools in Greece. The Averofion was basically tuition-free, with students paying according to their family income. It was maintained by the contributions of the town's elite. The teachers were highly qualified, and some had earned a PhD. I recall Dr. Haviaras, the modern Greek literature teacher and later the headmaster, who became the cultural attaché at the Greek embassy in Khartoum.

The free education meant that all Greek children went to school. The elite sent its children to mission schools as the Lycée, the Saint Mark, the Victoria College and more so schools abroad.

The level of education among Alexandrian Greeks was much higher than on the Greek mainland. Relative to the size of the population, the Greek community had a remarkable number of people who had completed university studies in Greece or other parts of Europe.

The Averofion offered the classical Greek curriculum, with a strong emphasis on modern and ancient Greek. Two of the most notable Greek writers—Kazantzakis and Cavafy—were, however, completely dismissed. In the early '30s Kazantzakis had flirted with communist ideas (he first renounced Nietzsche for Buddha, Buddha for Lenin, then Lenin for Odysseus), but the label remained in the eyes of the Greeks and the church; his writings were not taught to high school students. And although Cavafy's poetry was widely available in the '50s, being a well-known homosexual, he was totally banned due to the moral norms of the period. Classes at the Averofion averaged 20 students, and always started with a prayer. Religious studies—*Thriskeftika*—were part of the curriculum, and were taught by a lay preacher, who was occasionally seconded by a priest.

French was the first foreign language offered, followed by English. Arabic was not even an elective, and would be added as a requirement only after 1961.

The Salvagion, an imposing school building located in Mazarita, focused on teaching commercial subjects such as finance, accounting, and bookkeeping, meant to prepare students for the burgeoning of the brokerage and cotton exporting houses. Today it would be considered a trade school, less demanding than the Averofion.

Schools were not coeducational, as was the case of the Lyçée. The girls' high school was also endowed by the Greek elite of the time.

A school for the elite

Well-to-do families of Egypt, not only from Alexandria but indeed from the entire Middle East, sent their children to Victoria College, a British cultural outpost. Future kings (Hussein of Jordan, Faisal of Iraq), princes, prime ministers, cabinet members and influential members of Middle Eastern society passed through that institution, in which 30 different nationalities belonging to 10 different regions were represented. The distinguished roster included future Egyptian ministers, doctors, intellectuals, authors, and performers (such as the actor Omar Sharif and the movie director Youssef Chahine).

Writing about the VC in 2006, Samir Raafat would observe that "Victoria College was regarded a symbol of British cultural and political prestige in the Middle East. Physically, Victoria College was a reproduction of an English public school, with its own collection of houses. Physical training and out of class activities were more than ever a principle element on the academic curriculum. Yachting, squash, boxing, riding, swimming, tennis, and fencing were now as important as association football and cricket.... The British institution was expected, unofficially, to mold future generations and convert young minds into pro-British elements from amongst whose ranks would rise regional leaders and senior administrators. Given that objective, it was not a bad course to bring Cheltenham and Harrow to the Domaine de Siouf. Oxford and Cambridge could later do the rest."

There was a perception from us at the Lyçee that the girls at the English Girl's College were continuously at a picnic. Perhaps there was an element of envy there as their school boasted a swimming pool—something I learned from my brother, who dated a teacher from that school. They participated in numerous sports, like students do in American private schools today: hockey, lacrosse, swimming. Their motto was "A healthy mind in a healthy body." Team sport activities were absent at the Lyçée, with disciplines restricted to couple of hours a week, more like the ancient Greek activities limited to running, jumping, throwing—balance beams, pommel horse, long jump, pole vault. I was skilled at climbing ropes. I tried to persuade my parents without success to allow me to climb a palm date tree. I was slightly quicker and slightly stronger than the others, not necessarily better but often ahead by just a little bit.

At that at that time, tennis was the fashionable sport among the upper and middle classes, while at the English girls' college, hockey and lacrosse were in vogue, as they remain in 2015.

I befriended a honey-skinned girl—almost the tone of burnt sugar—with frizzy dark brown hair, who joined our class in the middle of the trimester. She was rather quiet, wrapped in an aura of mystery; she struggled in French but was fluent in English. Her features were strikingly different, and she bore such an unusual name: Tanusha. We were curious. Where did she come from? The Sudan perhaps? Her name sounded Russian.

The Malay Peninsula, she told me; her parents had fled Kuala Lumpur to avoid the Japanese occupation. The Malay Peninsula—where was that? Another war on another continent? I opened my Atlas, a child's version, to locate that faraway tropical land. She was the first Oriental—the word "Asian" was unknown to us then—whom I ever met in my life.

One day I reported to my mother that a teacher had been inspecting my nails and the pockets of my *tablier* to ensure I was not hiding any gum; she then looked through my hair, searching with her fingers and nails, raking my scalp roughly. Mother immediately began searching me for lice, suspecting that the school would never check students' hair unless a lice epidemic was already underway. There was a common myth that "dirty people" got it, but the truth was that lice liked clean heads. How humiliating it was when in front of the entire class you were told you were a carrier of lice. I told Mother that Jocelyn, a redhead, and I were the two students clear of any lice, but that was not good enough for my mother, who immediately placed my head over the sink and combed my hair with kerosene; if there were any lice, this would kill it, and it was the only remedy she knew. Fortunately, that process was never repeated.

A birthday invitation

A girl named Simone once invited me for her birthday. She lived with her parents and three siblings in what was the servants' quarters of a house down my street. I met her occasionally in my wanderings, as she walked with a younger sister in the neighborhood. She was not a student at the Lyçée, and I did not know if she went to school. Why was she inviting me?

There was little furniture in that dark basement of her house—a couple of wobbly wicker chairs, a newspaper-covered table with a stump of a candle in a tin container as its centerpiece. I was shocked by the seaminess of her life. Was she a refugee? It was a far cry from the elegant villas of my classmates where we celebrated birthdays, engaged in games and charades, played the piano, sipped hot chocolate, and savored glazed chestnuts, *marrons glacés*, and a birthday cake with pink sugar lettering, frosted flowers and curlicues, and other elaborate decorations.

At Simone's the birthday cake was a small loaf of sponge cake covered with a spoonful of apricot jam, without even a birthday candle. Her mother remained silent most of the time. Simone asked shamefully if my parents could spare some heating oil for the evening lamps. You do not have electricity? I inquired. She remained silent—their electricity was cut off as the bills were unpaid. I was mortified; how could I ask my parents for such a thing as oil? I gave a few disjointed words as an answer.

I knew nothing about poverty. It was the first time I had stepped outside the boundaries of my middle-class environment. As I recounted my outing to my mother, it did not take her but few minutes before locating a large tin canister; she filled it with oil, then gathered in a basket cheese, husk, biscuits, fruit, candy, and her own apricot jam to be gifted to the Carsentis. She understood the family's predicament, which in my innocence I did not realize. I do not know what further help my parents provided, if any, although they were always very generous. A few weeks later the family stopped by to thank us, letting us know that they were departing for Palestine, the Promised Land, soon the new state of Israel. Later I would eavesdrop on the conversation of class-mates and my ears would ring with new words like "Zionism" and "kibbutz."

A basket of eggs

Sometime my new friends would visit me at home. One of them was a Jewish girl named Mimi Salama who joined us to dye Easter eggs, returning home with a small basket of multicolored eggs—a Christian symbol! A few years later it was my Muslim friend Aida Sinbel who partook in this endeavor. We all shared each other's feasts—Easter, Ramadan, Yom Kippur—in a prevalent broadmindedness which is difficult to find today. There were Greek Orthodox, Greek Catholics, Maronites, Roman Catholics, Copts, and Protestants of all denominations, besides Jews and the local Muslim population. This broadmindedness, however, was limited to schoolchildren like us, and was not shared by my parents and their generation, who lived in a very Hellenocentric environment.

I was surprised when one of my classmates, Anne Geisenberg, wore a large cross and began calling herself Geisenberger; those two extra letters added to her family name altered the sound of her name from a harsh metallic guttural "G" to a softer tone. She proclaimed to everyone around her that she was now a Catholic. Was the discordance of her faith a measure of the anxiety she contracted from the proximity of war?

Can you choose your religion, I asked my parents? "Nobody chooses their religion," they answered me carefully. "We are all what we are born to be. The important thing to remember is that Christians, Muslims, and Jews have just one God. It does not matter how we worship Him as long as we have faith."

The school was governed by a code of discipline, which was archaic; we had to respect any form of authority, even a guardian. There was a ban on chewing gum and on ballpoints. We used a pen with a metal nib; an inkpot was placed on every desk, and the ink stained my fingers and my notebooks. How was I to erase those stains? A delicate rubbing would end up making a hole in the notebook paper, and diluting the ink with a spit of saliva would leave a larger smudge. In later years a fountain pen was allowed. My emerald-colored Pelikan pen, gifted by my godmother—the *stylo* as it was called—was the envy of the class.

Our notebooks had to be covered in blue paper. Would beige paper do? Absolutely not. Perhaps it was a way to augment the school's earnings, as we had to purchase the blue paper and the labels from the school store. A label bearing my full name, properly capitalized, was to be glued on the upper left corner of each notebook to indicate the subject, year, class, and volume. The blue paper moreover had to be tucked in—tightly— not glued with gummed paper. An old family friend whom we respectfully called Uncle Thrassos sat paralyzed in a wheelchair; he volunteered every year to cover my notebooks.

When the headmistress entered the classroom, we all stood up in attention. Every other week she distributed a report card with our grades, to be seen and signed by our parents.

Schoolbooks were not current, and a book written in 1930 would be used for two more decades. We were able to purchase second-hand books at a small bookstore in town called Carnezie's for our school assignments; there were also books available on a wall displayed on a main street in

Camp Cesar in the beginning of the school year. We tried to purchase those with fewer markings, and sold them at the end of the schoolyear.

"Are we expected to haul those thick books to every class?" remarked my friend Jocelyn. "They are so heavy!" "Use a *chariot*, a wagon," proclaimed Madame Chausson, the Math teacher. The following day Jocelyn arrived purposely late in class, holding a string; trailing behind her were her books on a skating board! We all burst out laughing. Jocelyn was called to the headmistress' office; fortunately there was no corporal punishment in our school. Punishment meant standing in the corner of a classroom, staring stupidly at the wall for an hour so. Or you could be detained during a break, staying in the classroom alone while others went out to play.

Stars and silkworms

During break time, we played marbles, blind's man bluff, and all those games which schoolchildren have played throughout the ages. Another outlet was collecting and swapping cards bearing photographs of movie stars, which were inserted at that time in Egyptian Coutarellis cigarette packages. Returning from his favorite coffee shop in the evening, Father would bring me a card. He did not smoke but many of his friends did. Saturdays were special as I would get a double ration of two cards. The Sunday cigarette pack was opened in advance for my benefit. I hoarded my treasures and the inventory kept growing. A second album had to be purchased to fill it with movie star pictures of the time: Greta Garbo, Marlene Dietrich, Claudette Colbert, Bette Davis, Louise Rainer, Spencer Tracy, Vivien Leigh, Gary Cooper, Jennifer Jones, Esther Williams, Bing Crosby, and so on.

As with any form of collecting, possessing a rare item was a form of distinction. Movie star cards were traded. I was tempted more than once to trade my Laurence Olivier card for a dozen others. There was a buzz in my French high school that I owned "Hamlet," with the aura of hipness that graced anyone who possessed one of those rarer cards. We were obsessed to some degree, not much different from America today where kids trade or sell baseball cards.

This trading experience introduced us to the law of supply and demand; to the pleasure of collecting was added the awareness of value and profit. The collection remained in Alexandria, most probably on a dusty shelf, feeding silverfish after I left for graduate school in America.

My brother was frustrated as he never found a piece of shrapnel in our garden to brag about. During the bombings in Alexandria, they had invented in their school an unheard-of game—during the school break they would compete to see who had brought the largest piece of shrapnel found in their back garden. Akis never found one, although some classmates did. I wondered if these came from their gardens or had been fetched by a friend living close to the port, the target of the bombings.

Another source of enjoyment, which started as a science project, was to follow the life cycle of silkworms. We kept those whitish silkworms in old cardboard boxes. They were fed exclusively with fresh mulberry leaves that they devoured in large quantities. A friend, the owner of a country estate in the area of Siouf, had mulberry trees on her property and would bring us a weekly supply of mulberry branches loaded with fresh leaves. We kept them in our bathtub and generously supplied a couple of classmates who lived close by. We followed the silkworm's growth as they reached up to a couple of inches; they wrapped themselves up in a cocoon of a white, pinkish or light yellow color, the size of a peanut shell, from where butterflies finally emerged. We swapped the colored cocoons with the white ones. The pinkish ones were rare and more in demand.

Collecting stamps

I received my first stamps in a large box, a gift of Aunt Katina. Someone had lived in Africa and had gathered those colorful stamps, tiny pieces of paper printed in foreign languages. Most were oblong, but there were square ones, while the most intriguing were triangular in shape. I spent countless hours unscrambling those stamps, classifying them by country, inserting them in smoky yellowish envelopes. I did not own any fancy albums like those available today, with printed labels and rows of little plastic containers in which to align one's treasures.

This cataloguing provided my first geography lesson, the urge to visit faraway places that developed later into a lifelong wanderlust. There were stamps from Equatorial Africa, from countries that since then altered their names, rejecting their colonial past, countries that unified or more likely were further split.

The stamps bore pictures of wild animals, of strange trees, of bushmen tall and upright, wearing Bermuda shorts, a fez, carrying a rifle, and looking at a vista so different from what I knew. One stamp series carried labels in two languages—"Belgian Congo" on the bottom and *"Congo Belge"* on the top. I got confused. Why two European languages? My parents reminded me that the Congo was a Belgian colony, the languages Flemish and French. Besides a geography lesson, I was getting my first political awareness of countries with two national languages, two sets of inhabitants with their own distinct cultures. Fifty years later the Congo split into two independent nations, while Belgium has yet to find its identity.

Why were the stamps of Egypt printed in French with *"Poste Egyptienne"* while those in English kept the Anglo-Egyptian protectorate sign? We lived in Egypt, and those stamps should have been printed in Arabic, I thought— the first nationalistic feeling I had for the country in which I was born. My parents reminded me that we were Greeks, that Egypt was a protectorate, and that the British were here to keep us safe. In the early '50s, the British flag was lowered from the military camps of Egypt, the protectorate with King Farouk as puppet ended, and all of us became refugees in our ancestral land.

No Christmas cards reached us when I was growing up during the Second World War. Even later, air communication was limited and letters and cards came by slow boat. When an overseas letter arrived, I was eager to unglue the stamps from bulky envelopes, cutting the surrounding paper, immersing them in water, carefully removing them without damaging the perforations, and then drying them on newspapers.

Father used to purchase commemorative stamps for my collection as soon as they were issued for circulation. Events of King Farouk's life—the birth of his children, his marriages, signing treaties—were immortalized in those stamps, providing additional revenues to the government. Stamps endorsed on the first day of their issuance at the post office had a premium and Father was ready to acquire an entire series, the price ranging from a few piasters to several Egyptian pounds.

A cholera epidemic

Once a year, all pupils were required to be vaccinated for typhoid. Cholera was endemic in the countryside, but in one particular year—in 1947—it flared into an epidemic. A number of cases had been reported, a few disguised by the authorities as simple dysentery. There were more than a thousand deaths reported from cholera that year, but not a single European died or got cholera. The epidemic caused the most damage in the countryside due to poverty and poor hygiene, and the lack of clean water. Jehan Sadat noted that the number of cases was minimized by the newspapers to avoid arousing public alarm.

As a precaution, it was announced that there would be another vaccination day; the oral vaccine for cholera would be available only after 1980. Only Sylvia Peta and her younger sister were excused, the procedure to be performed by their physician father.

Who did not dread those needles, as long as metal nails? Disposable needles were unheard of; after an injection they were placed in a container filled with water and boiled for ten minutes. The French doctor, humped and with a white goatee, looked a hundred years old through our eyes. They ran out of needles again as I waited in line for the sterilized ones to cool off so the nurse could handle them.

I could have developed a fever after the inoculation and been unable to attend school the next day, but I didn't want that to happen, as I loved my school and I loved my teacher. I was fascinated by my teacher's brilliant red lips; she had lipstick on, something my mother never used. (Nivea cream and a lemon-scented fragrance were the only cosmetics she used in her entire life.) I wish I had a lipstick like my teacher's Max Factor. In front of a full-length mirror I tried in vain to color my lips with a red Crayola. I planned to pick some red roses and bring them to my teacher, thinking that she liked red.

One day we were told that anyone who visited Liliane Spector, another schoolmate and neighbor, should report immediately to the local hospital. Liliane was bitten by her puppy, which developed rabies; anyone in contact with that puppy had to be cared for immediately. A series of injections in one's stomach was part of the treatment lasting for three painful weeks. Liliane was in tears, not only from discomfort but from losing her beloved puppy.

I was glad to be spared this torture. Since that episode I have been scared of dogs, and it is unimportant if they are cute little poodles lazing on Oriental rugs or mangy cur dogs roaming around dustbins. I try to avoid them, while cats purring on my lap have always been part of our household. As for my mother, a tiny yellow canary that twittered all day long was her joy; she fed it with morsels of egg yolk.

Aviva Mulhman was a stocky little girl with brown hair. She was myopic, one of the few wearing glasses, and she sat in the front row. She did not attend class for a few weeks; she must have had the mumps or measles, contagious ailments, we supposed, and was required to stay home. One day our teacher informed us that Aviva had passed away, from bone cancer. The pain had been excruciating. It was my first time to hear of this dreadful illness, which would affect so many in my family in later years.

Another dangerous disease feared in Egypt was bilharzia, caused by a fluke which breeds in polluted water. My parents refused to use hotel towels, unsure if they had been washed in clean water!

Leeches and other common cures

In a flashback, I recall Aziza, our washerwoman, sitting on a stool, her arm extended over the kitchen table with four or five leeches hovering over it. They were covered by a glass to prevent them from sliding. They would remain there for 40 to 50 minutes sucking blood, getting fatter by the minute while Aziza's blood pressure was brought down. When replete the leeches quit sucking; removing them after they were fed was simple, as they stopped snagging, but those slimy creatures were still difficult to hold with tweezers. Often a small amount of seepage would follow, to be controlled with medicinal alcohol. Were the leeches' punctures so deep? It was their saliva, reportedly containing 140 enzymes with an anticoagulant effect, which caused the seepage, besides lowering blood pressure.

The use of leeches was a great alternative for treating high blood pressure years ago. From China, India, and ancient Greece, folk medicine found its way to Istanbul during my mother's upbringing, thus the procedure she inflicted on Aziza.

I had completely forgotten about leeches until recently when, walking in a Papua New Guinea jungle to observe birds of paradise, I thought initially that mosquitoes were biting me, but it was something else. Leeches had crept up on my leg, sucking my blood, and without tweezers I had to detach them with bare fingers.

Many cultures still use medicinal plants and herbs to treat infections, and Mother had a repertoire to treat minor ailments.

If I had a deep cut, even a minor scratch, Mother would place a piece of moldy bread or cantaloupe over it to prevent a bacterial infection. Bread molded in a couple of days as preservatives were unknown and never incorporated in the bread dough; as for penicillin, it was still unheard of. In the late 1920s, Sir Alexander Fleming had observed that bacterial growth was inhibited around blue-green mold. What later came to be known as penicillin was extracted from a cantaloupe mold! Folk medicine had been using it for centuries.

Mother believed that natural herbs were most appropriate to be used when we were sick. Although she would take me to the doctor she often proceeded with natural remedies. When we suffered from stomachaches she gave us tea made from cumin or chamomile. Constipation was relieved by aloe, bitter apple leaves, or her rose-petal jam. Yogurt would be used to draw the heat of a sunburn after a day on the beach. When I was run down she prepared a brew of boiled hollyhocks which, according to her, strengthened the blood.

In our garden we had planted a variety of hollyhocks. They flowered and bloomed easily during the summer. Their color varied from white to pink and cerise red. Mother would select from the red petal flowers before they wilted, place them on a large cookie sheet or a newspaper, and leave them out to dry in the sun for few days. (This process is done in minutes today in a microwave oven.) The fragile, desiccated petals were then placed in an hermetically closed container and kept in the medicine cabinet. When someone had a sore throat, or just felt fatigued, Mother used them for preparing tea: heating the kettle, pouring hot, never boiling water, over a couple of teaspoons of the dry petals, then leaving the brew to sit; the brownish liquid was then filtered, and while still warm used as a gargle. For a sore throat, it was the best remedy besides being an effective antibacterial gargle wash. It always worked.

What I dreaded most, when I had a cold, was when Mother decided to alleviate the symptoms with *vendouzes*, i.e. cupping, her favorite remedy. We never heard of Tylenol or acetaminophen gels for relieving a cold or a respiratory infection.

She would first rub my back with a hint of olive oil—baby oil most would likely be used today. A dozen glasses, ordinary tumblers from the kitchen cupboard, were assembled; a small piece of cotton slightly moistened with rubbing alcohol was fixed to the interior of these tumblers, and then set on fire using a match or a lighter. The flashing cotton ball was then removed and the tumbler, still hot was inverted on my skin. I would plead with her to use thinner and smaller glasses as the process was less painful.

Air inside the glass heated with that flame drew the skin slightly upwards, creating a vacuum; the glasses were left for five to ten minutes. More than mere discomfort, it was painful and agonizing, and minutes passed until the glasses were removed. As a minimum a dozen would be used to cover my entire back. (Today pressurized plastic cups are commercially available; smaller in diameter than a glass, two dozen or more would be required to cover one's back.) The *vendouzes* process was immortalized in the film of *Zorba the Greek*, a Cretan story based on a Nikos Kazantzakis novel, starring Anthony Quinn. *Vendouzes* have also been used to improve circulation; the purple spots they left on the bodies of Olympic swimmers in the 2016 Rio Olympics raised many eyebrows.

As antibiotics were still not available in Alexandria, mother would end by rubbing my back with diluted iodine. Skin markings, due to the rupture of capillaries, were common. After the cups were removed, they would leave simple red rings, but more often it was dark red welts that would take a week or more to disappear.

Was the process effective? We always felt better afterwards. Natural cures and folk remedies have been carried down from generation to generation and in many cases are still more effective than chemicals and synthetics for stimulating blood circulation and producing a certain amount of detoxification.

The evil eye

Someone once told me how nice I looked in my pretty new dress. In a few minutes, I spilled ice cream over it.

Did that person give me the evil eye? The week before, I strained my ankle. Mother was concerned, seeking not only to ward off the evil eye but to uncover the person responsible.

In so many cultures, the evil eye is considered a curse. It was first recorded 5,000 years ago by the Mesopotamians on clay tablets. At every stage of human history, man has looked to magic objects to defy evil forces, and talismans with letters, numbers, or abstract signs have survived to this day. Go to Turkey or Greece or any of the Middle Eastern countries, and you see children, especially young girls, wearing—as a necklace or as a pendant —a blue-colored charm or amulet. What does blue mean? In any of those countries, water is precious—with water things grow and without it, things shrivel and die. The blue color reminds people of fresh, cool water. The tradition is still strong as I observed recently in Greek and Turkish villages —newborn babies, animals, and even doors of homes would have a blue amulet. In Syria I saw a Christmas tree with dozens of blue-eyed amulets as decorations.

I never had to wear an amulet, but to unearth the person who gave me that eye of envy (in Arabic, *ayin hasad*) was more complicated, and Mother used her folkloric knowhow to do it. She selected a bunch of aromatic cloves from a jar nested in the spice section of the kitchen cabinet. She held it with tweezers or pierced its bottom with a needle, and placed it close to a flame from a match. At that particular moment she thought of a certain person. If the clove crackled or popped, the culprit was the person she entertained, and the evil eye was cracked. If there was no sound, the person she had in mind was innocent. She continued the process, imagining every relative, friend, teacher, neighbor, or classmate we knew; fortunately she went through that process only a couple of times during my childhood. My father did not believe in such folk remedies or superstitions, and if we were sick, he called our physician.

At the Salle des Fêtes

The Lyçée was an imposing compound, a building clean and fresh, painted in mustard yellow, gleaming like gold in the mellow sun. The classrooms were large with ample light streaming through large windows. Classes there were not overcrowded as they were in public schools. Its interior was opulent, with a large quadrangle, la grande cour, open for class recess and gym classes. The science and chemistry laboratories were well endowed, outstanding for their time, while the Salle des Fêtes, the auditorium, was where school plays were mounted, movies shown and visiting artists performed.

While in town, the Comedie Française mounted, at the Salles des Fêtes, excerpts from the plays of Corneille and Moliere. I still remember a Chopin recital given by the blind Greek virtuoso Georges Themeli who brilliantly displayed his talents. Gina Bachauer, considered the greatest female pianist of the 20th century, was stranded during the war in Egypt, where she gave hundreds of concerts for the Allied troops. Although I never attended one of her concerts, I met her at a private home where she entertained the guests, mostly playing Greek folk songs, and when she found that it was the host's birthday she gave a rendition of the popular "Happy Birthday" tune.

One event that stands out in my memory was a documentary film on the trek of French mountaineers to Annapurna, one of the highest peak of the Himalayas. The natural beauty of the area, the glacial mountain ranges, white snowcaps, and thundering rivers in narrow gorges transfixed me;

Julie's father, Panayiotis Leotsinidis, 1925

Julie's mother, Urania Leotsinidis, 1925

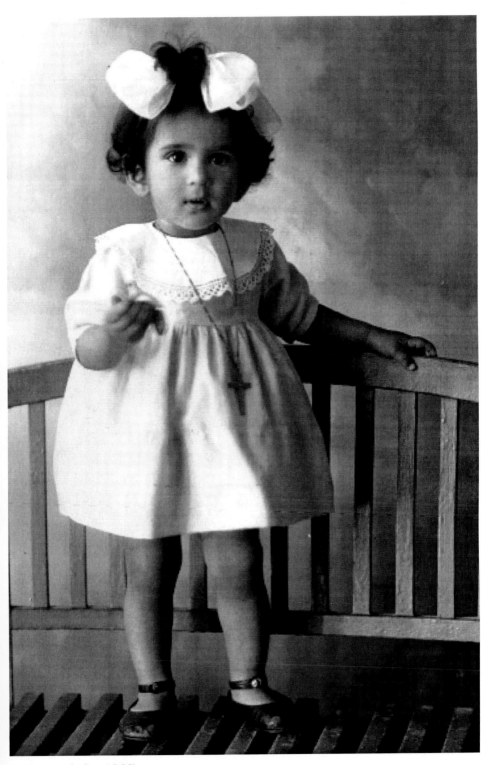

Julie as a baby, 1937

With her brother Akis, 1937

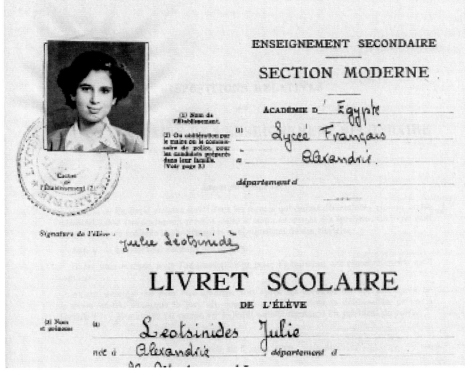

Julie's Livret Scolaire, 1952

Receiving an award at the Lyçée Français, 1952

In a peasant dress at a Student Association event, 1953

With tennis teammates at the University of Alexandria, 1955

Partying with Akis and friends, 1956

Julie and her friend Aida Sinbel, 1955

With Arthur and her parents at Beau Rivage, 1960

On her first job as a scientist in Minnesota, 1960

With her family before departure for the USA, 1956

With Mme. Jehan Sadat, 2010

At the Arab Quarter

Bread sellers along the Mahmoudiya Canal

Cherif Pasha, with the Bourse on the right

Alexandria's Corniche

The Ecole Grecque

The Lyçée Français

The Muhammad Ali Theater (credit to Mogaio, Wikipedia CC license)

151   ALEXANDRIA. — Entrance to the Nouzha Park. — , — LL.

The entrance to Nouzha Park

The Pastroudis patisserie

Ramleh Station, with the Grand Trianon in the background

Stanley Beach

A street scene with a tram from the 1960s

The French Gardens between Muhammad Ali Square and the Eastern Harbor

The Kozzica, Alexandria's Greek hospital

A hilltop view of Alexandria

The Citadel of Qaitbay

I learned that people called Sherpas existed. Cultural productions like this opened a new dimension in my wanderlust. I vowed that I would view one day the majestic Himalayas; Nepal with its mountain range was among the first travels I would take with my husband.

At the Salles des Fêtes, we gathered at the end of the year for the "honorable mention" (*tableau d'honneur*) for those who attained distinction in their grades, followed by the prize awards. My heart would pound with excitement, always fearing that perhaps, after all, I would not get a prize, but I managed to finish every year on a high note. I heard my name—Julie Leotsinides—and I stepped up to the stage, where stacks of books were lined up on a long table. Madame Campion, the headmistress, handed me a bundle of books, all tied up with a silk ribbon, and shook my hand. Later that day, I trooped home to show off my bounty: six picture books of the splendid castles on the Loire and a fat Larousse dictionary; decades later that Larousse still stands on my office bookshelf. My parents beamed, thrilled with my performance at school.

Flicking recently through the yellow pages of the Larousse, I found dried pansies pressed between them. It was customary for school kids to collect the largest, most colorful pansies and preserve them, and now they bring back memories of happy times.

Leader of the pack

In school, I was an Akela—the leader of the pack in Kipling's *Jungle Book* —leading a troop of Cub Scouts aged seven to eleven. I was just sixteen years old and together with another Girl Scout took my troop camping on a wealthy landowner's property in the delta, a three-hour bus drive from Alexandria. I was not seized by any anxiety over my responsibilities. I had the confidence of youth. I had no first-aid experience; health insurance was unheard of and telephone communications non-existent. The verbal permission of parents was sufficient to take off and climb on the school bus for a camping expedition in the Egyptian Delta.

My culinary ability was limited to boiling water in a giant cauldron for cooking spaghetti. Many parents however visited their children, bringing an ample supply of provisions and tray upon tray of delicious pastries.

In the morning we wandered, exploring, walking on the flat rich fields with their bountiful crops, for which the black silt of the Nile provided ample nutrition. We compared city life as we observed the bilharzia-ridden *fellahin* at their back-breaking chores, rattling along in bullock carts and prodding the ponderous beasts to move faster, raggedly dressed children whose faces were liberally plastered with mucus and dirt, and the blindfolded cattle, turning the slow globe of the water wheels. My assignment was the teaching of Morse signals and the making of complex nautical knots. In the evening, cross-legged around the campfire, we rehearsed the songs to be performed in front of parents few days later. Cicadas whirred, and birds chattered and rustled. Everyone who attended the camp was rewarded with a pin, a memento of youthful days and of fun times. We were carefree and happy, with no accident to report. It was summer and the clear nights were dusted with stars.

Delivering something based on value was an Akela motto. I volunteered to spend New Year's Eve at an Arab orphanage rather than the school dance. I had a rewarding experience when a young Copt girl handed me few coins to light a candle at her church and pray for her health, a simple request that could not be fulfilled by a Muslim.

But I was not always so well behaved. Akis and I liked to pull pranks on April Fools Day. Once we rang up our Aunts Katina and Elpiniki to tell them that our cousin George from Chios, the son of the doctor, had arrived unexpectedly, and that they should come as we were having a welcome party. Within an hour they both arrived, wearing their very best clothes—jewelry unearthed and dolled up—only to realize that it was April Fools Day! We did that every year to a teacher, a neighbor, or a friend; Akis was good at this, and I was his willing accomplice.

Passing the Baccalaureat

The Lycée girls' section was separated from the boys' by dormitories for boarders and apartments for expatriate teachers. In the last year of high school, classes were small and co-educational, and the majority were boys.

We had to choose from among three distinct sections: Philosophy, a traditional section favored by girls; Mathematics, favored by boys; and Science, my choice, which I never regretted.

There was attrition through the years as the French grading system was harsh. Term reports in secondary school recorded pupils' marks, in Cartesian fashion, to the nearest two decimal points. Every one of us knew how to compare ourselves with the average. Every two weeks, a report card had to be signed by one's parents. When a classmate forged her father's signature, she was asked to stand in a corner while the disciplinary action was discussed; she was expelled for a day. What a dishonor!

For the school-leaving Baccalaureat exam, 16 out of 20 was considered outstanding. In primary school, a *dictée* to test spelling was marked by progressively deducting points for every error, which could crash the grade down to zero, even into negative territory. There was tremendous stress and anxiety among all of us, resulting in a lack of confidence. It seemed like the system existed to discourage instead of stimulating us. I dreaded sitting for that French exam. The passing rate was low, and the grading was done under the supervision of the Education Attaché of the French Embassy. The results were published in the French newspapers a few weeks later. The foreign community followed the names of the successful candidates in the *Progrés Egyptien* or the *Journal d' Egypte*. The names were not given alphabetically, but rather by standing, by grade ranking: *Trés Bien, Bien, Assez Bien, Passable* (Very Good, Good, Fairly Good, Passing Mark.) You bore a stigma if you did not make it; better luck repeating the exams the following year.

I always excelled in Geography, History, Literature, and Italian; I scored a fair ranking in Philosophy and in Natural and Physical Science, but came down in Algebra and was nearly in the bottom of the English class.

I was uncommonly fortunate, for not only did I top my high school, but I received the highest grade among all the candidates in the entire country! Mr. Bonnicci called my father to congratulate him on my accomplishments. His son did not make it. The Baccalaureat, the terminal French high school diploma, was accepted with no further tests for entrance to Egyptian universities and automatically to all universities of France, except the Grandes Ecoles where a further selection process was required. There was an unwritten rule that Jews were not admitted to Egyptian universities.

Our teachers were French expatriates, all *agregée*, licensed by the French Ministry of National Education. A sprinkling of highly qualified local teachers holding the equivalent of a master's degree in their discipline supplemented the expatriate staff. The former were under contract, trapped in Alexandria by the war, wondering how their families fared in Occupied France. Communication with Europe was sporadic, and only through the Red Cross did one get a laconic message restricted to news of the passage of a loved one, a friend, or a relative.

The names of our teachers, all stellar professionals—Chausson, Heranger, Enright, Russac, Courtin, Vigoni, Chevrier, Doazan, Bascouret, and so on—still resound in my memory decades later. How could I forget our *proviseur*, the headmaster, Mr. Louis Marchal, whose accolade still gives me pride years later. I was the best "little geographer" he had encountered. I clearly recall his commanding nose and deep-socketed eyes—a figure of trust and authority. I knew the names of every river of Europe, of every mountain chain in the world, of every African capital, and that Houston was a major oil exporting port (I recall the audience being stunned at a public oral exam at the Baccalaureat by my mentioning Houston, which most of them audience did not know). I was seeing the world through Marchal's eyes—the wonders of the planet, the beauty of the city planning of a Paris or a New York. The benefit of attending the Lycée was not restricted to acquiring fluency in French; rather, it involved one's immersion into a culture distinct from my Greek upbringing. Like most other middle-class Greeks, my family led a parochial life, avoiding closer relations outside the narrow circle of churches, clubs, and societies. I found myself exposed at the Lycée to diverse people, to a cosmopolitan spirit, encouraged to develop an interest in the outside world, freeing my mind to wander and to dream.

I remain grateful to my parents for their foresight in enrolling me in such a remarkable school. They wanted me to learn foreign languages, and the Lyçée had a formidable reputation. Most likely they did not recognize the influence of a culture that was not Hellenocentric nor realize its effect. I came to be less of a Greek but more a citizen of the world, better prepared for the responsibilities that lay ahead as my husband engaged in a diplomatic career, representing the United Nations Development Program in various countries around the globe.

War comes to Alexandria

The city's highest minarets gleamed gold in the last rays of the sun. English and French warships lent a flickering grayness to the harbor. Their anti-aircraft guns moved slowly—tilted—then settled back into brooding stillness. They were practicing drills for the German bombers, which had resumed, with increasing force, their nightly raids over the Western harbor.

The harbor was encircled by batteries and anti-aircraft guns, while scores of barrage balloons were raised every evening and lowered in the morning, forming an effective screen against low-flying planes. To ward off enemy submarines, the harbor was closed by a floating boom, but there is still a danger from aimless bombs and parachute mines.

Sirens whooped and wailed, warning us to get off the street and run to a shelter. Our shutters were covered with large strips of blue paper tacked to the wooden frames; the window panes of the living room's French doors, which opened to a large balcony, were coated with cobalt blue dye; the street's square-sided gas lamps, manually lit at dusk by a gas company worker holding a long stick crackling with sparks, were also painted blue, as were the headlights of cars.

Masses of sandbags were piled high in front of apartment buildings, major shops, and hospitals. Located on a hill at Moustafa Pasha—the site of a Roman army camp centuries earlier—the British army barracks were surrounded by barbed wire.

In the skies over London and the southeast of England, the Battle of Britain was raging. Alexandria was just the only other city in the world to share London's distinction of being the victim of the Axis' air assaults. Capturing the Suez Canal was Hitler's objective; it meant cutting off the shortest route to the Indies and occupying the rich oil fields on Arab soil. From there he could move on to the oil fields of Iran and Iraq, threatening the Soviet Union and the oil deposits of the Caspian Sea to the south.

The sirens alerted us to scramble half a block away from our two-floor villa to the okela, a white ten-story apartment building whose basement was considered the best shelter in the neighborhood. There were few shelters, makeshift affairs that had to serve whole blocks of buildings. The walls of the shelter were packed with sandbags, piled one on top of the other. There was a hodge-podge of seats scattered about: old wobbly chairs, benches, stools and an occasional camp bed for children to sleep on. The room was sunk in darkness, with only a couple of yellow candles lit. All moved like ghosts in the dark. Someone suggested lighting the kerosene lamp and fiddled in the dark to trim the wick; another called for "some hot lemonade with a shot of brandy." You could hear whispered prayers as if each individual was praying to his own personal God, his own prophet or saint; "Virgin Mary, help us"; "Holy Mother and San Antonio, work your wonders"; "Allah, the merciful, have pity on us." But there was not room enough in that shelter for God, the prophets, the saints ... and the bombardment went on and on. In hushed tones, neighbors exchanged the latest news from those fortunate enough to own a battery-operated short-wave radio. A thousand conversations took place, seeking out each other like taproots for moisture. From time to time it would go quiet, and then we would hear a whistling sound, followed by a deafening blast. A bomb exploded nearby.

Each night we filled the bathtub to the brim just in case the town's water system was destroyed, being a target of the raids. Both the water company and electric company were controlled by the British, and were usual targets.

Mother carried a small leather bag, a first-aid kit with medical supplies for an emergency. As we sensed the bombs overhead, she swung it back and forth and murmured "*Sta psarakia, sta psarakia!*" meaning "To the fish, to the fish!", wishing the bombs to fall on water and not on land. Grave dark faces silently prayed, and rosaries that had been tucked into sleeves came into view. When the bombs fell, the noise was like a thunderstorm, and you could hear bits of shrapnel falling in the streets from the anti-aircraft guns.

A radio broadcast or the morning newspapers informed which neighborhood was hit and if there were any casualties. One night a bomb fell right in the heart of the Greek district of Ibrahimieh. The entire shelter shook, and people were screaming, praying, crossing themselves. We heard next day that two brothers, the sons of a friend, had been killed that night, rare casualties among the civilian population. Mrs. Polixeni, their widowed mother, was inconsolable, her grief exploding into a blind rage against the world. My parents attended the funeral and extended the spiritual renewal of condolences. I was too young to realize the misfortune of the family. Through the war the bombs' target was mainly the French and English fleet moored in Alexandria's harbor.

Casualties among the Alexandrian civilians were minimal, but wounded soldiers and sailors from the African front were evacuated to Alexandria. Prominent citizens threw open their homes to convalescent soldiers. Society ladies who formerly would not have been caught dead receiving anyone below the rank of an admiral or a general, or an ambassador or a banker, volunteered open their doors once or twice a week, prviding meals and entertainments for servicemen.

Many services clubs sprang up all over the city: the Greek Club, the Cyprus Club, the United Forces Club located in the plush former Karam palace, and so on. The Britannia Club—trumpeting "proof of British ability"—was on fashionable Rue Fouad. It had been furnished and decorated by Alexandrian residents, among them Baron Menasce and Oswald Finney, two of the most prominent members of the community, one Jewish the other British. Contributing thousands of books, they created the best reference library in Alexandria. The *Egyptian Gazette* reported on the Britannia Club's "comfortable chairs, shaded lights and a dainty little sitting and tea room for the use of women members of the Forces."

Aunt Katina volunteered at the Greek Club, which she endowed with a good share of her husband Basil Misserlis' library. The initials "BM" on the leatherbound books would puzzle residents, being the same as those of Baron Menasce!

To the shelter

The air raids came daily as the port was a prime target. Sometimes we would spend whole nights in the air-raid shelter. As soon as darkness fell, the first siren would be heard, a strident, hair-raising howl, followed by the blackout.

One evening Aunts Katina and Elpiniki joined us for a card game. Aunt Katina left her petits points behind. A pot of tea and homemade cookies were offered, while Father asked for his usual yogurt sprinkled with honey. All of a sudden the house shook; a strange rumble in the distance could be heard, but this was not the usual roar of anti-aircraft guns. Sirens wailed a few minutes later.

"We better shut the lights," said my father. "Let's not get into trouble." Mother carefully peeked through the curtains; the entire cluster of homes in Camp Cesar, our neighborhood, was in the dark. Were we rushing to the shelter?

We lit a candle, and Mother fetched the blue glass kerosene lamp from the kitchen. Muhammad, our servant, had forgotten to fill it with oil, a chore to be handled now by candlelight. The pungent odor of burning oil from the feeble wick in the lamp permeated the dining room. The rumble continued, tanks thudding and whining their way a block from our home at a major intersection. It was probably an army movement, a convoy of many, trucks that the authorities did not want us to see. The British that night were likely, feverishly moving ammunition and men from the Suez to the frontlines. Was there a raid? Was the mission that evening to create clouds of smoke around the port of Alexandria to camouflage the Royal Navy ships anchored there?

Across the room, the talk was of war. The exploits of the Greeks were recounted with pride. We heard about the sinking in the Atlantic of the 49,500-ton *Bismarck*, the largest battleship ever built by Germany, due to the unrelenting attack from the British gunners who fired with deadly accuracy. My brother had acquired an encyclopedic knowledge of the armature, guns, speed, and tonnage of many ships engaged in World War II and loved to chatter about it. We celebrated the sinking of the *Bismarck*, the *Tirpitz*, and the *Graf Spee*, the blockade runners of Malta, but we never lost sight of the fact that the war was at our doorstep. The tea got cold;

Father's yogurt remained untouched; we started talking in hushed voices.

While our water supply came from Alexandria's municipality, Aunt Katina was pumping water from a well on her property. Unlike many others made of mud, this well was of stone and mortar, but always needed repair; no stainless steel pumps were available at that time and the local pumps often broke down. She asked my father for advice as the engineer who had maintained it for years had left the country. "Have you heard who has left town?" was a question that popped up frequently in conversation.

That night, my brother claimed that he could not complete in the dark a school assignment due for the following day. The planned card game was indefinitely postponed. We began to adjust ourselves to deepening darkness. Were my aunts staying overnight? Was it safe for them to return home few blocks away? Might an unexploded bomb be waiting in their path, or a large piece of shrapnel? The crackle of falling shards sounded like a hailstorm. Aunt Elpiniki was worried about her stepson Anthony, who had volunteered and joined the Greek Army; he would later serve on the Italian front. The conversation ceased and everyone sat frozen in fear. As long as there was school the next morning I was content. I did not sense any danger; for me having no lights for a while was just a game.

Nights around the radio

Half an hour later, the pounding noise of engines receded, and we heard the all-clear, heaving a sigh of relief as we turned on the lights Mother looked through the curtains to make sure that the lights were back in the neighborhood.

"Are there any more biscuits?" I asked, obsessed with food.

In some ways I miss those nights—not the war, but those Alexandrian nights when the family was together, gathered around the Telefunken radio for news and whispering in the dark as though the enemy was listening, with the smell of kerosene and burning oil hovering over us like incense.

At first the bombings were very disconcerting as they made such an awful racket, but then we got used to them. The blackout precautions made our home uncomfortably hot, so we started like the others to sit in our garden in the starlight and the moonlight as the enemy passed overhead. Dozens of searchlights were prowling the sky, beaming back and forth, vast illuminations accompanied by a giant display of firecrackers. Sometimes we used binoculars to see the searchlights catching a glint of silver in their crossbeams. Then the anti-aircraft guns opened up with a terrible loud roar when a plane was caught by the lights. The searchlights, located on the outskirts of the city, scoured the sky. It was a sight both splendid and terrifying.

In his 1989 book *City of Saffron*, Edwar Al-Kharrat would recall those raids thus: "The sky above me had become terrible, enormously high, harboring death in its bowels, rushing, heavy final, inevitable. The all-encompassing brilliance of the moon was cruel. The searchlights made long moving swords of cutting light, coming both from the edges of the city and from the center; they turned in the clear silken blueness, crossing and parting veering away and swinging together again so that the ends met for an instant and fixed upon a small shining dot; branching out once more to probe the inscrutable belly of the sky, scouring it again for the ducking, weaving spot of treachery. The burst of ack-ack fire, thin, and piercing and continuous, rattled ceaselessly, exploding in great metallic red flowers whose sparks scattered suddenly and as suddenly were extinguished. The roar of the aeroplane engines was far and high, but audible between the bursts of fire from the anti-aircraft guns, in the silence which made the city seem more fragile, even more laid bare, from Anfushi to el Mandara and el-Montaza, etc. All the treasures of Alexandria lay prostrate and naked, veiled only by the work of beams which stabbed the sky."

The war went on for another two years, but moved farther and farther away from Alexandria. The raids became less frequent and finally ceased all together. I remained oblivious to the horrors and misery caused by war. The raids were for me child's play, despite the fact that war was raging on our doorstep, 60 miles from Alexandria. I never felt physically threatened. Only years later would I realize how much that experience, that war, shaped me.

A friendship in wartime

"Is the electric company the target again?" My father posed the question to his friend Mr. Diakoyannis, who called in that evening. They agreed that Mr. Bonnicci, a family friend, a Maltese carrying a British passport, must have had his hands full again. The electric company, like the western harbor, were usual targets.

Mr. Diakoyannis was a Greek from Rhodes, a Dodecanese island, occupied by the Italians since 1922. Like most of Greece, Rhodes had been part of the Ottoman Empire. He held Italian papers and had been summoned by the military authorities, who confiscated his papers, considering him an enemy of the country. Could my father handle his business? The conversation lasted far into the night. In their friendship they were able to share their private thoughts and ideas, to test them with one another.

"I should not come and visit you," said my father. "There is danger, as I have a family. But I'll record in your office what you need. I am not shirking that responsibility."

These were serious remarks in overheard conversations—fugitive memories that would make more sense to me only much later. As Durrell would write in *Justine,* "Far-off events, transformed by memory, acquire a burnished brilliance, because they are seen in isolation, divorced from the details of before and after, of why and when, the fibers and wrappings of time."

Mr. Diakoyannis would spend four years interned at a concentration camp in the desert, to be released only after Italy capitulated. "It was hot, overwhelmingly hot," he recalled years later.

When Nasser sequestered all foreigners' bank accounts, my father could no longer cover the rent of his office on Rue de France, and Mr. Diakoyannis offered him a room in his suite of offices. He had taken Egyptian citizenship to be able to make a living. His wife later helped my parents after they moved to Greece to gather relevant documents from Alexandria's municipalities, allowing them to receive a modest social security income from the Greek government.

The war hits home

The city was in panic. The railways were jammed with evacuees. People headed for Cairo, for Upper Egypt, even the Sudan. The Nazis had marched relentlessly across Europe and North Africa, and all of us in Alexandria were much affected. Jewish households were especially frightened at the prospect of Nazis storming Egypt. The Germans will arrive and cut our throats, they said.

Thousands of troops were stationed around the city to protect it. The British Empire descended upon the town. Tall Australians and New Zealanders distinctive in their shorts and wide-brimmed khaki hats, South Africans with rugged farmers' faces, frightening East Africans, haughty Sikhs in turbans, Indians smelling of curry and the English permanently drunk in Stella beer. They crammed the streets and shops, altering the atmosphere of the city. The British flag was proudly hoisted at their barracks in Moustafa Pasha, for us foreigners a sign of protection.

There were so many nationalities in town: Frenchmen, mostly sailors with their pompom hats; Greeks sporting the royal insignia on their caps; taciturn Poles; and Tito's Yugoslavs with red stars in their bonnets, well disciplined and always in groups. They gave us a living geography lesson. Durrell would note that the moneychangers counters were crowded with service people turning their francs and pounds into food, wine, silk, women, boys, and opium.

Horse carriages were in great demand, and so difficult to find; bars and nightclubs opened on every street corner. They were always crowded. The local market was bursting with goods stolen from Naafi (the British Navy, Army, and Air Force commissary), of course with the complicity of British soldiers. Mother no longer used her regular dishes, preferring dishes with the brown Naafi insignia, although they were of inferior quality. Was she keeping the better china for better days?

As a sign of the new wealth, fat American cars caused the city's first traffic jams. My brother had fun guessing their make from a distance: Packard, Chrysler, Ford, Oldsmobile, Studebaker.

Often soldiers had too much to drink, and they lay sprawled on the sidewalks. The military police became a familiar sight, driving up and down Alexandria's Corniche hoisting anyone who had passed out in their paddy wagons.

Taxi drivers thrived, enjoying a golden age. Young shoeshine boys, the *bouyagis*, polished shoes, pouncing on every unsuspecting soldier. They had developed clever schemes to alleviate these visitors of their cash, and became accomplished little swindlers.

In the avalanche of languages, French started fading. The taxi driver, the shopkeeper, the cinema cashier, the waiter, the tram inspector, the shoeshine boy, and the landlady of the "Pension" all started to speak the "special" English of Alexandria at war, as Edward el-Kharat would observe.

At school we were more attentive in English lessons. We started being envious of the pupils of the Victoria College and of the English Girls College. Hadn't we picked the right ticket for the future?

The war hit home. There was severe rationing in Alexandria and many necessities became difficult to find. The price of everything was rising and many shops remained closed for long periods each day. One evening I knew that a discussion was imminent; I half expected to be sent away but my father said I could stay.

"I'll go to the market tomorrow," he announced. "I want to do everything possible for the family's comfort."

He was leaning against the dining room table. I did not realize at that time that he was sixty. Perhaps if I had, I should have considered him old, very old, for sixty is a gigantic age to a six-year-old child. I have no pictures of him from that time to remember him by, but I recall that, that evening, he looked tired, showing all the baggage of having been born in another country, of having faced war, of having been expelled from Asia Minor.

Over the next few days Father came home from the market with a porter carrying large hemp bags with flour, sugar, lentils, coffee, and was of cotton oil, plus several large tins. Never betraying whatever she may have truly felt, Mother moved efficiently and calmly store it in the *sandara*—the attic above the kitchen—and in a huge oak armoire in my brother's bedroom, now serving as food storage.

We had hoarded enough supplies for couple of years—but what about soap? We could make our own soap using an old village recipe that Mother remembered from Istanbul, mixing cotton oil with potash. Large wooden trays, partitioned with wires, served as containers where the oil with the alkali mixture would be poured, then left under the sun at our terrace to dry. In few days, the soap would be ready!

Gasoline to light the Primus and cook the family meal was in short supply. Restaurants had a hard time getting supplies to regale their faithful and hungry clientele with. But there was a flourishing black market, and those who knew the city or had the right contacts were able to get their hands on crucial items. Those dealing with the British commissary thrived. In Alexandria, patisseries such as Delices, Pastroudis, Athineos, and Groppi in Cairo could still offer enjoyable pastries made with clarified butter. For how long, however?

At home, a small makeshift tin oven, blackened through years of use, required two Primus stoves. Mother was such a gifted cook that every meal she prepared in such a rudimentary environment—from a simple Greek dish to elaborate stews or pasta dishes—emitted a tantalizing aroma. I did not learn how to cook from my mother, as I spent my time studying. But I recall how she made the traditional Christmas cookies, a task that I have become an expert at, learning by trial and error. Mother shared her precious recipes. I penned them down in beautiful calligraphy in Greek. Years later I would try to make sense of quotes such as "a handful of flour" or "melt two piasters worth of chocolate." But there were occasions when a tray of baklava was to be baked and a proper oven was required. In such cases, Muhammad would carry the *sania*—a large round tray—balancing it on his head to the neighborhood bakery with its wood- and charcoal-burning oven, accompanied by Mother to ensure that Ahmet, who was in charge of fueling the oven, did not "accidentally" burn that costly dessert. A small tip was imperative.

One afternoon when I returned home from school, I saw that Father had brought home an Egyptian pound note with a swastika, imprinted with lettering in German and Arabic. Where did he find that banknote? With the imminent arrival of Nazi troops, it had been reported that new banknotes would be circulated, for use in all financial transactions; an artificial exchange rate would be established, devaluing the Egyptian pound. Because of this imminent possibility, my parents had been hoarding coins in gold and silver for some time.

Mother collected silver coins. The half-franc—equivalent to two piasters— the 20 and 50 piasters as well as the pound were available in silver with the visages of King Fouad, King Farouk, and later even Nasser. When we received change, it was mostly in silver half-francs, which we handed over to my mother. When she had a hundred or whatever number, she rolled them into paper tubes, and over the years she must have hoarded 50 pounds' worth of these small coins. They must have sold those coins, just as they sold the little gold bracelets I had as a teenager, when they needed the money.

During the war years, my parents wrote letters to relatives in Greece. They took months to arrive, and often got lost. Letters were censored, with a black felt pen concealing certain lines. Were there any codes used? Who were the censors? The censorship provided job opportunities for some Greeks. But were not alone. Our Swiss neighbors had the same experience, with letters received from home written in German censored as well. There was a purple stamp on the envelope with the inscrition "Postal censors," with some Arabic lettering.

The messages conveyed by the International Red Cross always brought sad news, such as the death of a family member or a dear friend. I recall how grieved Father was to learn of the death of Mr. Vlamos, a class-mate from Izmir and the owner of a pharmacy in Piraeus.

Cairo, open city

While Alexandria was in panic, life in Cairo was very different. In 1940 the Egyptian government declared it an open city, meaning that it would not be defended against enemy occupation and was therefore entitled under international law to immunity against bombardment and attack. Cairo blazed with lights for the rest of the war and its open-air restaurants and hotel-roof cabarets glittered.

Millions of Egyptians, indeed people all over the Arab world, would gather around battery-operated radios to listen to the live monthly concert of Um Kalsoum. She performed from the Ezbekia Theater in Cairo on the first Thursday of every month. Her songs were of love and sorrow, and her white handkerchief was her trademark. Her voice was considered magical, her prowess extraordinary. She could hold a single note for a minute and a half. During her concerts she would sing only three songs, lasting five hours. She would sing the same refrain, altering the nuance slightly every time. Anyone who lived through the war years in Egypt would remember the country at a standstill, listening to the country's nightingale.

For most Europeans her songs were repetitive, but not for her devoted followers from all over the Arab world. Lebanese businessmen and sheiks from Kuwait and Saudi Arabia flew in every month to hear her. Enter a taxi-cab today in Cairo, and the chances are the driver has an Um Kalsoum CD.

Cinema was a magical extension of the times. Aunt Katina escorted me to the movies; my mother spoke neither French nor English and watched only Greek movies. We stood up for the National Anthem as King Farouk's image filled the screen, followed by the 20th Century Fox newsreel, a ten-minute documentary of weekly events; finally, the movie was shown.

Giant colorful billboards at Ramleh Station advertised these movies. American movies were the most popular, although the great belly dancer Samia Gamal and handsome young Omar Sharif competed for attention. I did not know how many times I saw *Gone with the Wind* or watched Esther Williams jump through flower hoops on her water skis.

Summer in Sidi Bishr

In the summer of 1942 my parents rented a vacation home in Sidi Bishr, as they would do for the next three years until the end of the war. Previously, summers were spent in Greece. But the Europeans were in a panic because the Germans were approaching, and we decided that it was better to leave the city.

Sidi Bishr was a deserted beach town on the coast a few kilometers from Alexandria, no more than a 40-minute drive along the Corniche from Ramleh Station; but as we did not own a car it was a major journey. We took the red-labeled Victoria tram that followed the direct coastal road, with its many stops along the way, then transferred to a local bus which deposited us close to our rented bungalow.

The very names of the tram stations echoed like poetry. Mazarita's name derives from the Italian *lazaretto*, and there stood one of the early quarantines of Alexandria. Tradition claims that St. Mark's martyrium was on the Chatby littoral. There was in fact a large church that was destroyed in the early part of the 13th century, its position marked on two early maps (1472 and 1603). Chatby, where my school, the Lycée, still stands, has yielded traces of ancient roads and drains; Camp de Cesar suggests a Caesarean encampment; Cleopatra was for someone who never lived there; Sidi Gaber, a major railway station, was celebrated for its mosque; Laurens was a French cigarette manufacturer; Rouchdy was where the British consulate stood at the very top of the hill on whose slopes were many beautiful villas and where, during the wartime summer months the High Commissioner resided. Stanley Bay; San Stefano; Glymenopoulo; Sidi Bishr; Victoria—a litany of haunted and haunting names.

Our friends Bertha and Peter were neighbors in our Camp Cesar home but also in Sidi Bishr. While we rented a bungalow, they owned their summer home, an extensive property with date palms—seven of them, a number I recall as I wanted to climb all of them.

Bertha was a very strong swimmer, despite the fact that she was handicapped, having been born with an atrophied hand; she used an artificial arm but hated it, as these prosthetics were hardly as good as those available today.

Summer meant beach activities almost daily. Cabins painted in yellow and green, arranged around a cove in a huge semi-circle, like in a theater, were rented for the season. The sand at Sidi Bishr was so white and so fine that it slipped through your hands like powder; the emerald green washed on the beach, but further ahead the water turned turquoise and closer to the horizon a peacock blue. From that sandy beach we had a view of King Farouk's Montaza summer palace, located in a grove of palm trees in the distance.

I tagged along, always behind as I was so much younger than my brother and our friends. We searched for crabs, sea urchins, and brightly colored fish in some of the shallow ponds; Once Akis picked a shell, and the long fleshy foot of the mollusk appeared, gripping his finger, as if holding on to life itself. We swam, threw rocks at the blowhole, collected pumice stones. My brother skimmed pebbles across the water surface. I searched for flat slate stones for him, as they were the best; but Akis could reach thirteen ripples, and invariably won our competition, being so skilled.

When we got hungry we would sit under our colorful parasol, open our picnic basket, and devour the delicacies Mother prepared: flaky cheese or meat pies; we may even have a slice of the marble cake that Mrs. Rustelhorz had prepared. Our thirst was quenched with slices of red juicy watermelons or sweet honey-tasting melons. If we did not bring anything there was always a passing vendor; my favorite was the waffle man with his crunchy *fresca*, the honey-covered wafers that were a typical Egyptian snack found along the Corniche during the summer months. From time to time a *gala gala* or magician would appear. In no time, the other kids with whom we sought urchins joined us as curious onlookers, especially when he made tiny chicks appear out of his mouth, or pigeon eggs disappear behind his ears. Once he had quail eggs popping out of my own ears!

In her book *From Camp Cesar to Cleopatra's Pool, a Swiss Childhood in Alexandria* published by the Bibliotheca Alexandrina in 2008, Esther Zimmerli Hardman would recall similar scenes, prompting my own recollections.

On the beach, girls sported two-piece suits, a novelty at that time; bikinis would appear a few years later. Not many Egyptians frequented the beach, and those who came just sat fully dressed in front of their cabins eating pistachios and melon seeds, looking at the blue sea, taking the fresh breeze.

A diversion in the afternoon was a promenade along the Corniche with my parents. There was an iron fence through which the sea could be seen, not like the concrete fence I saw in 2014. It was a human fence made for the people. Now the Corniche seems to be made for traffic and you take life in your hand as a pedestrian.

My parents walked on the pavement while beyond the iron fence I was allowed to walk on the sand. One day I sprinted towards the water without a care, and my mother ran behind me, caught me, and gave me a good spanking. I burst out sobbing. The sea was high again, my father remarked; the wind was calm; the emerald green waves were rolling on the sand.

On the Corniche's pavement, an Arab vendor roasted salted peanuts, made a cone with newspaper, filled it, and for one piaster or half a cent, it was yours. Farther down, from a sidewalk stall, the aroma of roasted corn permeated the air. A hawker grilled cobs of corn on top of a copper stand, a common sight throughout the city in the summer; the kernels were tough, unlike the succulent white corn found in America. It was getting dark and I stared at the flickering lights of little fishing boats far out in the water. Then I glanced at the clear night sky dusted thickly with summer stars. Years later, I am still enthralled by these memories.

I do not recall exactly how long we stayed in Sidi Bishr, but then school started, so it must have been no more than three months.

The Germans at the gates

Everything seemed normal, but it was not.

That summer of 1942, panic broke out at a higher intensity when Alexandrians saw the Royal Navy's Mediterranean fleet—which had moved its headquarters from Malta to Alexandria in the mid-1930s—sail for the safety of Haifa, and then through the Suez Canal to the Red Sea. Gen. Erwin Rommel, the "Desert Fox," was advancing on Alexandria, and was a mere 60 miles or less than an hour away. He was anxious to reach Alexandria, to rest for a while in that mythical city.

Rommel boasted on the air that he would be at Groppi's, the famous Cairo patisserie, by five in the afternoon. Mussolini, meanwhile, sent word (we heard it on the radio, translated into many languages) that Egyptian women should prepare their loveliest dresses for the bash he planned to throw once the Nazis controlled Egypt. Rommel was seemingly unbeatable, his army ensconced in the town of El Alamein. He was confident he would be able to vanquish Cairo in time to enjoy afternoon tea at Shepheard's and a pastry at the legendary patisserie.

Shops, bars, and cafés were closed, their iron shutters rolled down; the streets were empty and from vacated houses the unanswered ring of telephones carried through Alexandria's empty streets. The stock exchange was closed; it would reopen only at the end of the war. There was a hysterical edge to our life as the battles grew closer. The future of Egypt and the Suez Canal hung in the balance.

The situation took a critical turn with the approach of Rommel's army. Many Jewish families and members of the elite Greek families fled anywhere they could—to the Sudan, Ethiopia, Chad, the Belgian Congo, Syria, Palestine, or even farther afield. We bid farewell to our friends, the Poulaki family, who departed for Tanganyika.

The Finneys, the unofficial head of the British community and the wealthiest people in town, departed by air to Cape Town, reportedly "showering gold pieces, literally gold Louis francs and English sovereigns, among their friends" at their last party before their departure. My brother would later work in one of their enterprises.

The streets were full of burning paper blowing in the wind as everyone torched compromising documents, even love letters from soldiers and sailors

Among those who did not flee Alexandria were the middle-class traders like my father, who had invested heavily in merchandise since the beginning of the year at the prospect of increasing import restrictions, and who were prevented from leaving by the lack of ready money, while the limited incomes of small tradesmen and artisans of the lower middle class made even the thought of flight impossible.

But not everyone recoiled from Rommel's advance. Bearing gifts of fruit and cigarettes, some Italian residents of the city were stopped by British guards as they tried to drive through the front to welcome the confidently expected Axis army. There were stories of cafés along the Corniche placing orders in local butchers for wurst. My father noted that several establishments had already posted signs saying "Welcome Rommel!"

Our friends the Rustelhorzes, a Greek-Swiss household, were looking kindly at the arrival of the Nazis. Madame Christine Rustelhorz was a Greek from Izmir, the widow of a German Swiss businessman. Their three daughters Louise, Alexandra, and Bertha and their young son Peter affirmed their allegiance to the Nazis. As Rommel was advancing, they hung a German flag, red with the black swastika symbol in the middle, over their balconies. My parents never forgot that.

Victory in the desert

The Alexandrian air shook with the hurricane roar of thousands guns off in the Western desert as the British unleashed their artillery and the Eighth Army went on the offensive in the Battle of El Alamein. I had never seen so many planes before in the sky. I was told they were bombers with their fighter escorts, and they were moving in every direction the whole time. The area off Mex where my father owned a tannery was thick with small torpedo craft and tank landing craft returning from their night business. The moon went from full to new through the twelve-day battle. Everyone was chattering, waving to one another, exchanging grimaces of hope and resignation while all the while training our eyes towards the western horizon where our fate was being decided beneath a terrible halo of light. We twisted the knobs of our radio—the station which we could hear often was German—alert for any magic words. We stayed silent and waited. Economic life stagnated. Father remained in Sidi Bishr, his office closed, with business at a standstill; we lived on our savings. Prices rose.

The British held off the Germans at El Alamein in July 1942 and Alexandria was spared, but the decisive engagement was fought in November, with the arrival of Field Marshal Bernard Montgomery, a stubborn, shrewd, and methodical commander who not only resisted all

German-Italian assaults but also succeeded in breaking the front and forcing Rommel to retreat. The Battle of Egypt, as Churchill called it, marked a turning point in the Allies' fortunes. In one fell swoop, the British dashed Germany's dreams of seizing Cairo and controlling Egypt and the Suez Canal. Rommel and the Afrika Korps started on their long retreat that within little more than six months would take them out of Africa. A jubilant Churchill, who had visited Cairo several times during the war, declared that "Before Alamein we never had a victory, and after Alamein, we never had a defeat." Egypt, the land of miraculous unfoldings, had brought the Allies luck.

Church bells rang to give thanks to the victory in the Western desert. The Alexandria Municipality joined the celebratory mood when it announced a proposal—never approved—bestowing the name "L'Avenue Montgomery" on the Rue des Soeurs. Victory reopened the Mediterranean to the mail, so that letters no longer took months to pass through Cape Town.

We cheered the allied victories of El Alamein, and we celebrated the sinking of German vessels, but the war that had come so close to us would linger for another three years.

Cracks in the varnish

Egypt breathed normally, and both in Cairo and Alexandria, *haute* society —British officers, Frenchmen, Australians, Greeks, Jews—converged in the cafés, the clubs, and the patisseries, confident for the first time that the war would go their way. While the Nazis had been routed from Egypt and were suffering one humiliating defeat after another in North Africa, the rest of the world was still at war. Refugees continued to pour into Alexandria and Cairo. Everyone was making fast decisions as if there was no time to waste.

In the Greek community there was the perception that Egypt would remain miraculously safe for them, refusing to adapt to the Egyptian reality that sooner or later would have presented itself; they remained hopeful, reluctant to face the truth.

Beneath the varnish of the newfound peace, cracks appeared. Communities that had been created over more than a century through tolerance and cooperation began falling apart in successive departures. Our Armenian neighbors left. They emptied the house of their belongings, sold some items at an auction, and sent others off to customs in trunks. The USSR sent two ships to welcome those who wished to settle in Soviet Armenia, with the promise to return them if they were not happy. The *Pobeda*, the Russian vessel that took them, was a white modern passenger liner, so different from the gray warships that had crowded the port of Alexandria during the war. They never returned, and we never heard from them again.

After the battle of El Alamein there were 30,000 German prisoners of war impounded in a desert camp at Marsah Matruh, 60 miles from Alexandria. The three young Swiss girls regularly went to visit them, bringing small gifts; the prisoners needed to send letters to their families back home and the Swiss girls were eager to oblige. I doubt that there was postal communication with Germany but the Red Cross, complying with its international obligations, transmitted the messages to their families in Germany. The war would last another three years. The Alamein cemeteries which I visited in 2007 were immaculately maintained: 6,200 casualties at the German cemetery, and 2,500 at the British. Impressive monuments with each side honoring their dead, so many crosses bearing their names and the title of the corps they had served in. I read their names; they all seemed twenty years old, all so young. Others remained anonymous.

V.

DARK CLOUDS OVER EGYPT

LIFE IN EGYPT had changed drastically since the heady aftermath of El Alamein. The colonial British were bitterly resented by the Egyptians, for whom "Egypt for the Egyptians" became their cry; foreign dominance had to end, war or no war. For Egyptians it was painful and shameful to see another flag instead of their own hoisted over their land. It was evident that it was not only a military occupation, but a many-faceted one: a monopoly of the government and an alliance with the Palace and the pashas. With the war ending, colonized peoples all over the world desired independence, and Egypt was no exception. But for the foreign communities and for the Jews, *les Anglais* were considered protectors and benefactors.

Did the British care about the Egyptians? Madame Jehan Sadat would note that, as a colonial power, they had built airports and roads from Cairo to Port Said and Suez that all Egyptians used, but these had been primarily meant for British military use. For all the years they had been "protecting" Egypt, they had done little for the majority of the people. In the country-side, half of the children died before the age of five; 70 percent of the adults had parasites from drinking Nile water. The British had not set up a single school, nor drilled wells for the *fellahin* to have clean water. The British had not even trained the Egyptian civil service as they did in India.

Indeed very little had been done by the British beyond peacekeeping. In Egypt at that time, 6 percent of the people owned 75 percent of the land, thus leaving under a fedan (1.6 acres) for most others to live on. The population was doubling itself every second generation. Meanwhile there was, in Durrell's words, "a steady growth of a vocal and literate middle class whose sons were trained at Oxford and who find no jobs waiting for them when they come back here."

A major characteristic of Egyptian nationalism was the growing envy and hate of foreigners, the half a million or so non-Muslims in the country. In particular, anti-Jewish sentiment grew in Egyptian intellectual and nationalistic circles, reflecting their sympathy with the Arab struggle in Palestine.

The foreign community was running the economy. The capital that flowed into the land (i.e. for cotton growing) was safe as long as the British were there, but now it was at the mercy of paunchy pashas. The Greeks, the Italians, the Jews, and the Copts began to feel the sharp edge of that hate; many wisely left, but others could not. They had made huge capital investments in cotton, in cotton oil refining, in cotton textile manufacturing, and in sugar and alcohol production; these could not be abandoned overnight. "The foreign communities are living from prayer to prayer and from bribe to bribe. They are trying to save their industries, their life-work from the gradual encroachment of the pashas," wrote Durrell.

Popular sentiment was mounting against King Farouk. He did whatever the British asked him to do as long as he remained on the throne. Instead of helping his country, he helped himself and indulged all his wishes and fancies. He made a law that no one could use the green color for a phone as he had installed green telephones in the palace bedrooms; he bought two yachts, 13 airplanes, and dozens of automobiles.

The King had become a symbol of corruption. The once slender young monarch whose reign had begun with such promise was now widely reviled for his dissolute lifestyle and grotesque appearance. He became paunchy, balding, and bloated. Perhaps the greatest irritant was the creation of Israel in 1947. In the ensuing war of 1948, Egypt fought and lost against the new Jewish state, and the loss continued to rankle.

The King was personally blamed for leading his country to defeat, and his detractors included the military officers who were actively plotting his demise. Some of them also resented the fact that the Farouk remained close to the Jews of Egypt who were now seen as the enemy in the same way that Israel was the enemy. One of these officers was named Gamal Abdel Nasser, who declared ominously that "It is time to restore the country's dignity and cleanse its honor with blood."

At home, it was a time of wrenching questions and vague desultory answers. My brother's education was a major dilemma. Akis had completed Greek high school as an average student who needed coaching in many subjects; tutors went in and out of the house. He enjoyed sailing at the yacht club, mastering two-masted vessels and venturing from the western port to the open sea. With his friends, he went hunting and partying at the Greek club or at friends' homes. From an early age, Akis would have preferred to stay in Egypt, be an apprentice in our father's office, but Father was adamant: "There are too many dark clouds in Egypt."

A way out for Akis

Akis did not have the entrepreneurial spirit required to take over my father's business. Father did not encourage him to follow a business path; he never took Akis along to any business meetings, and did not want to groom him to be a businessman and entrepreneur. A profession seemed more suitable, and like any Greek middle-class parent, Father dreamed of sending his son to study at a European university. The war meant lean years for business and the world was changing.

Having taken French and German in high school, the choice for Akis fell between France or Germany. German and Austrian universities were highly regarded, but Germany had just emerged from the war, impoverished and badly weakened. Leipzig, a favorite for Greeks, was now in the hands of Communist East Germany. The choice fell to a provincial French university, not Paris with its many temptations; my brother's grades anyway were not high enough to merit admission at a top French school. Studying in England was not even considered, in spite of the formidable reputation of British universities. Akis spoke little English; learning that language in the late 1940s was relegated at that time for immigrants bound for the United States or Australia, the destination of working-class Greeks.

Another dilemma was finding a way to get funds out of the country for his university studies. The Egyptian government had banned all shipments of currency abroad. The punishment was imprisonment and eventual expulsion.

For that, Father had a solution. I accompanied my father to the office of a friend, a bookbinder whose son, one of Akis' classmates, also intended to study in Europe. We took along a few books, some old, some new, some tattered. Why did we have those books bound, I asked myself, as we never looked at them; we should have bound my mother's Greek cook book instead, as it was falling apart. I was left behind closed doors. Little did I know that Father had brought along gold coins and small ingots of gold. They were to be enclosed in the new heavy book bindings. Smuggling gold inside toothpaste tubes, in the soles of shoes, or in heavy binding of books was the resort of many in those pre-X-ray-scanner days. The customs officials were not yet as thorough as they would become in 1956 when the mass exodus of foreigners took place.

We were hardly alone in this subterfuge. Foreigners with embassy contacts did their smuggling through diplomatic channels. Brokers with European representatives deposited their profits abroad, mostly in Switzerland. Wealthy individuals were able to ship clothes, carpets, antique furniture, and pieces of art, leaving behind a poorly kept villa filled with junk, moth-eaten rugs, and books. The Menasce family was transferring money abroad, and they gradually moved their priceless Chinese jade and other art objects out of Egypt.

The affluent members of the Greek community did smuggle significant assets out of Egypt before the mass exodus of 1956. In a recently published account, a Mr. Christodoulou admitted that before leaving Egypt perma-nently, he "had bought the house in which we now live in Athens" with a "little money" that they had sent out secretly. The same individual described how he prepared to smuggle out 40 gold sovereigns and several gold bars. The Egyptian authorities arrested 59 Greeks who participated in racketeering rings as they smuggled substantial quantities of jewelry and hard currency.

A state of distress

It had been the custom of the family during the war years to spend three months in Sidi Bishr. Usually we went the first week of June, at the end of the school year. But when the heat in Alexandria was unbearable and with the war having ended, we broke from our tradition, and funds were now earmarked for my brother's education.

We still had Greek friends spending the summer in Alexandria while my privileged high school classmates holidayed in Europe visiting relatives, exploring the continent's sights, and returning with fascinating tales. For us there was no more travel to Greece; the annual pilgrimage to the homeland before the war had ceased. The suite reserved for Father on the Adriatica Line vessels was no longer available as a perk, as his business with the maritime company had dwindled. The Greek islands, the spas of Loutraki or Methana, were now too costly. Many of my father's friends had perished during the German occupation. Family connections were strained, and our links to the homeland had weakened. Staying at home, life seemed to lose much of its luster, and I was envious of my traveling classmates.

I would look back at those years with a mixture of bitterness and longing.

I could sense these were troubled times, but no one seemed willing to explain why. I could not ask my father, who was half a century older, why we could not go to Greece for the summer while others were going to Europe. None of us expected the fall of the monarchy. I could not understand why my father had fallen into such financial distress. Were the bribes required to get an import export license too high? Was it the loss of his vessels during the war? Was it because he could not unload his merchandise from India or Madagascar, stuck in the free zone of the Suez Canal?

One day I spotted a secret look passing between my parents, a look which puzzled me but told me nothing. I could hear them talking about the new requirements being imposed by the government, but the subject was soon dropped and they moved on to other things.

Another evening, while in my room, I heard them talking on the verandah. There was a palpable difference in their tone of voice—no arguments, but no laughter either, certainly not the usual daily chatter. Something was wrong, a sense of urgency I found odd.

I got up from my chair and leaned out through the open window to listen. I was very still and I could hear every word of the conversation. Father was attempting to persuade Mother that in view of the poor business lately, they ought to cut down on expenses. Miss Ftiara, my private tutor for Ancient Greek lessons, was very expensive; my brother's membership in the yacht club had to be discontinued.

There was that frightening silence, a grim, uneasy sort of silence, that paralyzed me; these conversations were the first hint of the changes to come.

I was tearful standing there, insecure and wishing passionately for life to stay as it was now—no, not as now, but as it was yesterday when I could have gone playing tennis, attended a birthday party, and practiced solfege at the piano even if I did not care much for the piano lessons. I did not know then the many years of struggle my parents would face; all I knew at that moment was a vague fear.

In later years my mother pierced together most of it for me. Father's import export business had collapsed during the war years, meeting with all kinds of problems with labor, exports, and bad representation abroad. Export licenses for foreigners were difficult to renew, and a huge *baksheesh* or facilitation fee was very likely required to get one. The two vessels Father owned had been sunk or rendered worthless by the heavy damage done by German torpedoes in the port of Piraeus. Lloyd's insurance was invalid for acts of war.

Closed during the war, the stock exchange reopened its doors, but the momentum was gone. Egypt fell into a recession. Economic life stagnated while prices soared.

Kyria Argyro, the seamstress who had crafted so many lovely dresses for me, was hired no longer. We still sported the compulsory uniform at the Lyçée, but there were no new clothes for me. My mother just remodeled outfits from Aunt Katina's discards. My world was changing. I was gently dissuaded from having friends over for tea and cake or for an impromptu recital around my piano. I was always chatty and extroverted and expansive —I have not changed!—able to make friends in a heartbeat and to conduct animated conversations with the most diverse figures; but alas, my social horizons were closing.

So many of our friends were leaving the country, abandoning Egypt for some unknown lands.

Concerned for its own circulation, the Greek newspaper *Tahydromos* urged its readers to stay, predicting better years ahead, but the admonition soon turned hollow. Even if the Greeks had helped operate the Suez Canal after the British were thrown out, the goodwill did not last long. The Egyptians could well run the canal on their own without help from any foreigner.

A revolution rocks Egypt

Between 1951 and 1952, Egypt was rocked by violence as anti-British sentiments intensified. The government canceled its 1936 treaty with Britain, and thousands of Egyptians employed by the British walked off their jobs. Skirmishes arose between Egyptian auxiliary police and British troops. The British cordoned off the Suez Canal zone. An attack by British troops on a police outpost resulted in numerous deaths, and provoked a firestorm of protest.

The Free Officers Movement, led by young middle class officers including Muhammad Naguib and the charismatic Gamal Abdel Nasser, kept up the pressure on the British, and plotted at the same time to overthrow the monarchy. On January 26, 1952—known since then as "Black Saturday"—Cairo erupted in massive rioting.

Six months later, on July 26, the hopelessly corrupt Farouk was deposed and forced into exile by a military coup. A revolutionary council took over the government. A new regime was in place, and Egypt would never be the same again—not for the Egyptians, and certainly not for those like us who had been, more than ever, pushed to the fringe by the revolution.

Within days of Farouk's abdication, an edict came eliminating royal titles such as those for pashas and beys. The new military rulers wanted nothing even vaguely reminiscent of the royal family and proceeded to eradicate any trace of the monarchy. Within a couple of years, even the street names that paid tribute to various royals would be changed.

As Lucette Lagnado would observe in *The Man in the White Sharkskin Suit*, renaming streets became obsessively popular after the revolution. Never easy to navigate, both Cairo and Alexandria became a confusing mess of official names and unofficial names, old names and new names.

Malika Nazli (Queen Nazli, the King's mother) Street became the Street of the Rebirth of Egypt and then finally Ramses Street. Stately Rue Fouad, a tribute to the late King, was renamed 26th of July Street to commemorate the day the monarchy fell. For most Egyptians today the name of Rue Fouad Street remains. Farouk Street, rather humble considering its namesake, where you went to buy clay pots and pans for the kitchen, went through different iterations when Nasser and Sadat were in power, and ultimately became Sharia el Geish, the Street of the Army.

This is not unusual, as many countries breath their history and engrave their past into their landscape, like the boulevards and train stations in Paris (Gare Austerlitz, Boulevard Haussmann). No French town is without an Avenue Charles de Gaulle.

The edict banishing the *tarbush* was the most telling sign of the new order. The red fez, or the *tarbush* as it is called in Egypt, is a cone-shaped hat made of red felt, sporting a silk black sash. During President's Nasser's modernization campaign, it was banned by him because it was considered a symbol of Turkish dominance. He went so far as to ban photographs of King Farouk wearing the tarbush. Silver coins with this image disappeared from circulation, and became collector's items.

After it was declared illegal, the *tarbush* was relegated to actors in Egyptian black and white movies. Doormen and attendants working in posh hotels around Cairo also wore them to greet tourists who wanted a taste of the real Egypt. Among young, modern Egyptians, the *tarbush* has been replaced by the baseball cap.

Nasser vowed to restore political independence, revive the economy, and address social equality after ridding Egypt of foreign control. The involvement of young officers inspired similar revolutions across the region.

Nasser wanted to build the Aswan Dam, and it became an obsession with him. He wanted to tame the waters of the Nile that gushed out into the sea; a giant dam could be built, according to the experts, the flow could be controlled, the desert irrigated, bringing prosperity to the people. Neither the Americans, nor the British, nor the World Bank were willing finance it. Nasser nationalized the Suez Canal and turned to the Russians. The rest is history.

The Nasser regime continued to apply pressure on foreigners. Import-export licenses required fat bribes, and the stock market was eviscerated. My father's office was scrutinized by government representatives. These henchmen asked why there were such detailed maps of Egypt and Greece hanging on the walls—he had to be a spy!

A stroll and a snack

In the 1950s, with limited income, my parents had to content themselves with a modest lifestyle. On Sundays, when the wind was down, they would stroll along the Corniche past the elegant restaurants and the grand hotels, watching the blazing sunset; there would be no more tea at the Beau Rivage. All the latest models of cars would stream past them, while nearby, perched on his horse, the coachman of an *arabeya* would crack his whip on the poor creature's back.

Occasionally I joined them taking the coal-fired train to Abukir—famous for its Battle of the Nile, also known as the battle of Abukir Bay, where British forces under Nelson defeated Napoleon in the most decisive battle of the great age of sails—where we enjoyed our own snacks rather than patronizing even a rustic restaurant. I was always thrilled to take the train to Abukir, although I had taken it many times before. Despite my mother's warnings, I would not sit still but just had to thoroughly inspect the knobs and handles and the tattered upholstery of the seats, and often I poked my head out of window to watch the countryside flying past us.

We returned covered in black soot, as those little trains were packed to capacity. For me it was an adventure to stand in the corridor among the crying babies in that hot train and look at the passing countryside. My mother hurried me along the platform so we could return home and clean myself up. I kept looking regretfully back to the great monster which had transported us back to Sidi Gaber station.

Other times we took the little Victoria tram, our main transport, which with its clickety wheels brought us to the sandy beaches of Sidi Bishr, where we spent part of the day before visiting friends who owned a country home.

Nouzha Gardens was another destination where we sat on rickety wooden green benches, nibbling on roasted peanuts. Humble Egyptian families camped on the ground under oleander trees. By the rotting Mahmoudiya Canal, we watched dirty-nosed underfed children diving for coins in the ooze or eating leftover slices of watermelon from a garbage bin. We wandered among the idlers of the city anonymously. Memberships in the Greek clubs and the Greek community association were left to lapse. Outdoor cafés and the Western pastry shops were now too expensive. But still, my parents walked with pride in their step, sustained by a deep and enduring love.

A complex of misfortunes

One day, treading a slippery patch of cement, Father hit the pavement and broke his arm—a simple fracture which today requires no more than a couple of hours in a hospital or emergency room. He was ushered into the Kozzica, the Greek hospital founded by an Alexandrian industrialist, Theodore Kozzica. The hospital was partitioned into floors for first-, second-, and third-class paying patients, plus the "Open Clinic," the super-luxurious hospital private ward suites. These were expensive, and with their white walls and moneyed patients, it certainly gave the Kozzica something to boast about. To find work at the hospital was the goal of the more ambitious foreign doctors.

Father was admitted to the second-class section. Nothing distressed me more when I heard the whispers from a friend visiting: "Panayiotis

Leotsinidis in the second-class section? I was looking for him at the Open Clinic!" Father was in agony, not from pain but from a constant and uncontrollable itchiness caused by the plaster cast. The plaster used for his arm cast turned out to have contained bedbugs which hatched after the cast was put in place. The plaster had to be cut, the bone reset. I wondered if he had received the inferior treatment reserved for those who could not afford the better hospital floors.

Father was silent; he always kept to himself in good and bad times. Now he was even more reclusive. His import and export business had collapsed during the war years. Export licenses for foreigners were difficult to renew, and a huge *baksheesh* or facilitation fee was very likely required to get one.

On top of his problems, Hassan, a member of his custodial staff, sued him, claiming that he had not been paid for 25 years. The Mixed Tribunals had ceased to exist, ending protection for foreigners, so Father had to face the Egyptian courts. The office bookkeeper had faithfully recorded the wages Hassan had been paid for all those years, but it was in cash, the norm of those days, and no signed receipts are available. Amid yellowing papers, years later, I stumbled on a ledger that chronicled my father's payments to Hassan. I never found the outcome of the lawsuit and what, if anything, was negotiated.

Our savings were getting exhausted. Did we have enough funds to live on? Was my father's lack of funds a bit of an exaggeration?

An unlucky complex of misfortunes had engulfed him once again—in Asia Minor in the 1920s, and now in Egypt in the 1950s; Father was already in his sixties, and ruined. Could he ever recover? He never did.

Jobs were now strictly restricted to Egyptian citizens; no foreign firm large or small, no degree from a foreign university, had any cachet. Egypt was now, indeed, for the Egyptians. Foreigners in Egypt, and Greeks in particular, found it difficult to adapt to the country's postcolonial conditions.

Akis gets a job

After obtaining a Chemical Engineering degree, Akis had spent a year as an apprentice in Wiesbaden, Germany, at the renowned Baddish Aniline industrial complex, specializing in inks and dyes. Ali el Kouni joined him there as he was keen to learn the textile dying process. In Baddish Aniline, Akis specialized in inks. His apprenticeship would prove useful years later in America as he became an authority on the use of inks for newspapers, color magazines, and even textile printing. Later, Ali would establish a small textile factory. Towels made of Egyptian cotton were in demand and Ali profited from his enterprises. (Under Sadat, Ali would become a member of parliament.)

While in Germany, one of Akis' co-workers handed him a grayish square of soap, claiming it had been made from Jewish corpses. There was no proof that Nazis made Jews into soap in mass factories, although such a soap was provided as evidence at the Nuremberg trial, having been manufactured in Danzig from human corpses. Hoax or not, my brother accepted it and presented it upon his return to Egypt to the local synagogue of Camp Cesar. A memorial service was held where we were invited, and my brother was profusely thanked. It was the first time I attended a synagogue service.

Back in Egypt, and for the first time, it was necessary for Akis to get a job and collect a steady paycheck, but Egyptian citizenship was now a prerequisite. Some documentation was needed to acquire this status: a birth certificate to accompany the formal application, plus the usual hefty fee. Weeks passed as we waited anxiously for that precious citizenship. The paperwork remained stuck in the drawer of some bureaucrat; as it turned out, a case of Scotch whisky was what was needed to hurry things along.

Akis landed a job at the Finneys' yeast factory laboratory, where he remained employed for five or six years, becoming the breadwinner of the family. Early in the morning, a chauffeured car picked him up together with another employee who lived in our area, and dropped them off in the evening, a Finney's fringe benefit. With my brother holding a job, the matchmakers begin approaching him the way once they did with Barbas, but his heart remained with Francine, his French girlfriend, always carrying her picture.

Mrs. Finney, widowed now but still an astute businesswoman, often visited her diverse enterprises. The plant employees ogled her Rolls Royce, taking note of the different colors of her automobiles; my brother counted four, but he may have missed one or two.

Although Akis' Egyptian citizenship opened the door for employment, a new challenge emerged as he heard, "Your name is not Muhammad!" The law did not require one to be a Muslim, but by the late '50s it was the unwritten rule.

A wave of foreigners was departing from Egypt, their future uncertain but surely bleak if they stayed. For many generations, foreigners like me had been born in Alexandria but in some ways we never adapted and never learned the language, and now the rise of Egyptian nationalism had rendered our situation untenable.

Akis was caught in a bind. As an Egyptian citizen, he got a job; however, he was now restrained from leaving, an exit visa being required and difficult to obtain. An exception existed if one was traveling to the Soviet Union, as Nasser had befriended the Soviets who were building the Aswan Dam.

But a way out would be found. We tried to cope with a new situation as best as we could. An option to consider seriously was a business trip that had been planned to Berlin's Soviet sector. It was then the only way out, and Akis took it. He landed at Schonefeld Airport in East Berlin from where, with just an attaché case, not even a suitcase, he crossed over at Checkpoint Charlie to West Berlin. He entered West Germany on his old Greek passport. An American visa, secured in advance, was issued in West Berlin; a phantom job, conjured by relatives in America, facilitated the process.

So in 1957, my brother started a new career and a new life in Chicago, his hometown for the next 55 years. He even discarded his nickname Akis for the more westernized Byron, which was his middle name. He never wanted to be reminded of his tumultuous last years in Egypt; he always remained afraid, and insecurity shadowed the rest of his life. His friendship with Ali el Kouni remained undiminished, sustained by regular correspondence. Years later, Akis returned to Egypt with his Greek-American wife and their son to visit his native city and to have a reunion with his friend Ali.

A dream of Paris

As for myself, after graduation from high school, it was time to consider entering a university. Our system was different from the US, where students apply two years in advance to a number of universities and visit their campuses; besides school grades and extracurricular actives, they have to achieve a certain level in aptitude tests. I had topped the Baccalaureat, achieving the highest grade among candidates in the entire country. I would have been easily accepted at any French university. Classmates with lower grades were admitted to the Faculty of Medicine in Paris, and I was very envious of them.

Chemistry was my favorite subject; I do not know if I was just emulating my brother or if indeed it was a genuine fascination for the subject. Class experiments conducted on the fluorescent properties of algae had triggered my interest and imagination, but more likely was just my limited horizon at that time. I had no guidance, no mentor, no one to talk to. For years, indoctrinated at the Lycée and immersed in French culture, my dream was to study in Paris. Reluctantly, I would have considered Grenoble, a city up in the Alps. The initial response of my parents was that I was too young, too immature, to live alone on the continent. The harsh truth was that my father could not fund my education in a European University.

I cried and pleaded to no avail. My dreams were crushed. I would not easily forget that evening when harsh words were exchanged. Sixty years later, those words have not been eradicated. I went to bed that night knowing that rebellion was useless. I was only a teenager and would not be listened to, even if I had the words to explain the agony of my mind. I was aware at the family's financial strains but I had the illusion that there was a cachet of gold sovereigns set aside for my university studies. I was too young and naive to grasp the tumultuous events the country was going through; the daily edicts affecting foreigners. My father gave me several very good, cold, material reasons, but came no nearer to understanding my distress. I was determined that I would somehow strike out on my own one day.

My mother, who had little formal education, had never raised her voice above a whisper, never put forward an opinion for fear she would be frowned upon. But now she became adamant that a solution should be found for me. "A piece of land in Egypt could be nationalized overnight. (How right she was!) Whatever amount of stocks one owns, they will last only a certain time. Look at our stocks—they are good only as wallpaper. One day, gold will buy you nothing. It may be taken away but there is a golden bracelet that lasts forever, and it is called education. There is no time to think of grandeur and of universities in Paris. There is a university in Alexandria, and you should consider it."

If higher education was in my future, entry to an Egyptian university was the immediate answer. At that time very few foreign nationals—less than 1 percent of the total student body—were admitted to Egyptian universities, a number that has since increased tenfold. There was a small quota for Greek students, but I do not know if there was a quota for French or British nationals, as none of them were at the Faculty of Science. Although I was a graduate from a French institution, I must have been admitted as a Greek. Foreign students today are not Alexandrian but come from Palestine, the Emirates, and the rest of the Arab world.

A major hurdle was that a graduate from a foreign high school had to take tests in the Arabic language, equivalent to graduating from an Egyptian high school. The only Arabic I knew was the colloquial version, the street language, enough to communicate with servants or to bargain at the bazaar. I barely knew the 33 letters of the alphabet, which I could not even enunciate properly. I could pen my name using Arabic characters, but they looked like a jumble of scattered tea threads. Arabic became compulsory at the Lycée and all foreign schools only after 1960.

An interview brought me to the office of the Dean of the Faculty of Science, who was holding the chair of the Botany department. He shook my hand

and indicated I should sit on the only chair besides his own that was not littered with paper. A telephone was ringing constantly. I sat on the edge of a chair; I was nervous, my heart thumping. I expected he could hear it. I did not plead, I did not cry, although there was a lump in my throat. I was proud. I had prepared for that day as I would for a final exam. I did not show any gratitude towards Egypt but was straightforward. I expressed my unquenchable interest in science.

(A similar scene would take place 35 years later when I was interviewed for a position at the Bell Labs of AT&T. I was desperate to get a job that included medical insurance so I could help cover my sick husband's medical bills; diagnosed with leukemia, he was unable to work. I was also then prepared for that interview and nervous. I was determined that there should be no question that Mr. Hani Tawil, a Lebanese senior manager, could ask that I did not have some sort of answer to. I was proud and was determined not to be found wanting in anyway. And then, to my chagrin or rather to my surprise, the very first question he asked stumped me: "What is your definition of success, Mrs. Hill?" What sort of question was that? What did he want me to say? Working alongside renowned scientists, members of the National Academy, even the Bell Labs Nobel Prize winners? Advancing science, presenting papers on my research at international conferences, developing patents to benefit the corporation and the entire telecommunications industry, commercializing my findings, and making something for myself? A few seconds passed, and I finally found my voice. "I am very successful, Mr. Tawil." He looked at me, surprised. "Tell me more," he said." I have a happy marriage," I responded. He nodded in approval. I got the job.)

An opened door

The dean remained immovable like a Sphinx, and not a flicker of emotion crossed his face. I had my filed application in English, rather than in Arabic. I remember his last words: "I do not need any references." A month later I heard that I was among the three foreigners admitted at the Faculty of Science. Egypt opened the door for me, providing a steppingstone for graduate work in America. The university was tuition-free, requiring just a few pounds for registration on the first year.

The Faculty of Science was in Moharrem Bey, in one of the poorest neighborhoods of the city; it required taking two trams to reach, but I could read and read during the tram journey. Classes were in English, as were the books. Science books were not yet available in Arabic. The teaching staff had earned their PhDs from Egyptian, British, or American universities. A sprinkling of Fulbright scholars would rotate from one semester to another. After the Lycée, I found the university courses surprisingly light. Instead of being immersed in the configuration of organic compounds or in the Second Law of Thermodynamics, I spend countless hours learning Arabic.

I did four years of intensive study with a tutor, and later with a professor from the Faculty of Arts who befriended me and volunteered to coach me gratis in classical Arabic. I had to master works of Taha Hussein, the most influential Egyptian writer and intellectual, and read the news in *El Ahram*, the leading Egyptian newspaper. The most demanding task I faced was mastering the "punctuation" of the poetry of Mutanabi, the 10th-century Iraqi poet whose works were considered the epitome of classical Arabic.

I failed that Arabic exam four times; the fifth time the powers of the university must have had pity of me and let me pass, entitling me to become a Bachelor of Sciences with first-degree honors. I doubt that my final essay in classical Arabic was any better than the first.

I joined the Faculty sports team in volleyball, basketball, and tennis, and was invited every year during academic breaks to compete against the faculty teams of the University of Cairo and Ain Shams University. We were thrashed on the sporting field but had a joyful time otherwise and a rare opportunity to discover the hidden gems of Old Cairo. As students, part of the Faculty team, we always traveled third-class. Dr. Fathi, a professor of General Chemistry, escorted us. He was a tall, athletic young gentleman, and we all had a crush on him. He had an allowance for our Cairo expenses; once, left with some spare cash, instead of returning the money, he treated us at a pastry shop, and in addition purchased for every one on the team a lottery ticket. No one became a millionaire.

The gems of Old Cairo

Medieval Cairo became my favorite part of the city, being way more interesting than its Pharaoanic aspects.

I lost myself in Islamic, medieval Cairo at Al Azhar through gates that welcomed conquerors, into a copy of the Damascus mosque with its vast courtyard and colonnade, but more austere, more Protestant, the difference between a baroque church in Rome and a Lutheran church in Harlem.

"A traveler is usually pleased if he finds a dozen buildings from the Middle Ages in a single European city. Cairo has them by the score, and it is an unequal treasure house of Islamic architecture," notes a guidebook to Islamic Cairo. Medieval Cairo was one of the cities of the *Thousand-and-One Nights*. It was in those narrow streets that many of those characters were supposed to have lived. They were imaginary creatures, but there were enough real heroes, rogues, rascals, and clowns who did in fact live there, to people another set of thousand tales, and to build a city that, unlike Baghdad and Damascus, was spared the devastation of the Mogul invasions.

University life

Across the road from the massive gates of the Faculty of Science straggled an uneven line of shacks that sold everything that cash-trapped students would need: foul-smelling cigarettes, strong sweet tea, biscuits and juices, calendars, and stationery supplies. The entrance to one of the shacks was studded with flies but it was popular as besides the fruits, biscuits, and juices, the stall owner supplied two roughly put-together wooden benches for the customer's comfort. They were always occupied.

In my freshman year, the university instituted military training especially for women. It was not compulsory but difficult to avoid. Along with another student, Toula Nemzis, a Greek junior, I volunteered. Uniforms were provided and we were handed cumbersome old rifles dating back to WWI and taught how to aim and shoot. I could practice on a rifle I could barely lift. To fight whom? Westerners? Jews? We never asked. Fortunately, the military training lasted only few months, and fizzled out. President

Muhammad Naguib, the predecessor of Nasser, visited our Faculty and with Toula I was selected to sing the Egyptian national anthem in front of him. We barely understood the words but we sang with gusto.

While at the Lyçée, Anne Geisenberger had changed her name in fear of the Nazis, and for nationalistic reasons a similar situation developed at the university. Classmates called Farouk the first semester of the academic year were registering the second semester under a new name, Gamal! The fee to legally change one's name was two Egyptian pounds.

Although the campus was not politicized there was a Communist faction that tried to lure me into their fold, offering to pay for my yearly tram *abonnement* or fare. I never succumbed.

While in college I befriended a young and vivacious Egyptian girl, Aida Sinbel, who half a century later remains my very dear friend. Her family welcomed me with open arms. Although Arabic was spoken at her home, most of our conversations were carried in French. With an extended family of sisters, brothers, cousins, uncles, aunts, there were birthdays, weddings, anniversaries, arrivals, and departure celebrations where I was included. Her father was a technocrat, one of those individuals who made the wheels of the government turn. He was the Director General of customs in Alexandria, one of the largest customs operations in the world. In 1956 he represented Egypt in the negotiations with England, France, and the United States after the nationalization of the Suez Canal by President Nasser. In later years under President Sadat he emerged as the Minister of Finance, representing Egypt at numerous international financial negotiations.

Aida's path and mine diverged; both of us did graduate work at the University of Minnesota and moved on in different careers, but have remained in touch through the years.

Besides Aida, I did not make other friends at the university, a sharp in contrast with my classmates in high school. The Greek students did not bond with the locals. It was not that individually we were not accepted, but a "new order" had emerged under Nasser. We were on the average more affluent, more sophisticated, more privileged; we lived in nicer neighborhoods. The stigma of cosmopolitanism was stamped on our foreheads.

With Aida I explored local neighborhoods in Moharrem Bey. Instead of joining other students the Faculty caféteria, where for three piasters we could enjoy a wholesome and nutritious meal, we meandered in the local eateries. I got exposed for the first time to the local cuisine: eating *ful medanes* served with *tahina* sauce, *mahshi* which were vegetables stuffed with rice and spices, chickpea-based falafel, and the marvelous *tourshi*, brightly colored Egyptian pickles. If we had any piasters left over, we indulged after school by stopping at Delices and treating ourselves to *millefeuilles* or any of the Western pastries.

I joined the Greek Alumni Association and was elected to its board, responsible with others for orchestrating social events: lectures, photographic exhibits, and the annual costume ball; the dances proved to be the most popular.

A summer found me as an apprentice at the Shell refinery on the Red Sea —a casualty of one of the Israeli wars, bombed and destroyed few years later. With its air-conditioned accommodations and hot water in every tap, the complex was surprisingly plush. I spent my time getting hands-on experience and can recall little besides work, punching a clock but marveling at the corals of the coast and the swarming population of rainbow-colored tropical fish.

A summer in Greece

Once, as a member of the Greek students' association, I spent a summer in Greece. Standing under the Parthenon, I felt the thrill of my heritage. It was not only the visits to archeological and Byzantine sites that proved worthwhile, but also the exposure to the Athens University students who served as our guides all over Greece. I realized that there was a world beyond the confinement of life in Egypt.

When the student who escorted us invited me to his home and introduced me to his family, he mentioned as an aside that his father was the head of

Arios Pagos. I was awed—he was the chief judge of the Supreme Court of Greece! Never in my wildest dreams in Alexandria did I imagine that I'd meet such a distinguished personality.

Who financed this journey remained a mystery; my parents could ill afford it. It was Uncle Michael Nyhas from Chios most probably; I was never told, and it is too late to thank him and express my gratitude.

A trip to Aswan

I had visited Luxor in Upper Egypt with students from the Faculty of Science, travelling by train on a 14-hour-long journey, sitting on hard wooden chairs in a third-class compartment. When you are young the quality of the seats does not matter.

Another time it was Aunt Aphrodite, my mother's sister who came for a short holiday from New York, who treated me to a Luxor sojourn; it was an experience to go on a sleeping car, in the luxury of Wagon Lits rail accommodations. Aswan was also new to me. We reached Aswan—an overnight train ride that today takes no more than an hour by plane from Cairo—in the middle of a heat wave, ready to explore the Pharaonic treasures of the country.

We were booked at the old Cataract Hotel. I wondered if the hotel had fallen under a spell. The Moorish-style hotel, which had famously hosted Agatha Christie (who wrote *Death on the Nile* here) and Winston Churchill, had the languid feel of a tropical village shuttered by its afternoon siesta. I imagined that with every passing hour, rooms would be closed forever and staff would turn into stone. When I walked next door to its plainer sister, the New Cataract Hotel, the ping-pong table on the verandah looked like it had not been used for years and a felucca on the grounds was abandoned as if a tidal wave had swept it ashore.

The Nile looked so still from my room that it well may have turned to clay, the captains of the feluccas on it like ancient mariners doomed to ply the river for eternity. In 40 degrees, no one was venturing out.

Everything was just as it should be; we had arrived at the Cataract just a few days before it closed for lengthy refurbishments. This was serendipitous because the *grande dame* hotel was at its best when its carpets were worn and the staff shuffled around with warm smiles but less than speedy efficiency.

Thankfully, we did not encounter signs like "Gentlemen are requested not to strike servants," as Jan Morris reported was common in her book *Pax Britannica*. But these hotels were proud of that connection to the colonial past, few more so than the Old Cataract.

We sat on the terrace to escape the heat; the café menu provided a history of the hotel in the purplest prose: "There is no exaggeration to consider the train and the British Empire as the natural parents of the Old Cataract Hotel. The hotel's unique architecture is a witness of the Victorian Age when British imperialism was at the height of its influence."

These hotels were more than historical curiosities. They helped slow the passage of time. We stayed in Aswan for two days but it felt I had been there for two weeks. We did little at the Old Cataract other than contemplate the beauty of the Nile, and enjoy the pleasing intensity of the dry heat.

At sunset, we went to the stunning temple complex of Philae. The temple had been relocated from its original site when the Aswan Dam was completed in the mid-60s. We dined at 1902, where a young Churchill and "the third son of Queen Victoria" attended the inaugural dinner that year, and marveled at the candy-colored cathedral like ceilings. The waiters wearing burgundy Egyptian-style robes with gold sashes seemed more like clergymen. The one who served me looked like a cardinal. As I spoke Arabic, he thought I was Egyptian and addressed me as "*Emira*." My vegetable curry was doused in bland curry powder. But how you not love a restaurant where you are addressed as *Emira*?

The following day we took a felucca, sailing downstream; that was my dream, a felucca to ourselves; we passed the house and the tomb of the old Aga Khan and continued around the rocky, dark brown granite boulders that were the Elephantine Islands. The troops of Ramses II, as well as those of Cesar, Napoleon, and Field Marshal Lord Kitchener, on his way to the

Battle of Omdurman to avenge the death of general Charles Gordon, all carved their names on Kitchener Island. Its botanical garden was covered with purple bougainvilleas, oleanders, and pomegranates as well as many rare species. It was luxuriant and well maintained, a two-acre wonder worth visiting all by itself.

Our captain had fresh lemonade and cool towels for us when we embarked for our return. It was a peaceful boat ride; a gentle breeze blew on the felucca triangular sails as we glided over the water. The only sound that interrupted the blissful silence was the creaking of old oars and the squeaking of ibis fighting over good nesting sites over the treetops.

Arriving at the hotel sitting under a swirling fan, it was time for some good old-fashioned English tea. Staying at the Cataract was seductive but, like so many things, dwelling on the past needed to be done in moderation.

A grant for America

A month after our graduation, an event would unfold, a defining moment in Egypt's history. The date was July 26, 1956.

It was the fourth anniversary of the overthrow of King Farouk. President Nasser gave a speech from the balcony of the Stock Exchange; a quarter-million Egyptians were packed in the square. During the two-and-a-half-hour speech, Nasser denounced imperialism and the colonial powers seeking to dominate Egypt. In particular he blasted the British, the Americans, and the World Bank who refused to build the hydroelectric High Dam in Aswan, as he had purchased arms from Russia. He announced the occupation and nationalization of the Suez Canal. The crowd roared. Traveling on his special train, Nasser took almost a week to get back to Cairo following his announcement, held up at every station by popular demonstrations.

A personal turning point was also at hand. I had applied to go to graduate school in America.

I had received with distinction the coveted French Baccalaureat; my initial dream was to pursue undergraduate studies in France where my brother had gone, and I was also envious of his traveling adventures in Europe.

But by now English had become the prevalent language, and was the medium of instruction at the Faculty of Science. Many of my professors had earned their graduate degrees in American universities and strongly recommended them as an obvious choice. This was the time after Sputnik, and America's technological competition with Soviet Union had accelerated; thus, science was well funded and scholarships widely available. With many European émigrés like Einstein on staff, American universities were flourishing, posting significant breakthroughs.

That summer, I received a travel grant and an assistantship from the three American universities where I had applied: the Massachusetts Institute of Technology, the University of North Carolina, and the University of Minnesota. They all offered me a tuition-free scholarship, supplemented with a stipend as a teaching assistant supervising the laboratory work of freshmen students. Those monetary benefits did not exist in European universities, at least not for a Greek with an undergraduate degree from an Egyptian institution.

There was also family in New York. My mother's sister, Aunt Aphrodite, visited us during my last college year and offered support. For an emergency I had an anchor, a family in America, but I made the conscious decision not to be indebted to anyone and to strike out on my own. So I did not apply to Columbia, which had also been recommended to me, being too close to the family.

I finally decided on Minnesota for my MSc in Chemistry. Two giants in the field of chemistry were on the faculty of the university there. The first, Isaac Kolthoff, was considered the father of Analytical Chemistry; even in Alexandria, we took his books as our discipline's bible. What a legacy he left —there are now over a thousand doctoral students who can trace their academic lineage to his laboratory. The other was William Limpscomb, an authority of crystallography, a subject that fascinated me then and still does. His course proved extremely useful in my first job in Australia, while investigating the protein structure of wool. Kolthoff was small, balding, plump, bespectacled, humorless, and rather taciturn, while Limpscomb was relaxed and put you at ease; he was also a clarinetist who performed on weekends at a Minneapolis club, and we sneaked in few times to hear him. He departed during my last year in Minnesota for Harvard, by which time he was a Nobel Prize winner.

I had never really heard then of MIT. During my first summer in America, I went to Boston and visited MIT and Professor Charles Coryell, who had offered me an assistantship. He asked me why I chose Minnesota, and I told him that, first, it was for Kolthoff, and then added bluntly that the assistantship from Minnesota was 50 percent higher than what MIT was offering. I recall gifting him with a box of glazed fruit from Egypt, which he immediately opened and shared with his graduate students.

Having chosen Minnesota, I took the long ride on a Greyhound bus from the East Coast through the prairies of the Midwest, arriving panic-stricken in the land of ten thousand lakes. I was on my way to an unknown future. Little did I know that my choice of school would change my life in the most marvelous way, as this was where I would meet Arthur Hill, an Australian foreign student and my future husband.

The holy oil

But my impending departure came at a huge emotional cost—especially for my mother, whom I would be leaving behind, trapped with my father in an increasingly untenable situation in Egypt.

My mother's dire thoughts came in a torrent. "Where can we go? Return to Greece? All our friends there have passed away. We can't go to Australia or America, we don't speak English. Who can protect us here now? The Egyptians are rising up. We are foreigners in Egypt just as we were in Turkey!"

Calm down, Mother I told her, calm yourself. I'll take care of you from America, I promise—I'll teach French to some children—

"How can I be calm?" she repeated. "You do not understand what is going on. We do not have very many valuables, but even what we have, we cannot get out of the country." She looked down, desperately mouthing inarticulate cries of help,

She then went to our little altar in the bedroom and took out a small flask of oil that was always kept there and asked me to join her at Taxiarchis, the Greek church of our neighborhood. There she knelt down and prayed sincerely for my protection. She had the priest bless the oil, for which I donated all my pocket money—five shillings, about a dollar today. Then she anointed her own brow with a bit of oil before doing the same for me.

Then we went home. I remained silent until I saw Akis. In a mocking way I mentioned the church visit and how the holy oil was going to save me. He was astonished and a little amused, because Mother rarely went to church. "What is going on?" Akis demanded. "Will prayers save Laki? Save her from what? Shall we be praying now every day?"

Mother was furious. "Our family came to this country thirty-five years ago, just to get away from those people." She made a sort of gesture of helplessness. She put her hands to her face and begun to wail. "Oh, God, oh God, my girl, my poor girl, she is leaving us!" She was very disturbed, wanting me close by and yet knowing that I had to leave a country where I had no future. I knelt down and put my arms around her to comfort her.

I felt very strange myself, loving my mother but also feeling that she had to had to be told the brutal truth. "You are ignorant," I told her. "Holy oil will not protect me." Impulsively I removed my gold bracelet from my wrist and left it there. "I won't miss it. I'll go to America and I'll l have more." They were harsh things to say but I was not sorry then that I said them; I was just eighteen, and full of self-importance.

I continued talking to my brother—in French this time, so Mother could not follow us. We must have mentioned her ignorance, her narrow-mindedness, her lack of education. I'm sure she understood that we were talking about her, and murmured prayers.

I should have asked forgiveness for what I said, but I never did. Years later it still bothered me, the words that I could not take back. Even when I visited my parents in Athens for years I never asked forgiveness. I suppose the best form of atonement I could make was to keep my promise—that I (and later my husband Arthur) would take care of them until their last days.

Farewell to Egypt

The farewells began a few days before my departure as family, friends, neighbors, and even a couple of my Egyptian classmates dropped by to convey their good wishes.

The evening before my departure, I went for a solitary walk along the Corniche, passing one beach after another. The air was cool, the traffic sparse—a few black limousines, probably those of cotton brokers or gamblers, cruised by. Every once in a while, I would stop and face the sea; I could hear waves thudding in the dark, spraying the air.

There were countless cafés still open that late July night, with nighttime revelers relishing the breeze. From somewhere, in scattered snatches, came a faint lilt of music, first from a guitar. Was it crackling from a radio? Then I heard singing; were they students gathered on the beach, enjoying the cool air?

Facing the night, I looked at the stars and thought of America. In so many ways I was thrilled to leave Egypt to attend a major American university for graduate studies, but I was also frightened to go to a country I knew so little about, and to compete with students better trained, accomplished, and informed than I was. I tried to make sense of my situation, to clarify and strengthen my own goals, my dream of acquiring a graduate degree in a field I loved. I could have stayed at home, had some kind of marriage, played safe, been retained in my family's affections. I dismissed the idea angrily, feeling a sense of things quickly moving past me. How could I give up on life's challenges before I had even begun?

The moon began to ease from behind the clouds. I looked at the flickering little fishing boats, the oval of the Corniche in a necklace of light. The world was timeless and boundless and I thought of "all the shipwrecked, homeless mariners who had come to this very land praying for a wind, only to grow soft and reluctant to leave when the time came," as fellow Alexandrian André Aciman would later put it. I thought of Ulysses who, with his crew, used their ordeals with sirens, monsters, and seductresses as excuses to stay where they were.

Perhaps seduced by Egypt's bounties, my parents chose not leave to Egypt after World War II, even when the tide of politics had begun to turn against foreigners like them. Now my father was too old at 72 to start a new career elsewhere—cash-strapped, not speaking English, and with many of his business associates, people of his generation, gone. They still owned their home and had a few friends in the same circumstances, so they lingered. Father had spent the best years of his life in Alexandria and had carved a niche there, waiting too long before deciding to return to Greece. But then again he had never really lived in Greece, being an "exchangeable" from the Ottoman Empire. Home was Alexandria.

Most of us non-Muslims of foreign origin had lived in Egypt for a long time, and some of us were born there. Alexandria was our home. We had chosen to trust in the hope of equal treatment before the law; we thought there would be no discrimination in employment or in running our own business; all that proved to be an illusion. The rise in Pan-Arabism and Islamism marked a deterioration in the relationship between the vast Muslim majority and the rest of us foreigners, irrespective of whether we were Christians or Jewish.

In a way, we had it coming. Greeks, like most all other foreigners, never did adapt to postcolonial conditions, never bothered to learn Arabic properly. Looking back, Nasser was right to regain that land for his people. Foreigners had been traders, perhaps even the economic brains of Egypt, but they plundered its resources to enrich themselves.

On this pre-departure eve, I found myself caught between the future and the past; the past meant the irreplaceably warm embrace of family in a place that had shaped whatever I had become at that point, and the future seemed nothing more than a hazy brightness, edged with uncertainty; but

I was nothing if not curious about the world, and even Alexandria with all its cosmopolitan charm had become too small for me.

In the morning I made way to the dock; the family and my friend Aida gathered at Alexandria's port; I was on my way to Piraeus, my first stop before embarking on the ocean liner the *Queen Frederica* for the New World. As we embraced I promised never to forget them. I would do my best; I wanted to be worthy of my father. The face of my mother was gray and brittle-looking; I did not think that anything in life would hurt so much as my departure. "Always a lady," she admonished me, as she had done so often in the past, then her parting words: "Even if I never see you again in my life, never come back without finding your destiny. *Na vris tin tihi sou.*"

I would leave Egypt, but very soon, so would many others.

The Greeks in America

While the Greeks, like Odysseus, have gone all over the planet in pursuit of their destiny, this diaspora followed different patterns in different places, resulting in interesting if not unique localizations. The Greeks who migrated to Egypt in the early part of the 20th century, for example, had a different experience from those who chose to go to America.

For Egypt, a *taskara*, a travel ticket, was all one needed to land in the country—no visa, no passport, no documentation, none of the barriers that mark a nation-state, as Egyptian nationhood was established only in 1929. In the US, a quota system was in effect, and by 1924 it was deliberately designed to discriminate against Greeks, as Greece remained initially neutral in World War I.

What made Alexandria distinct from any other center of the Greek diaspora was the city notables, the patrons who presided over their community and who ran the cotton exchange and the exporters' association. The destiny of the city was in their hands; with their generosity they financed philanthropic and cultural organizations. The city was not an American melting pot, but rather a society ruled by an upper class of men and women connected by acquaintance and business. The very idea of assimilation or integration to the society and culture that hosted them was foreign to the community spirit.

A newcomer in Egypt moved into Alexandria's city state unperturbed by the local authorities; in the US, by the mid-'20s, the government began an extensive campaign to "Americanize" the new arrivals and assimilate those who came previously. Greeks in America generally reacted positively to assimilation. Names were Anglicized; my Aunt Aphrodite altered the family name from Kaloumenidis to the more pleasing sound of Kallas.

It cannot be overstated that both in Egypt and the US, the overriding motive for Greek immigration was economic gain.

Greeks who emigrated to Egypt from the Ottoman empire generally had a higher education level than those who came directly from Greece, and many had considerable comprador experience. Alongside or below the rich cotton exporters and industrialists existed a mass of working-class people, a number of white-collar workers and professionals, and a leisured class, according to the criteria of the time, which created and played an important role in the life of the community.

The few women who were working in Alexandria were employed mostly as teachers. By and large, Greek immigrant women did not work outside the household; if a man's wife, daughters, or even sisters had to seek gainful employment, it was considered a poor reflection on his ability to provide. Although formally submissive to her husband, the wife was frequently dominant in the practical affairs of running the household and disciplining the children. Not only tradition but practical sense enforced this division of labor. It took a lot of time to cook, clean shop, and bring up children. (In Alexandria the wages were so low that domestic help was widely available.) A wife was to be treasured for her ability as a housekeeper—a *kali nikokira*—than for any marketable skills outside the home.

The Greeks who went to America were for the most part barely educated, most of them with little more than three or four years of elementary education; however, like everywhere in the world, they had high aspirations for their children. They were expected to go to school, work hard, then go to college. Parents sacrificed a lot to make it possible, and it is no accident that second- or third-generation Greek-Americans have achieved some of the highest educational levels of any migrant group in the United States.

In Egypt, learning Arabic, although beneficial, was not essential to get a job or to communicate in everyday encounters; French was the *lingua franca*, and employment was available in many Greek or other foreign enterprises. My parents limited themselves to colloquial Arabic while my aunt in America had to learn English and became a fluent English speaker.

In both countries there was the strong desire of parents to have their children learn Greek, and it was available at the educational establishments of the Alexandrian Greek Community. In America most immigrant children learned Greek in the evenings at churches, with classes given by priests. Greek was also taught at Berlitz; my aunt teaching there recalled her first students, two Jewish ladies who wanted to learn Greek so they could communicate with St. Peter!

In Egypt Greeks concentrated primarily in Alexandria, while in the United States they originally settled in urban areas in the Northeast and the Midwest before moving southward and westward. Greek towns appeared where a sufficient number of Greeks immigrants had located, as Greeks have a tendency to group together in certain areas. This was the case in Attarin and Ibrahimieh in Alexandria. In New York City which is still the largest home of Grecks, they established a "Greek Town" in Astoria.

Numerous organizations emerged to assist Greeks, not only to integrate them into American society but to establish a balance between Americanization and the preservation of their identity.

From their native land, Greeks brought an assortment of traditions, customs, beliefs, and superstitions such as the evil eye in every city of the diaspora. They dutifully observed the Greek Orthodox holidays, especially Easter rites, the most sacred in their calendar.

In American cities with sizable Greek populations such as Chicago and New York, Independence Day, March 25, is celebrated with much pomp, with a colorful program that includes a parade, public addresses, folk dances, songs, and poetry recitations.

The turn towards Hellenism in America became all the stronger with the arrival of new migrants after World War II. Among them existed a small coterie of Greek university students and professionals; never fully at ease with their American colleagues, they were also socially distant from the main body of their co-ethnics. They gathered to raise the cultural level of Greek immigrants through public lectures and to bring their Hellenic heritage to the attention of the American public. In a manner of speaking, they became Greek-American Hellenizers.

Lastly, while the Greek community of Alexandria disappeared by 1956, in America it came of age, and rode on the larger wave of social and political change, easing their integration into American society. This proved especially beneficial for women who were able to break free of the traditional patriarchal family structure within the Greek-American family. By the third generation, Greeks had risen way up the ladder, pursuing high professional jobs in medicine, law, and academia.

It is worth noting that there may have been Greek donors, even Greek philanthropists, in the latter part of the 20th century, but not a single individual who could be called a benefactor in the manner of a Rockefeller, a Carnegie, or an Annenberg. Greek moguls emerged in the movie industry, most famously the Skouras brothers—Charles, Spiros, and George, the sons of a sheep herder who emigrated to St. Louis—but no one approached the philanthropy of the Greek barons of Egypt who in today's money gave away not just millions but close to billions of dollars. Charles Skouras gave back to the Greek community by building in 1952 the beautiful Saint Sophia Cathedral in Los Angeles.

Greek-Americans have contributed to their new home in many different ways including academia, business, film, literature, music, and journalism, but most notably in politics. They include former Vice President Spiro Agnew, Massachusetts Governor Michael Dukakis, CIA Director George Tenet, and UN Ambassador John Negroponte, among many others.

In 21st-century America, it is rare to find Greek families in which children are brought up to speak Greek as their first language. Throughout the United States, the Greek community has moved from one made up of Greeks with American citizenship to one consisting of Americans of Greek descent.

An exodus of foreigners

While the historians may disagree about some issues, there seems to be a consensus that the inauguration of the Suez Canal in 1869 marked the beginning of the cosmopolitan era of Alexandria and the nationalization of the canal in 1956 its end.

Nasser had defied the world, an action opposed by the British and the French, and for security reasons the Israelis. The Sinai was invaded and attacks launched on Suez and Port Said. This was followed by a swift retreat, under heavy international pressure from America and the Soviet Union. It became a triumph for Nasser, whose position was immediately strengthened at home and throughout the Arab world.

Nasser's speeches brimmed with venom. He vowed to rid Egypt of all outsiders, to eliminate the Jewish state, and to stamp out the last vestiges of colonialism and the monarchy. Entire industries were nationalized as Nasser moved closer to the Soviets. People lost their jobs and livelihood overnight when the regime sequestered a business, placing Nasser's officers and loyalists in charge and insisting that most employees be Egyptian citizens. The maid, the porter, anyone could be spying for Nasser's henchmen.

An exodus of foreigners began in earnest. The British, the French, and a third of Egypt's Jews, those with foreign nationalities, were expelled, given 48 to 72 hours to leave the country. "There was not even time to cry," one of them would say.

Families fled to countries like Australia, Venezuela, Unites States, and South Africa. Young lovers chose to tie the knot. There was a feeling that one had to get out at any cost. Owners were forced to sell their furniture, jewels, and pictures for derisory prices to the new rising class that would replace them—the military. And they left with 20 pounds per person.

By 1960, the government sequestered Father's bank account; our home was nationalized, and my parents were given the equivalent of sixteen dollars a month as compensation. My piano was sold to an Arab; my little gold bracelets had to go as well. My parents were not officially expelled, but life became unbearable in Egypt.

Even those who had acquired Egyptian citizenship found it difficult to acquire an Egyptian passport. Many were born in Alexandria and had never seen their country of origin, but now they found themselves unwanted aliens.

"We have lost everything. We have nothing left," my father wrote me from Alexandria. I detected desperation, even hopelessness, in his words. The time had come for them to leave.

Escorted to the port, they were bound for Greece, their ancestral land. My father's gold watch, an heirloom from his own grandfather, was confiscated as he climbed the ship's gangplank. The splendor of colonial life was coming to an end and they were paying the price.

For the next fifteen years I would visit them in Athens, where they retired. My husband's generosity was boundless. They were well taken care of in their old age, even as Alexandrian memories remained painful for them.

VI.

AWAY, AND HOME AGAIN

I SET OUT for life far away from my Greek Alexandrian home for graduate studies in America.

For someone who had never seen snow and had only experienced the mild Mediterranean climate, I landed in Minnesota, that beautiful state with many pretty lakes but punishing winters.

English was my fifth language and graduate studies the first year were not easy. I loved science, particularly Crystallography and Quantum Physics where I excelled.

But nothing had prepared me for the country itself. It was so big and very rich. It was wild with many forests and water and lakes. Nature has been quite generous to America. And one of its most attractive traits was freedom—embodied in law and order. As long as you were clear about the laws, you knew where you were and what you could and could not do.

In Alexandria we lived surrounded by family and friends. This could be very confining as you could not develop as an individual. I preferred the American way, the individuality, the solitude. I was happy taking long walks or spending hours alone browsing bookstores.

I was deeply concerned about my family, even frightened; with the Suez Crisis in 1956 there was not even a letter exchanged with my parents for months. I felt ostracized by my college mates; I was different, and I had a foreign accent (which I still do). I had never seen a supermarket, had never sampled prepackaged frozen food. I had never seen television, never attended a football game, I did not know how to drive, and worst of all I had never heard of someone called Elvis Presley!

But I learned to fend for myself. The first money I earned in America was at a military dry cleaner, and my job was to match the pants with jackets. They were all uniforms, identical in cut and color, but I could match the numbers of the tops with those of the bottoms. For an eight-hour shift I was paid $10.

A life with Arthur

At the university I met Arthur Hill, an Australian foreign student who was president of the Foreign Student Council. A friendship developed between us with magical ease, then love blossomed. From an account of my life in Alexandria, our conversations moved on to travel, to all those cities we planned to visit on our return to his homeland. We talked of the gender of cities: Paris was female, London male, Rome hermaphrodite, Alexandria with its stunning Corniche was definitely feminine; and we laughed as we plotted an extensive 100-day trip on a budget of $20 a day. We thought it would be the only tour of our lifetime. We were married while still in graduate school, with 14 people at our wedding on a 4th of July. It was the year Hawaii entered the Union. I was certain the fireworks display was intended for us. No one thought our marriage would last, but they were all wrong; it was a golden marriage of 43 years, over which a new world opened for me, a world of travel, of books, of music.

After graduation, we returned to Australia, where Arthur had to fulfill his Fulbright obligations. We were fortunate to get the chance to travel around the world on the way to our new home. It was our first glimpse of Europe; we were able to visit my parents still stranded in Alexandria, to explore the Indian subcontinent, and to encounter Southeast Asia. We were captivated by Bangkok, an exotic city, a helter-skelter of palaces, temples, and bazaars interwoven with rivers and canals, the Thai capital of 55 years ago. Southeast Asia opened our curiosity, becoming in our memory a kind of semi-mystical golden age. It brought us face to face with our destiny. Arthur vowed to return, to find a job there, and to make it our home.

A few years later, he achieved his ambition as advisor to the Minister of Education of Thailand under the sponsorship of the Ford Foundation, a most prestigious and generous employer. I was not hung up on a career and I never regretted it. For Arthur it was a gamble to be leaving a tenured position at the University of Melbourne, and for me a position as research scientist at CSIRO (Commonwealth Scientific and Industrial Research Organization) for a contract assignment in Thailand. We shared an enigmatic desire that could only be quenched with travel. I accepted the move, the challenge, and the opportunity with alacrity; and an adventurous life began, which I recounted and celebrated in my first book, *A Promise to Keep*.

Return to Alexandria

It would be another quarter-century before I would set foot again in Alexandria. At some point, I told Arthur that I wanted to return to my native city, and that together we should visit places where I grew up and take in the archaeological sites of the country. Although we had stopped by Alexandria in December 1960 before my parents returned to Greece in 1961, it was in 1981, when Arthur had a Middle Eastern assignment, that we spent more time there, being based in Cairo for six months. My dream was becoming a reality. We would go sailing down the Nile together in a felucca.

That was very well said, but with his hectic schedule traveling all over the Middle East, for me to join him on his sorties was out of question. A woman did not venture as a tourist to Saudi Arabia. I was to join him only in Cairo, staying on my own at the Sheraton Hotel a good portion of the time. For me it did not present an issue. Cairo was a city I knew well, and speaking the language would make my wanderings so much simpler.

Stationed in Alexandria during World War I, the novelist E. M. Foster wrote that the best way to see Alexandria was to wander aimlessly. How right he was about the only way to introduce my city to Arthur.

In Alexandria, one of my main objectives was to show Arthur the Corniche, that sinuous, 20-kilometer ribbon of asphalt overlooking the Mediterranean. I wanted to rediscover secret corners where something remained of my childhood footsteps. I wanted to gently, gradually, rekindle the memories I had nurtured in my soul, "perhaps even to weep for lost days" as Harry Tzalas so elegantly put it: "Alexandria remains special to us, because we entrusted her with our childhood dreams."

I had often mentioned to him the stations of the Victoria line, that litany of French, Greek, Italian, Arabic, and English names. They were forever embedded in my mind, echoing with so much history. I had spoken of the lovely beaches where I experienced a joyful childhood, which through the years captivated my imagination; the cafés on the waterfront wafting with Greek music, the "casinos," and my beloved school, the Lyçée Français.

I still had family in Alexandria 25 years later—my godmother, Aunt Katina, cousin Anthony, and Jewish friends whose families had left the country years ago. Afflicted with Alzheimer's, Aunt Katina did not recognize me. She muttered a few syllables, repeating them again and again: "Maître Misserlis," the honorary French title of her husband, a barrister at the Mixed Courts. That was all that was left in her memory.

My godmother was now in her middle eighties, and in a state of panic as she was flat broke. Arab neighbors had robbed her at knifepoint of her precious jewelry, including her multi-carat sparkling diamond with its rare hue of the palest blue; all the silver in the house was gone. She regretted not having gifted them to me years ago. Her apartment was dark, the furniture draped with white sheets, with only the feet and chairs showing beneath. The Persian rugs were gone and a cockroach skittered across the parquet floor; it was pathetic.

On a dresser I caught a picture of Barbas, printed on an oval-shaped piece of ivory; it was the only picture of Barbas I had ever seen; he had keen penetrating blue eyes. Like my father, her family had lost everything in Izmir, now in Egypt; the only vestige of distinction left to my godmother was, ironically, the revolver with which Barbas committed suicide.

The Jewish families were destitute, and during our visits we were able to hand them a few hundred pounds, funds provided by their family. There was no mechanism to remit money through legal channels to Jews; all other intermediaries were unscrupulous.

Vanishing landmarks

I was warned from reading and from several acquaintances that Alexandria was not the city I had left 25 years earlier. Indeed, I had difficulty holding my tears when I arrived; my initial reaction was of disappointment, even despair, looking at a filthy, neglected city.

We climbed on the Victoria tram, it rumbled and squeaked, as it passed Mazarita, Chatby, Camp Cesar, Ibrahimieh, Sporting, Cleopatra, Sidi Gaber, Moustafa Pasha, Rouchdy. Nearing Rouchdy, clearly visible from the tram, once stood lovely villas, with gardens shaded by large trees, a few even with fountains. Now everything was gone. One of the larger homes has been converted to an Arab public school. We could see the girls in their gray uniforms playing in what had been a beautiful garden, now a desolate courtyard.

This is Fleming, I told Arthur, my favorite station, where my friend Aida's aunt was living and where we had so many festive celebrations. As the tram traveled to Victoria Station I pointed to vanishing landmarks.

The lavish villas with their magnificent gardens had been almost exclusively replaced by ten-story apartments, poorly constructed structures built at random. Our home on 25 Rue Memphis has been torn down; in its place stood a high rise, gray and dilapidated with a rubbish-strewn entrance way. I felt embarrassed telling Arthur that this was where I grew up.

Now back in Alexandria, I climbed aboard the tram, went to the Nouzha Gardens, drove along the Corniche, and went to the beach. I knew I was back in Alexandria but everything had changed immensely. I searched for a point of reference, trying to reorient myself.

As we were riding the tram, we admired those marvelous trees of fire, the "flamboyants," large trees which in the beginning of June burst into flower. Alexandria was still blessed by those beloved trees.

The boulevard Saad Zagloul, the great patisseries, the shops—they were still all there, somehow altered, somewhat aged, under new ownership, but still there.

In my imagination, Rue Memphis was a lovely wide street; it was so narrow now. I realized it was nothing more than an ordinary and narrow Arab street. Did nostalgia exaggerate its dimensions? Every square inch of land was now utilized for an ugly high-rise. I wanted everything to remain as it had been. I did not want to see the real Alexandria, preferring to go back in time to uncover the Alexandria I grew up in. But my urge to see our house again, to retrace the steps of a childhood would be rewarded only by the searing pain of seeing our villa replaced by monstrous multistory building. Although I revisited Alexandria again in 2006 and 2014, I never returned to Rue Memphis; memory was a much more hospitable place.

Once again I confronted those 19th- and early 20th-century buildings of Ramleh Station at the tram terminus. I recognized them, still standing, walls stripped bare of their paint. The signs above shop windows and entrances were all in Arabic. Billboards advertising movies were in the local language. Television antennae sprouted from every roof and in front of the windows and balconies hung lines of laundered clothes and linen. So many of the cinemas were gone as well.

There was not a single European on the tram, not a single one in sight on the street. I felt that I was in a totally Arab city; Alexandria over the last 25 years had taken on an Oriental character, and it could have been any other Arab city anywhere in the Middle East.

The Corniche remained with its unique features, and at night—with the twinkling lights and the palm trees waving in the breeze—the magic of Alexandria was still there. As Laila Orfali would note in *Voices from Cosmopolitan Alexandria*, "It is evident that the ghosts are still there in the air, perhaps or within me. I meet them in the streets and in certain shops that have kept their old names.'"

There were plenty of taxicabs, yellow and black matchbox cars. These had not changed; the drivers were all Egyptians, speaking their native tongue. I recalled our favorite Greek taxi driver, Michalis, whom we patronized years ago. The taxi stand at Camp Cesar was always populated with working class foreigners, mostly Greeks and Italians.

A vaguely familiar stage

We entered the historic Cecil Hotel, a crenellated Moorish palace overlooking the East Harbor a couple of blocks from our hotel. I had never set foot in it before, and I thought that perhaps it was best to start with a site not associated with my childhood memories. It turned out be just another place with a plush, slightly tired dining room, ornate with huge gilded mirrors.

The Cecil Hotel was built in 1929 by a French-Egyptian Jewish family, a romantic hotel patronized by the city's elite. It became a recurrent landmark in the *Alexandria Quartet* of Lawrence Durrell where Justine "would perhaps be waiting, gloved hands folded on her handbag, staring out through the windows upon which the sea crawled and sprawled, climbing and subsiding, across the screen of palms in the little municipal square which flapped and creaked like loose sails." The hotel also figures in *Miramar*, Naguib Mahfouz's novel set in Alexandria. "From my balcony at the Cecil I cannot see the Corniche unless I lean out over the railing. It's like being on a ship.... The sea sprawls right below me.... The sea. Its guts churn with flotsam and secret death."

It had so much history, with room rates to match. Somerset Maugham stayed there, as did Winston Churchill and Al Capone. In 1942, with the German army sitting not far away on the coast in the town of Alamein, poised for a final push to Cairo, the British Secret Service maintained a suite here for their operations.

We strolled along the Corniche, passing by the café my father frequented. Arab men were sipping coffee, some playing backgammon, others sucking on hookahs. Later on, it was the Rue Fouad (renamed Sharia Horreya) with its antique shops brimming with what was invariably called Louis Farouk furniture: chairs and gilded mirrors, abandoned after Nasser threw the foreigners out.

Ibrahimieh Market, where we shopped through the years, teemed with people as in the past: pyramids of cabbages, crates of egg plants, okra, and tomatoes, walls of stacked garlic, baskets of eggs of every hue, live rabbits, live chickens, fresh and dry fish (dry fish a novelty now), tripe and meat, sacks of rice and spices, heaps of succulent herbs.

Metal stands held biblical clay pots of water to refresh passersby. Those were the clay pots we used, standing on our balcony filled with water to be cooled.

The bounty of fresh produce in the market was reflected in Alexandria's restaurants, where we gorged on the local cuisine, the spiced meats, the flat breads, and the rich dips.

Everything has deteriorated, I remarked as we were exploring my cluttered city. It was like walking on a vaguely familiar stage, as we went from place to place and I would tell Arthur how things were 25 years ago. Hotels had been converted to commercial offices. Many of the pastry shops, however, had survived. At Delices, my favorite pastry shop, we sat under the canopy in wicker chairs overlooking the dark sea. For the price of a cup of cardamom-flavored coffee, we sat there all night talking about Alexandria, about a forgotten life where everyone spoke at least five languages, a lost world.

The memory of the Mediterranean

What was I looking for? Had I found myself? I had discovered the memory of the Mediterranean. Here, as André Aciman put it, "I would come to remember not so much the beauty of the past as the beauty of remembering."

"Do not look at the past," Arthur suggested, as if that were possible.

The next morning, we walked from Ramleh Station to Moharrem Bey where the Faculty of Science of the University of Alexandria stood; it seemed that I had completely wiped out any memories. We took a cab to look for my father's office on Rue de France, and found ourselves in what the driver told us was Midan El Tahrir. We saw a few pathetic palm trees shriveled by the wind; the area was littered with empty Coca-Cola tins (the old Sinalco bottled with fizzy orange juice had been replaced by Coca-Cola) and other refuse lying around. Where was I? I looked hard for something familiar until I recognized the statue of Muhammad Ali, and realized that we were in Muhammad Ali Square. No more were the well-kept lawns, no more the flowerbeds of red and yellow cannas. The imposing structure of the Stock Exchange, the fourth largest in the world and for almost a century the very heart of Alexandria's business, had been burned down in 1977 and completely demolished by 1981, now reduced to an empty lot. Then I remembered the Syrian pastry shops along the Square, where so often with my father, we purchased Oriental sweets, the *arissa* which I was still so fond of—but of course they were all gone.

On the Rue de France, many of the old buildings were standing, their shutters hanging off their hinges. I pointed to the second floor of my father's office; the building was still there, but somehow it was not the same. The green roller blinds of my father's office could no longer slide properly and thus remained stuck halfway.

There were many small sparkling stores around, which sold silver and gold. We purchased silver coins, collector's items, in every denomination we could find, from the half-franc equivalent to two piasters to the Egyptian pound, coins with King Fouad and King Farouk sporting their *tarbush*. We made up an assortment that I gifted to my brother, who could appreciate their history. There were stores selling rainbow bolts of cloth and everyday plastic kitchen items; but there were no Persian carpets, nothing from the Orient, in this utilitarian market.

We went from place to place in Alexandria, each one marking a different moment of my life. I was awakened to new memories and emotions, new images of myself. At each place there is me, I said; I see me again and again and me and me.

Patisseries still persisted, under different ownership, a little worn-out around the edges; you could still sit down for hours at these Art-Deco surroundings for a cup of coffee and a piece of patisserie.

Engulfed by emotion, I recalled what Omar Kareish said in *Voices from Cosmopolitan Alexandria*: "That life is over. It will never return. It was a mythical Alexandria. The circumstances that led to its rise no longer exist in the world." But somehow we still take refuge in the past and carry the city in our soul.

By now I had seen so much of the world. I had lived in so many Asian capitals, so many great cities, viewed so many lovely coastlines, so many glittering events, so many glamorous homes. But somehow here in Alexandria, that Arab city, was my home, my street, my school, my world.

The memories that moved me most were those of my school. I had a first glimpse of it from the tram from Chatby Station. We walked along until we came to the main gate, which was closed. This is my school, I said, overcome with emotion, and my knees nearly gave way.

Postscript to the Lycée

The Lycée of the Mission Laique remains the pride of the French educational system, operating 125 schools in 48 countries in 2013. The Lycée of Alexandria was one of the first to be established, celebrating its centenary in 2014.

Following the abortive tripartite invasion after the nationalization of the Suez Canal in 1956, the Nasser government expelled all British and French citizens, including all expatriate teachers. They were given 48 to 72 hours to leave the country. "There was no time even to cry," Mr. Marchal told me when I saw him a few years later in Paris.

Decolonization had started, and it was not easy for many of the British or French schools' teachers and administrators. Used to having the upper hand, they were suddenly faced with an uncertain future. The lucky ones would find comparable positions in other British or French outposts, but the world was changing.

The Lycée property, owned by the French government, was sequestered; for ten years the building remained empty and fell on sad times. When I visited it in 2006, the school was closed, a dilapidated building, with graffiti on the wall corridors, its windows smashed, the *grande cour* now a parking lot for Alexandrian buses.

In 2007 the Lycée reverted to an Egyptian private school. Comprehensive renovations were undertaken, buildings were partially rehabilitated and repainted, the mustard yellow giving way to a ghastly pink, but at least the windows were replaced.

It is no longer a French school; the prestigious institution that it used to be is gone. The school fees range from $500 to $1,500 a year, extremely steep by Egyptian standards. It does not offer the French Baccalaureat, but an Egyptian high school diploma.

The quadrangle was dusty and needed to be hosed. There were fewer trees, and the lavatories at the end of the quadrangle were all smashed; rusty yellow Alexandrian buses stood in another corner with their wheels removed. This was not the Lycée I remembered.

There was not a single expatriate on the staff, although a few teachers were trained in France, and I met a couple of them, including Mrs. Chewikar, the former headmistress who hosted me at her home. I must add that for all my predictable dismay at the loss of the cradle of my most cherished childhood memories, the hospitality of Mrs. Chewikar—who went out of her way to be my guide and to host me in her home—was a balm to my sagging spirits.

In 2014, I found myself in Alexandra, privileged to visit the Lycée once again, and to be entering the boy's section for the first time in my life.

Like royalty, I was ushered by beaming teachers from class to class, where highly sophisticated Egyptian children greeted me in French and English. I had returned to my school after sixty years not only as an Alexandrian living in California but also as a guest, a friend of the Bibliotheca Alexandrina, that palace of infinite modernity which the Egyptians understood long ago.

The kindergarten was cheerfully decorated. But near a blackboard in a tiny I climbed once again the steps of the stage, steps I had climbed many times before to receive high school prizes. I was asked to reminisce about my school of long ago. I was overwhelmed with emotion, and the tears flowed freely. I could not speak. For a split second in time, I was back at the Lycée in 1952 at the Salle des Fêtes. Unwilling to share the intimacy of thought, I recited, in French, an appropriate poem, a sonnet from Victor Hugo.

Long days in Cairo

For a couple of years in the early 1980s, Arthur was commuting to Cairo. He was heading a major project in the Middle East for ITT. One day he would be in Kuwait, the next in one of the Gulf States, or Saudi Arabia. His work also brought him as far as the Sudan. Cairo served as his base and I joined him occasionally if his stay felt too long an absence from home.

On one occasion, what was supposed to be a short two-week stay went on and on and stretched for seven months. The bureaucracy took over. Unlike our time in Asia, we did not get to establish a household in Cairo, but spent our entire time at the Sheraton Hotel. It was managed by ITT and we were offered the best possible accommodations.

As a city, Cairo with its teeming millions and dull beige buildings was very old and at the same time very new. Its older sections, its bazaars, and its mosques evoked pleasing echoes in one's memory of what one expected the East to be, while its newer parts throbbed with the energy of a people who have played a leading part in the progress of civilization. Now they were striving vigorously to overcome the difficulties of a developing country.

One evening on the third day of the small Bayram—the festival marking the end of the Ramadan—the office was closed as it was a holiday; downtown Cairo bubbled over with excitement. After an agonizingly slow taxi ride, we got off near the old Cairo Palace, an area packed with food vendors. Like Charlton Heston parting the Red Sea in *The Ten Commandments*, we carved our way through the crowd in order to reach the venerable Art-Deco cinema.

We could have settled for a more modern venue but decided to pay homage to one of the last vestiges of Egypt's cinematic golden age. The Cairo Palace was built in the 1940s at a time when the city was a worthy rival of Hollywood. In fact before the Americans had begun hand-cranking film through a camera, the Egyptians were learning the basics from the Lumiere brothers—early film pioneers who on their first trip abroad came to Egypt to capture its famous monuments on celluloid.

Arthur always tried to see a local film whenever he was overseas, usually one chosen at random. As I had never seen an Egyptian film before, this would be my first exposure to the genre. Our selection turned out to be *Sib Wane Sib* which, I would learn from the papers next day, was an unholy cross between *Home Alone* and *Adventures in Babysitting*. We decided to depart after an hour, our curiosity about Egyptian cinema satisfied. My Arabic had atrophied after 25 years and I could not follow the dialogue; with no subtitles we could not really follow this family comedy.

As days became weeks and the weeks turned into months, hotel food grew monotonous. We were longstanding residents now and did not need to look at a menu; the chef was most willing to prepare a simple dish of fresh noodles or poach an egg for our dinner. There were, however, many restaurants in Cairo, from humble affairs serving charcoal-grilled chicken or kebabs and *kefta* (minced lamb shaped into small cakes and served with pepper sauce) to luxurious international cooking.

Imported wines were very expensive, so we limited ourselves to the locally produced Gianaklis wine. I remembered the Gianaklis, a Greek family who owned vineyards in the Alexandria region for fifty years. Sequestered now, the vineyards passed into Egyptian hands, and only the brand name remained. The land was fertile, the climate perfect, but with no further investments, new developments in the winemaking process had not been adopted. It was not unusual to find, among a dozen bottles, at least one that had turned completely to vinegar. Unceremoniously returning a bottle of Gianaklis wine was perfectly acceptable; the sommelier was accustomed to it, no questions asked.

In the afternoon it was common to adjourn to a patisserie for coffee and gateaux; pastry shops proliferated in every corner. Fresh dates were available from September for a few months onward.

Egyptians are great sugar addicts; everything is sweet from their pastries to the tea and the fruit juices that are always served sweetened. A home invitation was rare; we were so hungry for home cooking. How tasty was the apple pie prepared at an American friend's home!

Service at the hotel was erratic. The waiters were eager to please, very courteous, but getting their attention and providing efficient service was not part of their training. I recall when a senior executive from ITT headquarters joined us for inner; to get a waiter's attention, he took the large silver candelabra gracing our table and held it up above his head. Three candles were flickering, and he looked like the Statue of Liberty with a three-pronged torch. Even this gesture did not catch the waiters' attention immediately.

Working hours in Arthur's office stretched from morning to noon; the Egyptian staff went home for lunch, and a long siesta followed. The office reopened at five, and work continued past nine in the evening. This meant that there were four traffic jams every day. By that time, I would walk along the Gezirah Bridge to Arthur's office, unperturbed, blending completely with the locals. It was perfectly safe.

Driving in Cairo was not an easy task; nerves of steel were needed. Traffic was chaotic. Arthur had a car and driver during the day, as he needed them for appointments at different ministries in different sections of the city. Cairo was in a continuous gridlock. The air was thick with pollution and dust drivers were unwilling to give way, especially in major intersections. The worst was at Tahrir Square, the giant Independence Place in the center of Cairo. I pitied the policemen who tried desperately to maintain order. As in many large overpopulated cities in the developing world, public transportation was crumbling. Buses were overflowing, with people overhanging from every door and every window; sometimes they sat on the roof. This was not in a rural area; this was in the center of the major capital of the Arab world. It was the noisiest city on earth, worse even than Teheran. Every driver had his hand on the horn, blasting his way through, a national pastime. One of the consultants, part of Arthur's team, could not stand the noise registered from our car; he would tip a pound—equivalent to couple of dollars—to the driver, with the stipulation that he would not use the horn. The incentive worked, most of the time.

Telephone communication was virtually nonexistent. Within the same area, calls would get through, but if the call had to reach the other bank of the Nile, it was another story. I recall when I tried one day to place a call to Roda, an island on the Nile in the middle of Cairo, just a couple of kilometers from the hotel. I was unable to get through; the telephone cables under the river must have disintegrated, having been laid there a half a century ago. I took a taxi, only to get stuck in traffic. It would have been faster to walk.

Another time, Arthur spent 24 hours in our hotel suite, waiting for the international operator to place a call through to the United States; it was so frustrating. Usually he would fly to Athens, a 90-minute flight, make telephone calls from the Greek airport, and return the same day! Wireless telephony had not yet been introduced.

Meeting "the Doctor"

I would recall in my book *Promises to Keep* meeting General Adel Meguid el Abd, the Deputy Minister of Manpower under President Sadat and Arthur's counterpart in Egypt. We called him "the Doctor," a title he loved. He was trained in Sandhurst, the United Kingdom's prestigious royal military academy, and moved up the ranks in the Egyptian army. During Nasser's time it was advantageous to learn Russian, which he did, and ended up earning a PhD at Moscow University. Americans were back in favor now and President Sadat was running the country, so the Doctor covered his bases and sent his children to study in the United States. His wife was the daughter of the past governor of Cairo, from a distinguished familyof Turkish origin, powerful and influential during the time of King Farouk and the British Protectorate.

The Doctor was tall, trim, and very fit. Every morning at dawn, he took his canoe and rowed along the Nile for an hour. His military training was part of his upbringing, and he was one the few Egyptians for whom punctuality was a prerequisite. He was very sensitive, and Arthur's diplomatic skills were constantly tested during many negotiations.

He traveled often with Arthur to Jeddah in Saudi Arabia. There, he would take an afternoon off, change his smart Western suits for a long white robe, and go to Mecca for prayers. He was a devout Muslim and never touched alcohol. Islam indeed was a sacred part of his life.

After a few months in Cairo, and with Arthur on business in the Sudan, I decided to return home. A major snowstorm hit the East Coast the day I arrived with 24 inches of snow. I regretted leaving the balmy weather of Egypt for the tundra of North America.

While in Khartoum, Arthur heard about the major snowstorm that blanketed the Northeast on the radio. African news does not usually report US weather, but this was a major storm. He was worried and called me. After his experience in Cairo, he was very doubtful that he would reach me. It only took him a few minutes and we were connected. I was thrilled to hear his voice, eager to tell him about being welcomed home by a snowstorm.

The next day, meeting the Telecommunications Minister of the Sudan, Arthur congratulated him on the Sudanese telephone efficiency. The minister laughed. "It does not happen this way. Everyone must be shoveling snow in New York, and they are not in their offices, so this is why our circuits are open."

Arthur stayed at the Khartoum Hilton. One evening he was having dinner at the coffee shop. At the next table sat a group of Americans who were having a voluble conversation. Being alone, he began eavesdropping, and the names of common friends were mentioned, names from our Philippine times. The group was having a meeting with the Agricultural Development Council of Sudan. He could not resist and decided to introduce himself and join them. One of the gentlemen immediately recognized him and said "My wife and I had dinner in your home in Manila." He recalled even the fact that another of our guests, Arturo Tanco, the Minister of Agriculture, was late to join us for dinner. What a small world! Arthur then remembered the occasion.

The Doctor had a vast network of contacts in the Middle East, and this was how Arthur met Prince Muhammad El Faizal, a grandson of King Abdel

Aziz, and brother of Saudi Arabia's Foreign Minister. They met many times at different locations: his palace in Jeddah, his Dakota apartment in New York, his castle in Ireland, and his stunning apartment at the Ile de la Cite overlooking Notre Dame Cathedral in Paris. The same decorator had furnished all locations, all very modern, with an exquisite collection of Oriental rugs thrown in.

Prince Muhammad was tall, broad shouldered, with the characteristic hooknose of his Arab heritage. He has studied at the Sorbonne and Harvard. In Saudi Arabia he wore the traditional robes, while smart business suits were his attire in the Western world.

While in Cairo he offered us his suite overlooking the Pyramids at the Sheraton. Fresh flowers were delivered daily and the telephone was ringing for the Prince, sometimes with a sweet young voice on the other line. When I greeted him as "Your Royal Highness" in the hotel lobby, many heads turned to look.

A new life after Arthur

Arthur passed away in 2002 from colon cancer. Until his last days he was cheerful. He told me to take a pencil and paper and tell our friends that "I had a good life and I have no regrets, because my wonderful wife who cared so much and still cares."

I was devastated. Arthur was my best friend, my only friend, the window through which I enjoyed the world. I live with the wonderful memories of 43 golden years of marriage. He touched the lives of so many people, and he lives on in their memories, which is the best memorial of all.

His advice was to enjoy the years I was left, do the kinds of interesting things we always did together and life would be "good for me."

I found scrapbooks, photographs, clippings, carbon copies of letters written years ago, papers that lingered in some forgotten file. I decided to sort them out and write my memoirs, beginning with my years with Arthur, as a means of both putting a close to one phase of my life and opening a new one.

I was on my way to becoming a writer. Now I needed some one to help me to pull my stories together to weave them, to smooth out the prose, never having penned anything beyond highly technical presentations. I found that help from friends in the Philippines, and I was introduced to Jose Dalisay, an award-winning novelist and professor of creative writing, who soon served not only as editor but as mentor, a sounding board for the next three books I penned. Mostly he emerged as a friend. I am grateful for his guidance with his encouragement and unwavering support a new career was launched.

My peripatetic life did not end with the death of my husband, nor my own retirement from the corporate world. I settled down in lovely Rancho Santa Fe, where I am involved in my local community, mentoring graduate students of the University of California in San Diego, and serving on non-profit boards such as the Scripps Cancer Center. I have adjusted to new challenges and continue to travel to remote places more confidently than ever before.

Back on my own

I did not forget Alexandria, where I returned as a business executive and as an invited friend, hosted by Madame Jehan Sadat. I returned link by link along the iron chains of memory to the city where I grew up. I roamed the city streets and looked at its vanishing landmarks. Today a magnificent edifice—resurrecting the spirit of the Ancient Library of Alexandria using 21st-century tools—stands overlooking the Mediterranean. In contemporary Egypt and outside government jurisdiction, it is a space of freedom where every point of view is discussed. I belong to the International Friends of the Bibliotheca of Alexandria and am its staunch supporter, grateful for the education I received in that country.

When I was planning a trip to Egypt in 2006, everyone—family members, friends, colleagues, even perfect strangers—told me that it was too dangerous. What about the Islamic fundamentalists? Don't go. You were there with Arthur during Sadat's time, when the going was good and there were fewer tourists. You were disappointed with Alexandria. Why do you want to go again?

This advice was ignored.

I was not interested in Alexandria as the focus of my travel this time, although I returned for a day. I had no more living relatives or friends. I was a widow now, retired from my job with AT&T; traveling alone, I had the luxury of time to see Egypt, accompanied with a knowledgeable Egyptologist to take me around. Visiting St. Catherine Monastery in the Sinai was a priority; it was inaccessible when I was growing up, when the only way to reach it was to trek the desert for 12 days in a camel.

It would be an FIT journey (Foreign Independent Travel) with my own car and driver and the most sybaritic accommodations possible. How fortunate when the tour operator Abercrombie and Kent, who put together my itinerary, assigned Zeinab Showkry as my guide. Zeinab was an attractive, well-connected woman who spoke perfect English and French; she would accompany me during my journey. We became instant friends.

She was an Alexandrian, a cat lover, well traveled, and prodigiously well informed about events in dynastic Egypt as well as the tumultuous events that shook Egypt in the 1950s. Incidentally Zeinab would be again my guide in 2014; she invited me to her Alexandria apartment for lunch, and showed me precious art pieces from India where she had spent a few years. She reminded me of the Pullman bus, the luxurious air-conditioned bus which I took with my parents a few times when visiting Cairo.

In December 2006 I flew directly from California to Cairo with Lufthansa, with a short stopover in Munich.

I was billeted at the Mena House which dates back to the 19th century; the hotel is actually in Giza, a suburb 45 nerve-wracking, knuckle-whitening minutes from the center of Cairo. Old-fashioned and set in beautiful gardens at the edge of the Sahara Desert, it reminded me of the Ammonia in Marrakesh. There are many modern hotels in Cairo but nothing quite as glamorous, with an unrivaled view of the Pyramids, which are literally across the street.

A frantic schedule

Our schedule in Cairo was frantic. Four days seemed like too much; after all I had been there so many times, although never in the company of a leading Egyptologist. As it turned out I was never bored for a moment. Cairo, the city itself, was fascinating and appealing, vast beyond belief, rivaling even Mexico City in sprawl, squalor, traffic density, and pollution —a kind of ultimate nightmare in which even the immense cemeteries of the Cities of the Dead were overpopulated by the living as well.

In former days, tourists in Egypt went up the Nile from Cairo to Luxor, or all the way to the first cataract, by boat. The only concession to fundamentalist terrorism was that tourists bypassed the long stretch between Cairo and Luxor; they now flew from Cairo to Luxor then sailed up the Nile to visit the main Pharaonic sites to Aswan, and returned in reverse order.

We flew to Abu Simbel, the gateway to Aswan Dam, and started by standing in admiration at the awesome temples of Ramses II.

In Aswan, we boarded the *Sun Boat III*, a vessel owned by the American tour operator Abercrombie and Kent. In all respects the *Sun Boat III* more than fulfilled my expectations. It was comfortably modern and charmingly antique with its carved wood and plush public rooms, giving off the unmistakable emanations of first-class travel in the old days, the Nile paddle steamers of Agatha Christie's time. The service was flawless and efficient, and the food excellent with an emphasis on large lavish buffets. The planning was perfect, splendid. Zeinab was exceptional, platinum-class, and the itinerary she took me on went beyond the postcard sites every one saw. I felt safe and secure.

The heart of this trip to Egypt was viewing the antiquities, and for several thousand years no words have been adequate to describe them or the awe they produce. In Luxor we stopped to see the Colossi of Mammon, the temple of Hatshepsut, and the tombs of the Valley of the Kings and then on the final day the temple of Luxor.

We had a private viewing of Queen Nefertari's tomb (for a $40 entrance fee, restricted to 150 visitors a day.) Taking a camera or video equipment was strictly forbidden and the penalty for sneaking one in was confiscation. Nefertari's tomb has been closed since 2007 to prevent further deterioration of the painted funeral scenes. Access is restricted to scholars; even then, they must be accompanied for limited time by a top Egyptian archaeologist, and the entrance fee is in the tens of thousands of dollars.

I was glad I saw Nefertari's "House of Eternity" last. All other monuments looked pallid beside hers. Seeing it made me realize that the obelisks, temples, columns, and statues, which we had grown to see as monochromatic stone, were in the days of the Pharaohs as colorful as a Disney cartoon.

That encounter with the old queen would soon resonate in another context. I had been interested to meet Madame Jehan Sadat, the former First Lady of Egypt, and interview her on the status of women in Egypt. It did not take long for Zeinab to facilitate that meeting.

Over tea, Madame Sadat asked me about my recent travels in Egypt, and as I mentioned the beautiful tomb of Queen Nefertari, Madame Sadat recalled an incident in the Valley of the Queens years earlier when she escorted Mrs. Imelda Marcos, her Philippine counterpart. While visiting the tomb of Nefertari, Mrs. Marcos remarked that she resembled that ancient queen.

Mrs. Sadat objected: "Nefertari is one of our most famous queens—an intriguing woman who played an unusual political role in the ancient capital of Thebes 3,200 years ago. There is no resemblance with you, Imelda." But Imelda insisted, "Look at her earrings, at the wide golden collar."

The Queen's paintings were alive in warm flesh tones and Imelda Marcos not only compared herself with the Queen, but insisted that she was the Queen. "Even her dress is similar to a Filipino dress. I am Queen Nefertari," she repeated over the strong objections of Mrs. Sadat.

Then, as they emerged from the tomb, Mrs. Marcos pull out her checkbook and wrote a check for one million dollars for the restoration of that tomb!

Mrs. Sadat was dumbfounded. "Yes, Mrs. Marcos, you are Queen Nefertari!" she found herself exclaiming.

The amount was more than enough not only to restore that tomb—a job undertaken by the Getty Conservation Institute of California—but also to restore other tombs in the valley.

The vivid wall paintings and delicate high relief can now be seen up close, without even the plastic shielding of other tombs, and it is easy to see why specialists call this the work of some of the most accomplished craftsmen of antiquity. Should we thank Imelda Marcos or the Filipino people for this contribution?

From the Nile to the Red Sea

It was the Nile itself, however, that for me that was the highlight, commanding attention, its banks thin strips of green vegetation that ended suddenly in desert sand dunes, making it clear what a miracle it was that a civilization could flourish for thousands of years entirely dependent on the river. The great pleasure of a boat trip down the Nile is to sit on the sun deck and look at the river and the life on its shores. Feluccas tack back and forth, much as they must have in the day of Ramses II; children play in the mud wave; a man on a donkey appears, leading two camels burdened with sugarcane, looking much as he might have in Biblical times; far in the distance at the summit of a huge rolling pink sand dune, a man on a camel, in desert garb, shades his eyes and looks down at us.

I could hardly think of a single disappointment with this trip. The only disconcerting element was the sheer number of tourists who seemed about to overwhelm the sites, their guides filling the temples with shouting matches as they lecture at the top of their voices in English, German, Japanese, or Russian, while tourists resolutely push, jostle and shove, popping camera flashbulbs despite signs in many languages warning them not to do so, and touch the carved stones, damaging them with the humidity of their hands. I had no doubt that the Egyptians were saying the equivalent about tourists four thousand years ago. You just had to get up earlier than all the others.

By the time we reached Sham El Sheikh after a flight from Luxor via Cairo, I was ready for a rest but was too tempted by the prospect of snorkeling in the Red Sea.

When I was growing up, Sham El Sheikh—near the southern tip of the peninsula that divides the two halves of the Arab world, separating Africa from Asia—was an isolated fishing village. Since then 138 hotels have sprung up in the area. The temperature at wintertime is always warm, enough to swim in January; the area has developed into a major holiday resort.

What began as an opportunistic development under occupation following the 1967 war with Israel has evolved from cheap hostels to the most sophisticated resorts within range of Europe. One critical factor is the direct service scheduled from London to Sham El Sheikh.

I climbed onto a glass-bottomed boat to view the coral reef which lay just below the azure surface of the Red Sea. The entire length of the peninsula is surrounded by terraces of coral 100 meters deep, providing food and shelter to a dazzling array of marine life. *Conde Nast Traveler* would note of the place that "There are corals of every hue and shape from flame-red to intricate yellow fans waving in the current. Fish are everywhere: delicate spotted striped angelfish, coral groupers, and one carelessly daubed parrotfish."

Years ago, on a holiday at the Great Barrier Reef with my husband, we did the same thing, viewing the coral through a glass floor. The reefs along the Sinai Peninsula are not as well known, but are also spectacular and in some respects way less commercialized than those of Australia.

Tea with the Bedouins

Madame Sadat would tell me that more than half of Egypt's tourism revenue was generated from this town alone, because of the attractions I noted.

I was billeted at the Four Seasons, just five minutes from the airport. Scattered across a hillside cradling the narrow beach were 34 villas none higher than two stories, and each with a view out to the Red Sea horizon.

Purple bougainvillea, pink hibiscus, and blue jacaranda clambered over sunny verandahs and shady terraces.

At the reception, I was welcomed in perfect Greek (the word was out that I was an Alexandrian Greek). Two large pictures of President Mubarak of Egypt and King Abdullah of Saudi Arabia looked down from the reception desk. Abdullah's portrait stemmed from the fact that the Four Seasons chain, a Canadian company, was co-owned by Bill Gates and a prince of the Saudi royal family.

The desert and its mysteries are never far away from the narrow strip of coastal resorts. Half an hour's drive inland conveys one to a landscape of spiky barren granite mountains. Acacia and scrub cling on in temperatures reaching 50C in summer, and a year can pass with not a drop of rain. Yet the wilderness is not as empty as it seems. Concealed in the shadows of rocky outcrops are the black tents of the Bedouins, woven of goat and camel hair.

My Abercrombie and Kent guide who incidentally spoke perfect Greek scored as he arranged tea with the Bedouins. As we approached their tent, the women scurried inside to veil themselves. After the ritual greetings, our hosts saddled up four camels for a trek (a guide for each one of us) but we both declined—I had seen too many traveling companions seriously hurt in camel rides. We sat cross-legged on the floor; a carpet was rolled, mint tea offered in stemmed glasses, and a bowl of fresh dates presented. There was little conversation except about camels while children dashed in and out, looking at that foreigner who spoke their language. As evening fell, the temperature cooled off, and the sun cast long shadows onto the orange rock. Gazelles fled into the darkening rim of canyons, while iguana regarded our passing with age-old disdain.

Six and half thousand Bedouins inhabited the Sinai—some in caves, others in villages, but most pursued the nomadic life of 15 centuries here. Their loyalty is to the tribe— one in six in the peninsula—not to the nation. The center of their life was the camel, a strong animal, worth a thousand dollars. A typical dowry was 20 camels. In this land, water was more expensive than gasoline.

As we returned, it was already dusk; a thousand filigree lamps lit up the resort, which became a romantic place tinkling with fountains and the distant hum of Tibur lute.

A mosque in a monastery

I did not come to Sham El Sheikh just to enjoy the luxury of the Four Seasons,but I wanted most of all to visit, in the shadow of Mount Sinai, the fortress-like monastery of Saint Catherine. The monastery established by Emperor Justinian in 527 stood at the spot where Moses supposedly encountered the burning bush. Believed to be the oldest Christian monastery in the world, its original preserved state was unmatched, and it was the only monastery in the world with a mosque within its walls.

When I later met with Madame Sadat for tea at her home in Cairo, she would recall visiting Saint Catherine's with her husband President Sadat. Seeing the glorious Byzantine icons and the library with documents relating to Christianity, they were surprised to find within the grounds of the monastery a small mosque. This gave President Sadat an inspired idea: "We should build a small synagogue on these sacred grounds, so three major religions could converge in that area." I admired his ecumenical outlook.

I met Father Makarios, dressed in a black robe and a monk's hat; he took it upon himself to lead me around. As a Greek Orthodox pilgrim, I was allowed to enter the holiest of places of the monastery, removing my shoes first in remembrance God's commandment to Moses. "'Put off thy shoes from off thy feet, for the place whereon thou stand is Holy Ground."

The monastery with its fortress-type structure survived largely undisturbed for 1,400 years by winning protection from the leaders of the day. Recognizing the significance of monotheism, the Prophet Muhammad issued a written promise granting protected status to the monks under Muslim rule. So did the Crusaders, several of the Ottoman emperors, and Napoleon. Muhammad's letter was taken away in 1517 by the Turkish Sultan Selim I and is now in the Topkapi Museum in Istanbul.

The monastery was a powerful building, a fortress with massive walls dominated by a tower, raising above the central place of worship the Church of the Transfiguration.

A guidebook noted that the monastery and its environs enshrine many of the most famous legends, such as that of the Burning Bush in which God was said to have appeared to Moses and commanded him to lead the Jews to the Promised Land. The harsh peak atop Mount Sinai is where God supposedly gave Moses the Ten Commandments, or the Tablets of Law. Also close by is the rock which Moses was said to have struck with his rod, drawing water. Tradition has it that St. Catherine's body lay for three to five centuries in the small mountaintop chapel after she was martyred in Alexandria and transported by angels to Mount Sinai.

We entered the Church of the Transfiguration, a sizable structure with a high ceiling, and dozens of oil lamps suspended from chains. A red carpet and many icons lined the walls. Incense drifted through the apse. Father Makarios pointed to the beautiful marble floor, a mosaic of marble crafted by Syrian artisans in the 6th century, when the monastery and the church were built.

In the abbey church, a gilded iconostasis hid the holy of holies. Concealed within its shadows were not the bones of a martyr, but the roots of a bush. I knelt in front of the silver-covered roots and found myself intoning prayers learned more than half a century ago in my childhood. It was a moving moment.

Outside a cut of the shrub thrived, emerald-green in the brown wilderness of the Sinai. If the survival of the miraculous bush was ever in doubt, the holy fathers were taking no chances with spontaneous recombustion. Beside the bush stood a fire extinguisher.

Father Makarios remarked that there were 20 Greek Orthodox monks in residence at the monastery—down from a hundred in better times—one Armenian, one American, and one Russian; they all celebrated the monastic hours. The monks were awakened each day by 33 strokes of the bell, one each for the 33 years of Jesus' life. They were the students and guardians of the greatest collection of ancient manuscripts outside the Vatican and a constellation of sacred icons unsurpassed elsewhere. A few years earlier I had viewed many of those icons on loan at the Metropolitan Museum in New York when it mounted a retrospective of Byzantine art. But nothing could compare to viewing them in situ at the new Exposition of the Sacristy and Treasure of the Monastery.

There were 2,000 icons on display, some from the early Byzantine period (the 6th to the 10th century); these are among the most ancient portable icons of Christendom. They covered the church walls from ceiling to floor. Some were in dark corners difficult to view and appreciate, but the most precious ones were in the Gallery, for which a small admission was charged.

Within its grounds were six wells, four springs, and a large garden rich in fruit trees—I saw citrus, almond, fig, and apricot—two mills, and an olive press. The monastery employed 400 Bedouins to take care of the gardens. It was for these Bedouins and for the Muslim cooks and servants that the small mosque was built on the grounds; the key to the mosque, however, was kept by a monk.

The monastery still attracted Biblical scholars and devout pilgrims, but mostly it was visited by tourists. Most of them came on a tour to the Holy Land, and were guided by a monk on arrival, with English and Russian the most commonly used languages. Russians who were Orthodox made up the majority of visitors. For the sun-seekers of Sham El Sheikh, the monastery was not a priority on their agenda. Non-Orthodox visitors were not permitted to attend Mass.

Its priceless collection of old manuscripts was restricted to scholars, but I was allowed to view photocopies of documents, displayed inside glass cases. Father Makarios did show me a fragile parchment text, a copy of a psalm.

Until a few years before my visit, reaching St. Catherine involved a 12-day camel trek, undertaken by only the most devout pilgrims. Today a car could reach the monastery from Sham El Sheikh on a modern paved road in three hours. The scenery was absolutely spectacular: deserts, mountains, canyons, and dried-up riverbeds or *wadis*. On our return we discerned a few Bedouin tents dotting the landscape. One Bedouin approached us, cigarette in hand, marketing a camel trek, asking 10 dollars for the ride. Most interestingly, behind his tent on the desert sand, a new Mercedes was parked. Business must have been good.

Even if one was not religious, one could find spirituality in this inspiring setting, a land sacred to a multitude of faiths, reaching out in every direction.

Since 2013, the monastery has been forced to close down its doors because of the deteriorating political situation in Egypt. It is opened for services only, no longer for tour groups or overnight guests. Some visitors climb Mount Sinai—a demanding climb, requiring a Bedouin as a guide.

With the Bibliotheca Alexandrina

I was introduced a few years ago to the International Friends of the Bibliotheca Alexandrina—better known as the BA—by my childhood friend Aida Sinbel Khalafalla. Before long I found myself invited to join the Friends at their annual conference and present the three travel books I had penned.

I accepted the invitation with alacrity. It was not only an opportunity to attend the conference and to participate in a number very interesting activities and to meet with government officials, business leaders, university scholars, prominent journalists and television personalities, and diplomats; it was also a return once again to my native city, an opportunity to take a fresh look at its people and to search for its vanishing landmarks.

The buildings occupied the site of the palaces of the Ptolemies, not far from the spot where the Great Library stood in antiquity. They reminded me of the Smithsonian, the Library of Congress, and the Kennedy Center rolled together. The BA is not just a library, but a complex that includes conference and exhibition halls, a cultural center, specialized libraries, archives, research departments, three museums, galleries, a media center, a planetarium (the only one in the entire African continent with panoramic shows produced locally), a design laboratory, a publishing house, and shops. We all felt immensely proud of this modern monument to human civilization.

The complex overlooking the Mediterranean was the brainchild of two academics of the University of Alexandria, who in 1974 came up with the idea of building a new library as a means of revitalizing their city. Sheer tenacity on their part gradually won over the authorities, and Unesco gave the project its support. It was designed after an international competition was won by Snohetta, a Norwegian architectural firm, while construction was undertaken by Italian, British, and Egyptian engineering companies.

The design is exceptional for its bold aesthetic *parti*. Besides Unesco, Arab countries contributed to the construction, while the land was gifted by the Egyptian government. Greece's contribution was well represented by the Onassis Foundation.

The Bibliotheca opened in 2002 and shone instantly with the hundreds of programs it offered. Using state-of the art digital technology, it aimed to be Egypt's window on the world and the world's window on Egypt.

The collection is far from complete—close to two million volumes have been acquired since 1990—but it can accommodate eight million books. A further feature is the display of fine Arabic manuscripts borrowed from libraries of Alexandria, and of archival material from collections such as that of the Suez Canal Company.

I saw all this at a conference at the BA in 2014. Enthralled as I was by the Bibliotheca itself, its sheer beauty could not allay the anxieties I held for the whole of Egypt, which had gone through difficult and turbulent times since my last visit, and now faced a severe economic and political crisis. What was the vision of the country in 2014? Would it go the Islamist route, or promote a pluralistic society? Democracy was messy around the edges in this part of the world.

But despite the massive political upheavals since the ouster of President Mubarak, I was glad to observe that Egypt as a whole had welcomed a new and dynamic President, President El Sissi, who exuded energy and demanded hard work.

As Bibliotheca Director Ismail Serageldin put it, "There is a new sense of calm and security pervading the country. Terrorism is being effectively curbed and the days of mass protests are rapidly coming to an end.... But increased calm and security come with a price in terms of pluralism, openness, and the kind of full respect for human rights and due process that one hopes on." Egypt was engaged in a balancing act, badly in need of some semblance of stability if it was to survive and prosper.

The BA Conference

The conference did not have any political overtones. Delegates from a number countries met with their Egyptian counterparts and were informed of the work undertaken by the Bibliotheca Alexandrina. Dr. Serageldin opened the meeting with a perfect roundup, a concise, precise rundown of the BA's impressive achievements in the past year.

The Governor of Alexandria joined us in one of the conference events. For the International Friends it presented an opportunity to lobby against the demolition of Lawrence Durrell's home. The governor, a combination of mayor and mini viceroy, an ex-Army general and a consummate politician with eyes of a sly, smiling child, invited us to the opening of a jewelry museum the next day; we eagerly accepted. It was a command.

The mini palace that had been turned into the Royal Jewelry Museum was bursting with local grandees and foreigners; we were not special there, just extras to gild the lily. When the governor arrived, it was total pandemonium; there was no ceremony, just bare-knuckle, hand-to-hand, sleeve-tugging advancement; I guess that was democracy, Egyptian-style.

I moved away and sat in the shade looking up at what was essentially a large Beaux-Arts, two-part villa, comprising a *haramlek* or women's quarters, a private block connected by a gallery to the *samlamlek*, a guesthouse or entertainment wing. It was the summerhouse of a cousin of the King, one among many in this quarter.

Princess Fatma Zahra, who escorted us, was a charmer; during Sadat's time, a law had confiscated everything from the royal family, but she must have gotten around him as he gave her the use of her own house for her lifetime, and now it was the Jewelry Museum.

Wearily I got up, chivied by the minders, and followed the crowd. I was surprised by the tasteful disposition of artifacts, a miniscule portion of the vast treasures accumulated by the dynasty that ruled Egypt from Muhammad Ali to King Farouk over 150 years and swallowed up by the Nasser regime. I marveled at the richness and refinement of an exquisite court more brilliant than Versailles.

A piquant reception was hosted by Mrs. Fahima El Nokrashi, one of the International Friends, one of many memorable events. Fahima divided her time between Germany, Cairo, and Alexandria. Her huge apartment, served by a large staff, could easily hold a hundred guests, just in the living room alone. This was the *haute bourgeoisie* and its manners on show, complete with paintings of her ancestors, three former prime ministers all lit by magnificent chandeliers; the apartment was indeed a museum. The doors of the dining room opened to a large buffet of delicacies.

Everywhere and nowhere

This time around, I traveled by train to Alexandria from Cairo rather than through the desert road, which I had taken many times before. I was looking at the delta landscape, once a major center of cotton growing. I noted how much the agricultural land had diminished and how built up the villages had become since I made that journey years ago.

Houses once no more than two stores high were now three or four. They consisted of upright concrete pillars, the spaces between which were filled with brick. Arriving at the outskirts of Alexandria I saw the same, the city expanding, growing even denser, the buildings exactly like the delta houses except that these were now much taller, rising up to ten stories, many with no elevator.

I looked to see if any of these new structures owed anything to the wider world, to the Mediterranean, but I saw nothing of the sort, only the simplest Egyptian notions of a box to live in.

From the fifth-floor balcony of my hotel, the Windsor Palace, I surveyed the cerulean blue sky and sea over the Eastern Harbor, trying to fill in all the landmarks: the Abou Abbas mosque, the Fort, where the Lighthouse stood, and there to the East, the Fourth Pyramid, the Bibliotheca Alexandrina, the reason we came.

It was the harbor that held my gaze, not just the bright fishing boats swinging around their moorings or the little dinghies dropping red buoys for a small-boats regatta later in the day, but the pleasing oval shape of the port, a small inner sea, ovoid, enclosed and cozy.

The hotel staff could not have been more accommodating and helpful. On one occasion, overcome by fatigue when I sent out my jacket to be ironed, I had left a 10-pound bill (i.e. $1.25) in my pocket. The jacket was returned intact in a couple of hours and the 10 pounds presented with a gracious smile. The hotel had old charm, with frescoes on the high ceilings, massive rooms, even a quaint old birdcage elevator which worked at its own whim. The noise of the traffic on the Corniche and a discothèque close by made sleeping difficult, but then that view of the Mediterranean more than compensated for my discomfort.

I could still see along the Corniche and few blocks behind the architecture of the late 19th and early 20th century buildings, exotic constructions that ran block after block but all of them needing a fresh coat of paint.

The panorama showcased a mixture of a dozen styles: neo-Byzantine, neo-Venetian, neo-Renaissance, Art Deco, neoclassical, and so on, expressions of the national sentiment of the architects who built them. My guidebook noted that "On one side of the street lay the whimsy of Art Nouveau apartment decor, on the other side the stylized towers of a Neo-Gothic office block. Strangely there are few Ottoman cupolas and Pharaonic friezes thrown in. They display the sort of eclectic Orientalism that Edward Lutyens, the imperial architect of the Raj, would have enjoyed."

The oddest thing about Alexandria's past was that while it was everywhere, it was nowhere. You had to look consciously to find it. The ground floors of buildings had been converted to garish shop fronts, their facades festooned with tangled telephone wires, their roofs hidden in a jungle of advertisements and signboards. What was visible was hardly recognizable. Decades of dirt and dilapidation had bestowed upon everything the same gritty film and suggestion of slow, unstoppable decline.

Movie theaters which I had patronized decades ago had been demolished. The Rialto cinema, an Art-Deco landmark on the Rue Safia Zaghloul where I had seen *Casablanca* during the war, had been torn down. So many demolitions had been done without permission by developers. Could it be stopped? Foreign posters and advertisements had vanished; everything was in Arabic; in my time, film posters were billed in several languages with Arabic subtitles.

When I was growing up, you could hear Greek or some other Mediterranean music from cafés on Safia Zaghloul and the Corniche. Now the music was dull and indifferent.

I also noted how deeply Alexandria had drifted toward a new conservatism, at least out in the open. In the '50s and '60s I could slip into a two piece bathing suit and walk with other bikini-clad girls on Stanley Bay beach. Now women wore head coverings such as the *niqab*, the black shroud-like garment with slits for the eyes. In the private swimming pool of the Four Seasons at San Stephano, however, foreign women lounged in bikinis.

Where Alexandria had once been known as Little Paris, home to a vast community of Europeans and Jews, today with a few exceptions, the European population was gone. In the late forties the city's population stood at 800,000, a third of whom were foreigners. Now, according to the Greek Consul General, it was close to 6 million, with foreigners accounting for just 600, mostly Greeks and a smattering of Jews. I did not count among "foreigners," i.e. the Westerners, Kuwaitis, Palestinians, and Arabs studying at the university.

Egypt's second city was now a bastion of adherents to an austere Saudi Arabian brand of Islam. Once sold widely, alcohol had been relegated to hotels.

Many of the changes came during the 30-year rule of Hosni Mubarak. Paradoxically, it was under his pro-Western, secular regime—a de facto one-party system where political freedoms were limited and the state cracked down on religious extremists— that swaths of Egyptians grew more religious and some embraced a less-tolerant Islam. Millions of Egyptians who went to Saudi Arabia, Kuwait, and other Gulf states to profit from their booming economies came home, embracing Salafism and the black veil.

A movement forward

However difficult Egypt's transition to its present state has been, and whatever the demands for democracy and for an end to corruption, etc., they also mean a movement forward in the evolution of the Egyptian identity. The new Egypt is still struggling to be more than a fresh assertion of the old. The country is caught between an assertive Islamism and the buoyant idealism of the young protesters at Tahrir Square who captured the Western media with their pursuit of free expression and political reform. The old and the new will continue to contend for the Egyptian heart and mind, but it is a struggle that reaches back into the past when, even in what we now call antiquity, Egypt became the birthplace of many things new and wondrous.

Along Ramleh, the two tram lines, the Victoria and the Bacos, still rolled along the same trajectory, but garbage now lined the tracks and the stations were filthy with debris. Once trams comprised first- and second-class carriages. Ladies attending the cinema for an evening show would ride in the first-class compartment, dressed in their finery, their perfume (Schiaparelli was popular at that time) permeating the tram. First- and second-carriages had been replaced with male and female compartments. The price of the ticket was no more than a four cents. A friend advised me not to speak in English but to converse in Arabic, explaining that the tram fares were heavily subsidized, and some locals might resent seeing a foreigner taking advantage of subsidized transport; foreigners took private cars or taxis. There was not a single European on the tram.

None of the women on the tram wore the black *nijab*, but they wore long wraparound skirts, their heads covered with a veil. Next to me sat a young girl with a very charming suntanned face, framed in a colorful scarf. Her features were full of character. I tried to draw her into a conversation, and she told me that her name was Magda, and that she was a student at the Faculty of Law; she expressed a desire to study in America but deplored the difficulty of obtaining a visa. Our conversation was brief as she got off a couple of stations ahead of me.

I was having lunch with Nicholas Deliyannis, a friend from Paris, at Muhammad Ali, the old Benyamin. It was highly recommended for its local cuisine, a very inexpensive eatery with no frills, no tourist rates, no tablecloths, and no linen napkins, but the food was delicious. What a bargain we had for three dollars—six vegetarian dishes, plus half a dozen pieces of pita bread. We could not finish them, even if they were all so good—including *turshi*, the bright pickled vegetables I enjoyed at the Moharrem patronized by locals, including women enjoying lunch there; we saw no other tourists.

Later we realized that Nicholas had left his attaché case and cell phone in the taxi. We had dismissed the driver as we were planning to walk after lunch. But then after lunch, we found the taxi driver waiting to return the forgotten items. He refused any tip. Where else could you find that kind of honesty among taxi drivers in the world?

There were white minibuses cruising along the Corniche; the fare was 60 cents for the entire 20-kilometer drive. They were packed, and there was no segregation here, with men sitting next to women. They stopped regularly along popular beaches, depositing passengers as new ones ascended.

Driving along the Corniche proved a great disappointment. The entire length of the beaches had been overtaken by private clubs. Architectural monstrosities obstructed the view: the Army club, the Navy club, the Air Force club, the engineers' club, the teachers' club, the doctors' club, the accountants' club, etc. Every branch of government and every profession owned one of those ugly structures, with admission restricted to their members. Alexandria had a special kind of magic found in a very few cities in the world—Havana was another one—and the magic had to do with the sea and shore. Doing away with public beaches, now the enclave of a military and professional private clubs, saddened me enormously. I asked why most of the beaches were reserved "for members only," and was stunned to be told that "local people" would make them dirty!

A few tiny patches of the Corniche remained open to the public, but they were crowded with garbage and huge piles of debris. In those few public beaches was where the main sewerage of Alexandria deposited tons of filth. But in one of those beaches, I saw a woman completely covered in her black *niqab* immersing herself in the water!

Young lovers still strolled along the Corniche in Stanley Bay, holding hands. The women wore scarves, but often brightly spangled and paired with make-up and tight jeans. Women dressed in black *niqabs* passed the other way, walking behind their robed husbands.

Attitudes towards cosmopolitan Alexandria differed widely among the Muslim majority. We are proud of our history, said a young teacher in a long skirt and a long veil. She would welcome a more liberal society, even bikinis, if not for herself, she said, laughing. At a sweetshop, 32-year old Muhammad Nasr believed that Islamic proselytizing rescued the city from its cosmopolitan past and would have to step again if it returned.

I looked for Alexandria's old bookstores, and was no longer surprised to find that my favorite bookshop, the Cite du Livre on the old Rue Fouad, was gone; in others I found only lamentable stock.

Around the antique market in the Attarin district of town, only a couple of stores had distinctively Middle Eastern items such as octagonal tables, inlaid mirrors, and antique brassware. Shop after shop was filled, instead, with European furnishings, heavy rosewood armchairs, garish crystal chandeliers, bulbous little chests, and paintings. There were assorted metal cups, trophies, antique evening purses, browned family photos in frames, cigarette cases, and trinkets so corroded it was impossible to tell what metal they were made of. Only gradually did it strike me what all this stuff was: the debris of the families who left Alexandria behind, in 1956. These were the true relics of the city's cosmopolitan past, now being bought up and absorbed into Egyptian homes, or bought for export and sent "back" to the West. These inanimate objects had been at home once upon a cosmopolitan Alexandria.

If there was any notable change for the better, it came in the form of the new Bibliotheca Alexandrina, the symbol of the city's rebirth alongside the recently opened 1921 Opera House, a newly formed orchestra, and a renovated antiquities museum. The Bibliotheca Director, a dynamo of a man named Ismael Serageldin, told me that after a long period of decline for Alexandria, his library had lined its shelves with books including Salman Rushdie's *Satanic Verses*, roundly rejected by Islamists. In the looting and violence that shook the city in 2011, the director was heartened by the reaction of local youths who formed a ring around the library and shielded it from attack.

A $140-million underwater museum was being planned to showcase Queen Cleopatra's palace, another tourist attraction. Its exoticism will contrast sharply with the 500-km coast between Alexandria and the Libyan border, where nothing but turquoise water and sleepy Bedouin tents can be found.

A Mediterranean sensibility

When I was asked what I thought about Alexandria I could only say that in my time there I missed the wider world. I rather liked that waft of a foreign breeze. But then I was not an Egyptian, and when they started chanting "Egypt is for the Egyptians," I knew even more clearly that it was not for me.

Taking a walk on the Safia Zaghloul, I found one of the old landmarks: the Brazilian coffee store. It was the kind of establishment good enough to have its collection of morning regulars (an early version of a Starbucks), and 60 years on I could still recall the wonderful aroma emanating from that store. The giant coffee roasting and grinding machines, all blackened now, were on display at the store's window as museum pieces.

Men stood around stools outside the coffee with their coffee in one hand and a cellphone in the other. Visiting Alexandria in 2008, the travel writer Nicholas Woodworth had encountered the same scene, seeing men "at the shop's open door, nursing their coffee and chatting away in Arabic, as easy and familiar in their manner as if they had stood there surveying life every morning for decades, which they probably had.

"But what struck me most as I approached these characters was their physicality. Their gestures were animated, their facial expressions were vigorous, their voices lively; they talked with their whole bodies. Suddenly I realized I had seen those men before.

"They were not sipping pastis or ouzo, but in their jokey bravado and mocking affection for each other, they were the split image of pastis drinkers I had seen in the back streets of Marseilles or Piraeus. They did not have a quiet bench to sit on, but in their sharp-eyed surveillance of the street, they were like the old gaffers I had sat with in Greek or Sicilian village squares. In their battering delivery they were the same ones I had heard in waterfront cafés from Piraeus to Valencia."

Woodsworth concludes his observations (later published in his book *The Liquid Continent*) with an insight I could not agree more with: "Alexandria may sit on the edge of Africa and, looking out to the sea, barely belongs to the continent in the prickly post-Suez. It may even have a harder time acknowledging its historical ties to the European land across the water. But of its essential nature there is no doubt. The city's character is not in its buildings, but exists most in its people, and they have no trouble expressing it. Their intimacy, a garrulous warmth and near-tribal sociability, belongs to the city and is shared by all others on this sea. It is not African, nor European, not Middle Eastern. But it is identifiable. It is Mediterranean."

Paying homage to Cavafy

On a late fall morning while I was in Alexandria, I decided to visit the Cavafy Museum, inaugurated in the Cavafy House in November 1992.

I had been a devotee of Constantine Cavafy (1863-1933) since my college years. I was given then a book of his poems and to my astonishment I discovered how much I enjoyed the poetry. Reading him once again, I rediscovered childhood memories of Alexandria.

> *The setting of houses, cafés, the neighborhood*
> *that I've seen and walked through years on end:*
> *I created you while I was happy, while I was sad.*
> *with so many incidents, so many details.*
> *And, for me, the whole of you has been transformed into feeling.*

> From *"In the Same Space,"* C. P. Cavafy

I inquired about the whereabouts of the Cavafy House, and most people whom I talked to were eager to help but were not aware of its location. Many were not even aware of who he was.

The Bibliotheca Alexandrina staff came to my rescue, giving me the address and informing me of the museum's opening hours from 10 am to 3 pm. The location was not too far away from my hotel, so I decided to walk.

After many a hit and miss—I thought I would have little difficulty navigating through the streets of a city that I knew well—I finally arrived at the street now named Sham El Sheikh after the site on the Bay of Aqaba. Originally the street was called Rue Lepsius, after a French engineer; in 1992 it was renamed Cavafy Street.

The path to the house is through a series of small roads and by lanes in a rather shabby area. Over the years the pavement turned into an undulating terrain of dents and bulges, mostly cracked. The whole street was blanketed by a deep drab, dirty gray. It was here, according to his biographers, at 10 Lepsius Street that the Greek Alexandrian poet lived for 35 years.

After his death the flat became a small pension of the kind described in many Middle Eastern novels, modest and seedy; most of the furniture was sold by his heirs; fortunately, his books, notes, and manuscripts were saved by friends and a noted scholar, Professor George Asides. The flat was taken over by the Greek Consulate and with noble intention made it a museum.

I located a plaque outside the house identifying Cavafy's home. Ascending the broad flights of worn stone steps, I reached the second floor. There I faced a large varnished oak door, hermetically closed, conjuring an image of refined splendor. A neighbor living on the same floor informed me that as no visitor had arrived that day, the museum attendant had left couple of hours earlier. I repeated my expedition the next day early morning; only to find the door as closed as ever. I had not paid attention at one of the bronze plaques outside the apartment door, stating that on Mondays the museum was closed. It took a third attempt to reach Cavafy's flat, and by this time I have mastered short cuts among Alexandria's alleys.

Here Cavafy lived with his books, paintings, and sparse furniture in an intimate and secluded atmosphere. The apartment of five or six rooms was large; the living room occupied the entire width of the house with a large sofa in the middle, interrupted by an Oriental rug. A balcony, the only one in the entire building, overlooked the street below; I could listen to the small vendors and smell the aroma of spices.

> *Then, sad, I went out on to the balcony,*
> *went out to change my thoughts at least by seeing*
> *something of this city I love,*
> *a little movement in the street and the shops.*

From *"In the Evening,"* C. P. Cavafy

The pieces of furniture were reproductions, recreated from old photographs and with the assistance of some of his living friends. The many black-and-white photographs displayed here evoked the milieu of his time. How difficult it was to recover the atmosphere of Arab-Byzantine clutter.

Where was the cane chair which "creaked all night," in which I fantasized the old poet of the city sitting and reciting *The Barbarians*? The cane chair, even as a reproduction, was missing!

The walls—originally painted green, red, mauve according to the museum guide—had been repainted white or in pastel; the poet's desk, the metal headboard bed, and a few pieces of furniture, Arabian-style, stood neatly in those rooms.

The room in which Cavafy lived had a number of articles and objects associated with him: a wooden trunk of that period, an old mirror which the poet used, the old silk carpet on the floor, and a number of lithographs of the poet done by author-painter P. Tetsis. The arabesque armchair gifted by the Greek Orthodox Patriarch of Alexandria and a console from the poet's house with his death mask brought the man alive in one's imagination.

Here, near the door, was the couch,
a Turkish carpet in front of it.
Close by, the shelf with two yellow vases.
On the right—no, opposite—a wardrobe with a mirror…
In the middle the table where he wrote,
and the three big wicker chairs.
Besides the window was the bed
where we made love so many times.

They must still be around somewhere, those old things.
Beside the window was the bed;
the afternoon sun fell across half of it.

One afternoon at four o'clock we separated
for a week only… And then—
that week became forever.

From *"The Afternoon Sun,"* C. P. Cavafy

Missing were the beautiful petroleum lamps that contributed to the aura of the apartment. The deeper distinction was of course the personality of the tenant that made it unique in the whole city.

I spent considerable time looking at objects around the rooms: drawings of Cavafy's mother Chariclea, his younger brother Paul, his eldest brother Aristides, and a stand with exquisite old icons.

The museum guide played a CD for me so I could listen to a couple of Cavafy's poems read by a leading Greek actress, Eli Campeti. I wished that a rendition of these poems were available in English or in other languages, preferably Arabic.

Between shabbiness and riches

Extensive bibliographical material—translations of Cavafy's work in many languages, books, and articles—provided a unique insight into the life and times of the poet. The enduring literary importance of Cavafy was also demonstrated in the room devoted to Stratis Tsirkis, the author of *Drifting Cities*, a trilogy set in wartime Jerusalem, Cairo, and Alexandria. The book *The Canon* by Cavafy contains the original 154 poems translated by Stratis Haviaras and is a treasured possession of the museum. Incidentally Haviaras was the headmaster of the Greek high school my brother Akis attended.

Clippings of newspapers and journals like *Le Monde*, *Le Soir*, the *Times Literary Supplement*, *La Vanguard*, and *Journal de Genève* added a touch of history to the place. The poet's publications, letters, correspondence, notes, and photocopies of his manuscripts were spread on glass-covered display cases.

Cavafy's home stood between the Greek Orthodox Church of St. Saba, the Greek Hospital, and the bordellos of the city. "Where could I live better?" Cavafy asked. "Below the brothel caters for the flesh. And there is the church which forgives sin. And there is the hospital where we die."

Alexandria has many strata of memory: Hellenistic, Roman, Islamic, Mediterranean. Cavafy began the whole approach of mining the city as a source of historical memory but he largely went unnoticed until E. M Foster shone the literary spotlight on him.

In Cavafy's poetry the contrast remains between the shabbiness of the city and the richness of its past. Introducing Rae Dalven's translations, W. H. Auden would note that Cavafy writes "of Ancient Alexandria, of unconventional love, of the clash between Christian and Pagan conception of life, he writes as no one else could have done, and his controlled intensity of feeling is set off by a wit which has the bouquet of an exquisite wine…. He has been the greatest influence from the past on contemporary Greek poetry and has already influenced poets in many other languages. His complete sincerity, his angular stance, his tenderness that is combined with accuracy of a surgeon, his awareness of the past in the present and of the present in the past, his meticulousness, his grandeur…. These are some of the qualities which no reader can fail to observe and which, singly and together, made him one of the greatest writers of our time.'"

I tried to imagine how Cavafy, a great poet dear to me, lived so many years of his life in this house and wrote poetry. For me the visit was a pilgrimage but also a reminiscence of Alexandria, a tiny speck on the map of the world from which radiates so many roads I traveled and on which I always long to return.

And so this is my story: growing up in Alexandria, which makes up the bulk of my book, and by itself perhaps not an uncommon story; a remarkable marriage, a rich and enduring partnership that spanned many decades and many countries; coming into my own, witnessing significant transformations of our time. What evolved in this book is an enumeration, a list of events, a selected collection of memories, an accumulation of images, dots of colors in an impressionistic painting. The picture shifts and changes much as life does, like fleeting revelations when the sun shines through the fog.

As Gabriel Garcia Marquez once wrote: "The life of a person is not what happened, but what he remembers and how he remembers it." So this is what I remember in this afternoon of my life, when the sun of the past shines extraordinarily bright, rendering everything with a kindly luminosity.

SOURCES CONSULTED AND CITED

Books

Aciman, André. *Out of Egypt: A Memoir*.
New York: Farrar, Strauss & Giroux, 1994.

Al-Kharrat, Edwar. *City of Saffron*, translated by Frances Liardet.
London: Quartet Books, 1989.

Awad, Muhammad and Sahar Hamouda, eds. *Voices from Cosmopolitan Alexandria*.
Alexandria: Bibliotheca Alexandrina, 2006.

Brinton, Jasper Yeates. *The American Effort in Egypt: A Chapter in Diplomatic History in the Nineteenth Century*.
Alexandria: [Impr. du Commerce], 1972.

Cavafy, Constantine P. *The Complete Poems of C.P. Cavafy*, translated by Rae Dalven.
London: Chatto & Windus, 1968.

Cavafy, Constantine P. *Collected Works*, edited by George Savidis and translated by Edmund Keeley and Peter Sherrard.
Princeton: Princeton University Press, 1992.
(All the poems excerpted in this book come from this edition.)

Durrell, Lawrence. *The Alexandria Quartet*.
London: Faber and Faber, 1974.

Empereur, Jean-Yves. *Alexandria: Past, Present, and Future*.
London: Thames & Hudson, 2002.

Forster, E.M. *Alexandria: A History and a Guide.*
Kindle Edition, 2012.

Haniotis, John D. *Your Guide to Chios.*
Athens: N. p., 1971.

Hardman, Esther Zimmerli. *From Camp Caesar to Cleopatra's Pool:
A Swiss Childhood in Alexandria, 1934-1950.*
Alexandria: Bibliotheca Alexandrina, 2008.

Hill, Arthur and Julie. *A Promise to Keep.*
Bloomington: Xlibris, 2003.

Hill, Julie. *The Silk Road Revisited: Markets, Merchants, and Minarets.*
Bloomington: AuthorHouse, 2006.

Lagnado, Lucette. *The Man in the White Sharkskin Suit.*
New York: HarperCollins, 2007.

Mahfouz, Naguib. *Miramar.*
Cairo: AUC Press, 1989.

Matz, Mary Jane Phillips. Verdi: *A Biography.*
Oxford: Oxford University Press, 1993.

Parker, Richard B. and Robin Sabin. *A Practical Guide to Islamic Monuments.*
Cairo: AUC Press, 1974.

Sadat, Jehan. *A Woman of Egypt.*
New York: Simon & Schuster, 1987.

Souloyannis, Efthymios. *Elliniki Koinotita Alexandrias, 1843-1993.*
Athens: ELIA, 1994.

Tzalas, Harry. *Seven Days at the Cecil*.
Alexandria: Bibliotheca Alexandrina, 2009.

Yannakakis, Ilios. *"Farewell Alexandria" in Alexandria 1860-1960:*
The Brief Life of a Cosmopolitan Community,
edited by Robert Ilbert and Ilios Yannakakis,
translated by Colin Clement, 106-22.
Alexandria: Harpocrates, 1997.

Magazines and Newspapers

Aramco World, September-October 1969
Aramco World, September-October 1970
Aramco World, September-October 1977
Aramco World, March-April 1994
Aramco World, September-October 1995
Cairo Times, 15 June 1996
Cairo Times, 11 May 2000
Conde Nast Traveler, October 2007
Egyptian Mail, 30 March 1996
Financial Times, 3 April 2015

Websites

http://www.academia.edu/919853/The_Purge_of_the_Greeks_from_Nasserite Egypt_Myths_and_Realities_Journal_of_the_Hellenic_Diaspora_35_2_2009_pp.13-34
http://www.bl.uk/onlinegallery/sacredtexts/codexsinai.html
http://www.egy.com/victoria/96-03-30.php
http://www.neo.gr/website/ergasiamathiti/
http://www.nybooks.com/articles/archives/1997/dec/18/shadow-cities/
http://www.nbcnews.com/id/49860648/ns/technology_and_science-science/t/mystery-our-memory-why-its-not-perfect/
https://prelectur.stanford.edu/archive/#aciman
http://www.serageldin.com/Attachment/eS-URLPqqJI_20150203160826989.pdf
http://www.theguardian.com/world/2013/sep/05/mount-sinai-monastery-egypt-closure
https://en.wikipedia.org/wiki/Shanghai
https://en.wikipedia.org/wiki/Benaki_Museum

Others

Lorenzo Montesini, Private Communication
Jehan Sadat, Private Communication